'It is all too easy to regard the Philosophers' Stone as an idle metaphor or as the product of a misguided and vain alchemical obsession. But *Jung's Alchemical Philosophy* demonstrates on the contrary that the Stone is something to take seriously with deep implications for our self-understanding and our connection to the cosmos. In this ambitious and comprehensive book, detailed discussions are given of Jung's extensive research into the relationship between the search for the Stone and the greater Self, and of subsequent contributions by James Hillman with an emphasis on the soul work symbolized in alchemical transformation and on imagination as an inherent ingredient in that same transformation. The larger philosophical significance of the Stone is pursued in a nuanced treatment of Hegel's notion of Absolute Spirit, drawing on the depth-psychological interpretations of Wolfgang Giegerich. Contemporary authors such as Derrida and Zizek are also woven skillfully into the larger tale. The book generates a complex tapestry of philosophical and psychological insights, demonstrating their dialectical co-valence. Written with a rare combination of precision and passion, this book expands the horizons of the always enigmatic relationships between matter and meaning, self and other, life and death. By the end, the reader comes to realize that the Philosophers' Stone is not something merely chimerical but a psychical reality and an inroad into soul and spirit alike'.

Edward S. Casey, *Professor of Philosophy, SUNY at Stony Brook, USA.* Author: *The World on Edge: Studies in Continental Thought*

'This edifying book has a double impact. The author is a philosopher and a psychoanalyst, and his book is at once a philosophical psychology and a psychological philosophy. In the first instance it reveals to its reader valuable and varied insights into the history and imagery of alchemy, demonstrating why the philosophy of alchemy has been crucial to the development of the theory and practice of psychoanalytic therapy. But this is not all. Philosophers think about thinking, and philosophy, as the book reminds the reader, is thought in the act of thinking about itself. So, in the second instance, this book shows its reader how to think about psychology *psychologically*, as opposed to thinking about psychology *personalistically* as medicine, science, spirituality, or problem-solving for ego and its difficulties. The book's doubleness rewards the reader with provocative perspectives'.

David L. Miller, *Watson Ledden Professor Emeritus, Syracuse University, USA.* Author: G*ods and Games: Toward a Theology of Play*

'Stanton Marlan's *Jung's Alchemical Philosophy* provides a wide-ranging and profound analysis of the transformative psychological understanding of alchemy initiated by Jung. In the process Marlan brings to light the alchemists' efforts to come to terms with such binary oppositions as nature and spirit, absolutism and relativism, thought and being, and most pointedly, image and idea. Marlan provides a perspective through which these oppositions can be reconciled and he opens a new philosophical vista on alchemy which expands upon and complements Jung's depth psychological perspective on the alchemical opus'.

Sanford Drob, *Core Faculty of Fielding Graduate University in Santa Barbara, California, USA.* Author: *Archetype of the Absolute: The Unity of Opposites in Mysticism Philosophy and Psychology*

Jung's Alchemical Philosophy

Traditionally, alchemy has been understood as a precursor to the science of chemistry but from the vantage point of the human spirit, it is also a discipline that illuminates the human soul. This book explores the goal of alchemy from Jungian, psychological, and philosophical perspectives.

Jung's Alchemical Philosophy: Psyche and the Mercurial Play of Image and Idea is a reflection on Jung's alchemical work and the importance of philosophy as a way of understanding alchemy and its contributions to Jung's psychology. By engaging these disciplines, Marlan opens new vistas on alchemy and the circular and ouroboric play of images and ideas, shedding light on the alchemical opus and the transformative processes of Jungian psychology. Divides in the history of alchemy and in the alchemical imagination are addressed as Marlan deepens the process by turning to a number of interpretations that illuminate both the enigma of the Philosophers' Stone and the ferment in the Jungian tradition.

This book will be of interest to Jungian analysts and those who wish to explore the intersection of philosophy and psychology as it relates to alchemy.

Stanton Marlan, PhD, ABPP, FABP is a Jungian analyst, President of the Pittsburgh Society of Jungian Analysts, and an Adjunct Professor in Clinical Psychology at Duquesne University, with long-time interests in alchemy and the psychology of dreams. He is also the author of other books on psychology and alchemy, including *C.G. Jung and the Alchemical Imagination: Passages into the Mysteries of Psyche and Soul.*

Philosophy & Psychoanalysis Book Series
Jon Mills
Series Editor

Philosophy & Psychoanalysis is dedicated to current developments and cutting-edge research in the philosophical sciences, phenomenology, hermeneutics, existentialism, logic, semiotics, cultural studies, social criticism, and the humanities that engage and enrich psychoanalytic thought through philosophical rigor. With the philosophical turn in psychoanalysis comes a new era of theoretical research that revisits past paradigms while invigorating new approaches to theoretical, historical, contemporary, and applied psychoanalysis. No subject or discipline is immune from psychoanalytic reflection within a philosophical context including psychology, sociology, anthropology, politics, the arts, religion, science, culture, physics, and the nature of morality. Philosophical approaches to psychoanalysis may stimulate new areas of knowledge that have conceptual and applied value beyond the consulting room reflective of greater society at large. In the spirit of pluralism, *Philosophy & Psychoanalysis* is open to any theoretical school in philosophy and psychoanalysis that offers novel, scholarly, and important insights in the way we come to understand our world.

Titles in this series:

**Metaphysical Dualism, Subjective Idealism,
and Existential Loneliness**
Matter and Mind
Ben Lazare Mijuskovic

Jung's Alchemical Philosophy
Psyche and the Mercurial Play of Image and Idea
Stanton Marlan

For more information about this series, please visit: www.routledge.com/ Philosophy & Psychoanalysis Book Series

Jung's Alchemical Philosophy

Psyche and the Mercurial Play
of Image and Idea

Stanton Marlan

Routledge
Taylor & Francis Group

LONDON AND NEW YORK

Cover image: Jimlop collection/Alamy Stock Photo

First published 2022
by Routledge
4 Park Square, Milton Park, Abingdon, Oxon OX14 4RN

and by Routledge
605 Third Avenue, New York, NY 10158

Routledge is an imprint of the Taylor & Francis Group,
an informa business

British Library Cataloguing-in-Publication Data
A catalogue record for this book is available from the British
Library

Library of Congress Cataloging-in-Publication Data
A catalog record for this book has been requested

ISBN: 978-1-032-10551-2 (hbk)
ISBN: 978-1-032-10544-4 (pbk)
ISBN: 978-1-003-21590-5 (ebk)

DOI: 10.4324/9781003215905

Typeset in Times New Roman
by Apex CoVantage, LLC

Credit line: Science History Images/Alamy Stock Photo

For my children and grandchildren:
Dawn, Tori and Brandon
Malachi, Sasha, Zia and Naomi

Contents

Figures

Tables

Acknowledgments

With great appreciation and respect, I would like to acknowledge a number of professors, philosophers, psychologists, Jungian analysts, artists, colleagues, friends and family, all of whom have contributed to my work. I am grateful to James Hillman, Edward Edinger, Murray Stein, Ed Casey, David Miller, Sanford Drob, Tom Rockmore, Wolfgang Zucker, William Wurzer, James Swindal, John Sallis, Robert Romanyshyn, Terry Pulver, Roger Brooke, John White, Maury Krasnow, David Perry, Jeff Librett, Keith Knecht, Leticia Capriotti, Lynne Cannoy, and Virginia Moore.

I would like to thank Alexis O'Brien, Editor, and Jana Craddock, Editorial Assistant, at Routledge for their professionalism and timely ongoing support. Special thanks to Jon Mills Series Editor of Philosophy & Psychoanalysis publications for his friendship, continuing interest in my work and encouragement to publish my book in his series. Also special thanks to my friend and colleague Claudette Kulkarni without whose help, dedication, editorial skill and hard work organizing and preparing this manuscript it would not have arrived in a timely manner for publication.

I am most grateful to my wife Jan Marlan for her love and untiring support and to my children and grandchildren, who continue to delight and inspire me and to whom this book is dedicated.

Preface

In this book, I will consider the enigmatic and mysterious goal of the alchemical process, the Philosophers' Stone. The Stone has for the most part been dismissed as a serious object of academic and scholarly studies and has been thought of as an illusory fantasy of the old alchemists in their impossible quest to turn lead into gold. At best, the results of the alchemists' quest for the transformation of substances have been seen from the perspective of the history of science as a naturalistic process and as a precursor to the science of chemistry. From this perspective, many of the religious and symbolic aspects of alchemical literature were passed over or reduced to code names for material processes. For many historians of alchemy, this approach left out or ignored important aspects of what alchemy was about. Considered from the wider perspective of the history of the human spirit, alchemy and its goal appeared not only as physical processes leading to chemistry, but also as a religious discipline whose goal was the transformation of earthly man into an illuminated philosopher.

The complex history of alchemy is a current and burgeoning field filled with tensions and controversy that may reflect the historical divides within alchemy itself and mirror what I will call a split in the alchemical imagination. For Jung, alchemy had a dual face. He saw it as both a quest to literally transform matter in the laboratory as well as a spiritual quest aimed at the transformation of the soul and thus as a religious philosophy. Studying alchemy from this perspective led Jung to see it not only as a precursor to chemistry, but also as a historical counterpart to his developing psychology of the unconscious. Jung's psychological perspective on the symbolic dimensions of alchemy opened a way of understanding the alchemical process that revolutionized our understanding of alchemy. While Jung's perspective on alchemy continues to influence the field to this day, his view has been challenged both from within and from outside the Jungian tradition. I will claim that current challenges to Jung's position take place in the context of differing philosophical convictions. Therefore, I propose that, along with natural scientific, religious, and psychological perspectives, the alchemical philosophers should be considered as philosophers working out a philosophical perspective. The goal of their work was the Philosophers' Stone – a philosophical substance. Placing the Philosophers' Stone in this context opens up many philosophical issues and tensions with regard to the study of the goal of alchemy, including the problem of binary oppositions, splits and gaps that are seemingly impossible to close, among them: chemistry and alchemy, scientific positivism and religious esotericism, psychology and philosophy. Alchemy itself has been seen as gold making, Self-making, and God making, and there are also the divides between phenomena and noumena, limit and transcendence, mechanism and vitalism, thought and being, image and idea, spirit and nature, soul and spirit, ontology and history, absolutism and relativism. I will consider these binaries in several contexts and among different thinkers and arrive at the conclusion that none of these divides can easily, if at all, be resolved into a simple unity or oneness.

Coming to terms with the idea of binaries and their resolution appears to be both an ancient and contemporary philosophical struggle. The work of many philosophers is relevant to this issue and lends itself to the concerns of this book. The Philosophers' Stone as the idea of the goal has been understood as a unification of oppositions into a oneness that was not a oneness mirroring the enigmatic dictum that the Philosophers' Stone is a "stone that is no stone." The attempt to penetrate further into an understanding of the unity of the Stone requires that it be understood not as a simple unity, but as a complex one. A philosophical way into this conundrum is an important focus of this book. In it I came to see what I consider a modern philosophical rendering that can shed additional light on notions such as the Self and the Philosophers' Stone.

Introduction

The Philosophers' Stone is considered the end product of the *opus philosophorum*. It has been described in numerous ancient manuscripts with considerable disagreement about its nature and appearance and about how it was to be discovered or made. It was identified with the transformation of matter and turning lead into gold, as well as philosophically identified with the transformation of "the earthly man into an illuminated philosopher."[1]

This miraculous Stone has a strange sort of complexity that once led Jung to confess that he "regarded alchemy as something off the beaten track and rather silly."[2] After an initial study of the images of the classical Latin alchemical text *Artis aurifera, volumina duo* (1593), Jung declared, "Good Lord, what nonsense! This stuff is impossible to understand."[3] Echoing this sentiment, Jung wrote elsewhere, "What the old philosophers meant by the *lapis* has never become quite clear."[4] And, in a similar spirit, alchemical scholar Lyndy Abraham called the Stone the "arcanum of all arcana."[5]

While the Stone was often identified with the *unus mundus*, the principle of one world, it has also been known by a variety of names, many of which were collected by Gratacolle in his "The Names of the Philosophers" (1652). Among the many names of the Stone, we find it referred to as "Chaos, a Dragon, a Serpent, a Toad, the green Lion, the quintessence, our stone Lunare, Camelion, . . . blacker than black, Virgins milke, radicall humidity, unctuous moysture, . . . urine, poyson, water of wise men, . . . Gold . . ."[6] And the list goes on, disseminating itself into a continuing complexity of images. The complexity reaches nearly absurd proportions in Dom Pernety's *Dictionnaire mytho-hermétique*, which lists about six hundred synonyms for the Stone or related materials.

DOI: 10.4324/9781003215905-1

Perhaps the description that most embodied the Stone's paradoxical nature is *lithos ou lithos*, the "stone that is no stone."[7] In this saying, the enigmatic quality of the Stone shines forth. How are we to understand this goal of the opus, which presents itself in so many images, contradictions, and enigmatic expressions and both presents itself and negates itself in a single gesture, as a multiplicity and yet also as a single substance or unity? Abraham has noted that:

> Despite the many names of the Stone, the alchemists stressed that it personified unity and consisted in one thing and one thing only. Morienus wrote: "For it is one Stone, one med'cin, in which consists the whole magistery" – and the *Scala philosophorum* stated: "The Stone is one: Yet this one is not one in Number, but in kind."[8]

The play between unity and multiplicity, the one and the many, identity and difference, manifests itself in many ways throughout the alchemical literature.

The making of the Philosophers' Stone was said to require an understanding "of the laws of nature so that [the alchemist] can reproduce God's macrocosmic creation in the microcosm of the alembic."[9] To achieve this union, one had to begin with the *prima materia* or "principal substance of the Stone"[10] which was known as philosophical mercury or, more accurately, Mercurius, a substance philosophically different from the physical materialism of chemical mercury. Within natural substances, the alchemists discovered "living . . . seeds" "necessary for the generation of the Stone in the *dialectic of creation*."[11] Just what is meant by these "living seeds"? "Jung has written that by the fourteenth century it had begun to dawn on the alchemists that the Stone was something more than an alchemical compound."[12] Jung here was alluding to the psychic and spiritual components of material reality discovered by the alchemical imagination. Abraham notes that

> the spiritual component of Alexandrine and Islamic alchemy entered Europe as an integral part of that science. Zosimos of Panopolis . . . had written that the alchemist must seek his origin in order to "obtain the proper, authentic, and natural tinctures" and that this was accomplished by "plunging into meditation."[13]

Jung finds innumerable alchemical references to support the idea that images of the Stone were to be discovered within oneself and that the imagination was a major component for the achievement of the alchemical goal.[14] In short, for Jung, alchemy and its goal, the Philosophers' Stone, came to be seen as a religious philosophy and as a precursor to his psychology of the unconscious. For Jung, the "living seeds" of alchemy were to be formed through philosophical and psychological awareness, though looking into the essence of the human soul through meditation, imagination, and dialectics. For Jung, advancing our knowledge of alchemy and the Philosophers' Stone required that we understand the alchemical philosophers as philosophers, as adepts dealing not simply with literal and material realities, but with philosophical substances and philosophical issues that had been of concern from time immemorial and throughout history.[15]

The importance of philosophy for understanding alchemy and the Philosophers' Stone is underlined by Jung who refers to the alchemist Raymond Lully as saying that "owing to their ignorance men are not able to accomplish the work until they have studied universal philosophy, which will show them things that are unknown and hidden from others."[16] And quoting Richardus Anglicus: "There is no way by which this art can truly be found . . . except by completing their studies and understanding the words of the philosophers."[17]

Jung's approach to alchemy has had an enormous effect on the historiography of alchemy. Some historians support Jung's spiritual and psychological understanding of alchemy, but others do not. Some current historiographers who are critical of Jung believe that the spiritual/psychological interpretation of alchemy is a bogus one, as is his universalist interpretation of it. What appears as a split in the alchemical imagination continues to pervade the literature of historians, psychologists, and philosophers alike.

Perhaps it is not surprising then that one of the most persistent philosophical themes that runs through my study of alchemy is the problem of opposites and the attempt to resolve them. Jung's notion of the Self and the Philosophers' Stone represent the end product and goal of the effort to resolve such opposites. For Jung, the Self was a modern psychological equivalent of the Philosophers' Stone, but both notions remain enigmatic and each has undergone continuing reformulations over time.

Jung's idea of the Self has also been challenged by a growing ferment within the Jungian tradition. James Hillman criticized the notion of the Self and in its place he developed what for him was a less "metaphysical" notion: the soul. He considered this a better phenomenological description of both what Jung was after and as a way of moving beyond the limits of Jung's perspective. Likewise, Wolfgang Giegerich via Hegel went further along this path by centralizing the notion of spirit and developing the idea of the soul's logical life. Each of these formulations has analytic and philosophical implications and offers different views of the subject/self and of human "nature" and "purpose." As such, these are not only psychological concerns but philosophical ones as well. These differing views, based on self, soul, and/or spirit, have implications for how alchemy and the Philosophers' Stone are understood as well. Following these threads and tracking the Philosophers' Stone into its various historiographic and psychological variations sets the stage for continuing philosophical reflection.

One of the major orienting concerns of Jungian psychology and of alchemy has been the unification of opposites and the attempt to come to terms with binaries. The notion of the Philosophers' Stone and the Self represent the goals of the alchemical and psychoanalytic processes respectively. Such goals have been understood and symbolized in many ways and refer generally to ideas of "wholeness." Jungian psychology as a modern discipline has contributed to our understanding of the process and goal of alchemy. While doing so, it has also gained a great deal from alchemy and has advanced our understanding of the psychology of the unconscious as well as opening up interesting philosophical issues. As noted above, Jung understood alchemy to be a philosophical endeavor and though I consider the Jungian approach to be a "philosophically" oriented psychology, I believe that further research into the philosophical meaning of the goal of alchemy would continue to enhance our understanding of it.

Both Hillman and Giegerich challenged the philosophical parameters of Jung's approach and for both of them, though in very different ways, philosophical understanding was implicitly and explicitly important in their reflections. While many philosophical orientations influenced Jung, Hillman, and Giegerich, Jung's notion of the Self was significantly influenced by Asian philosophy, whereas Hillman's idea of soul drew on neo-Platonic influences, and Giegerich's notion of the spirit was largely influenced by Hegel.[18]

When read in a certain way, Hegel's dialectic and his notions of "Absolute Knowing" and "Absolute Spirit" can be useful ideas, helpful to consider in connection with the idea of the Philosophers' Stone, as a unity that is complex and differentiated. While finding Hegel's philosophy to be relevant to my interest in the goal of alchemy, I have been suspicious of

Giegerich's "Hegelian" understanding of spirit as promoting a final sub-lation, as raising spirit above image and imagination, and of his seeing syntax and form as "true psychology" beyond the semantics of the ego, content, and "picture thinking" (images). For Giegerich, it is clear that spirit surpasses soul, as soul is seen by Jung and Hillman.

In my work, I have struggled with Hegel and with the way Giegerich adapts Hegel's ideas for his own philosophical position. Giegerich's inter-pretation appears to have precedent in Hegel's hierarchical placement of philosophy above art and religion, and thus also above imagination, image, and soul in Jung and Hillman's sense. I have argued against an interpre-tation of Hegel that promotes the elevation of idea and spirit in such a manner. As I have continued to read Hegel, I have also found a number of interpretations of his philosophy and ways of reading him that have prompted me to rethink and reinterpret his point of view and its relevance for understanding Jung, alchemy, and the Philosophers' Stone.

In my final chapters, I consider the work of Donald Verene, Karin De Boer, Kathleen Dow Magnus, William Desmond, Slavoj Žižek, Tom Rockmore, and Edward S. Casey; all of whom in different ways open up perspectives that are imaginative and challenging and that, along with and contrary to Giegerich's point of view, have allowed me to deepen my reflections.[19] Desmond has noted that in philosophy we must avoid quick and easy solutions and while I would say that philosophy helps to clarify issues, it also "does not dispel our perplexity but deepens it."[20]

I find such a perplexity in Rockmore's reading of Hegel's notion of the Absolute. For Rockmore, the Absolute cannot be seen as a completely ontological statement and, even though Absolute, it is also relative in its dependence on the historical moment and thus also always relative to time and place. For Rockmore as for Hegel, philosophy is ultimately tied to the history of ideas. For Desmond, "philosophy must acknowledge its own plurivocity;" it does not speak with only a voice "of a dominating univocal logicism."[21]

For me, the multiple voices are both within philosophy and between phi-losophy and its others – in my case, particularly between philosophy and psychology, spirit, and soul. My reflections in this book are drawn from my history and thus from both "fields." In writing a book on philosophy, I could not part completely with psychology, but I cannot write psycho-logically without also writing and thinking philosophically. In this ten-sion between "fields," I find Casey's reflections resonate with my struggle.

Casey writes: "Philosophy and Psychology – how will this strange twain meet? Or have they not always already met – but in a way unknown to each other?"[22] For Casey, these fields appear alien and have strict boundaries, but for him this aggravates the problem. Putting it otherwise, he asks "how are we to join – or rejoin, or to see as already conjoined – spirit and soul?"[23] With this question, Casey addresses my own concern about philosophy and psychology, as well as about the tension between image and idea, spirit and soul. In Casey's work, he finds a "place" where "spirit and soul not only *will* meet but . . . already [have] met" and are held together in meaning, imagination, and image, and in a linking between philosophy and psychology.[24]

In the following chapters, I intend to think through the problems and complexity of a number of divides in the history of alchemy and in the alchemical imagination. In this book, I intend to deepen the process of resolving these divides by turning to philosophy in ways that shed light on the Philosophers' Stone and Jung's notion of the Self.

Hegel is one figure whose ideas can be seen to penetrate into the dynamics of the Philosophers' Stone and to a complex unification of opposites that is resolved in his idea of Absolute Knowing and Absolute Spirit. Hegel's view of the Absolute is not best read as an ontological conviction or abstract theory privileging idea over image, form over content, syntax over semantics, and I will argue that while there is evidence in Hegel's work for privileging the first term of the above binaries, there are many readings of his work that demonstrate the profound and inseparable connection between image and idea, form and content, syntax and semantics, and the timelessness of the Absolute and its relative history in time and place. I believe it is this latter reading that deepens our understanding of what has been called the Philosophers' Stone and it is this kind of Absolute Knowing that has continued to inspire inquiry into the alchemists and into contemporary psychology and philosophy. The concept of the Philosophers' Stone is an ancient way of expressing what Jung considered to be the Self. Both the Stone and the Self can be given philosophical expression in terms of the notion of Absolute Knowing, but this knowing has been variously understood by numerous depth psychologists and philosophers in alternate ways. Part of my work in this book is to suggest that their alternative understandings can throw new light on the Philosophers' Stone, the goal of alchemy, and of Jung's psychology of the Self.

Notes

1 Abraham, *A Dictionary of Alchemical Imagery*, 145.
2 Jung, *Memories*, 204.
3 Ibid.
4 Jung, *Psychology and Alchemy (CW12)*, §555.
5 Abraham, *A Dictionary of Alchemical Imagery*, 145.
6 Gratacolle, "The Names of the Philosophers' Stone," 67.
7 Jung, *Mysterium Coniunctionis (CW14)*, §643.
8 Abraham, *A Dictionary of Alchemical Imagery*, 148.
9 Ibid., 146.
10 Ibid.
11 Ibid.; emphasis mine.
12 Ibid., 147.
13 Ibid.
14

> "Calid had stated that 'This Stone is to be found at all times, in everie place, and about every man." This tradition was inherited by the medieval alchemists and the alchemists of Renaissance Europe. Many were aware of the fact that the Stone or the matter for making the Stone was to be found in man himself. Ripley wrote: "Every-ech Man yt hath, and ys in every place/ In thee, in me, in every tyme and space, and Philalethes wrote that Morienus informed his pupil, the king, that he must 'descend/ I Into himself the matter for to finde/Of this our stone." Gerhard Dorn likewise indicated that panacea was the truth to be found in man. Colson's *Philosophia maturata* states that the Stone "is generated between Male and Female and lieth hide [sic] in Thee, in Me, and in such like things." In the production of the Stone, the alchemist was advised to employ his imagination as the major tool. Arnoldus is cited in Zoroaster's Cave: "Follow it with the Instance of Labour, but first exercise thyself in a diuturnity of Intense Imagination: for so thou mayst find the compleat Elixir; but without that never at all." (Ibid.)

15 See Panisnick, "The Philosophical Significance."
16 Jung, *Psychology and Alchemy (CW12)*, §365.
17 Ibid., §362.
18 It is interesting and perhaps not surprising since the goals of alchemy and analysis are concerned with the unity of binary oppositions that Hegel's *Philosophy of Spirit* and his *Logic* have been important to a number of contemporary scholars who bring his work to bear on both the Freudian and Jungian traditions. In terms of the Freudian tradition, see the work of Jacques Lacan, Slavoj Žižek, and Jon Mills. For the Jungian tradition, see Sean Kelly, Sanford Drob, and Wolfgang Giegerich.
19 Giegerich's appreciation and interpretation of Hegel is important for today's psychology, however, he is only one of several thinkers who have come to similar conclusions. Giegerich has brought Hegelian reflections to the work of Jungian psychology in *The Soul's Logical Life* and in *Dreaming the Myth Onwards*. Also see Mills, *The Unconscious Abyss*; Žižek, *Less Than Nothing*.
20 Desmond, *Beyond Hegel*, xi.
21 Ibid.
22 Casey, *Spirit and Soul*, xi.
23 Ibid.
24 Ibid., xviii.

Chapter 1

Philosophical tensions in the historiography of alchemy

The history of science and the history of the human spirit

Alchemy is a vast subject and the Philosophers' Stone is one of its most enigmatic ideas. The Stone was considered the ultimate achievement of the "Great Work" of alchemy and the elusive goal of alchemical trans-formation. The Philosophers' Stone has been described in numerous ancient manuscripts and in many recipes for its production, and with considerable disagreement about its nature and appearance as well as about how it was to be discovered and/or made. These disagreements have followed the Stone throughout its history and alchemists have argued with one another about the materials, procedures, and the reality of the Stone. In spite of overlapping claims, many alchemical treatises proclaim their own recipes as the correct one for the achievement of alchemy's sought-after goal. It was not unusual at the beginning of an alchemical treatise for the writer to begin by mercilessly denouncing other adepts, calling them charlatans, "puffers," and fools. In the midst of such controversy and confusion, the Philosophers' Stone remained shrouded in mystery.

Richard Grossinger has noted that "[a]lchemy is primeval. Those who would give its origin must also realize: there are no origins."[1]

> Alchemy is a form that comes to us from the most ancient times. Its survival bespeaks numerous redefinitions and rebirths, many of them known to us from texts (Egyptian, Greek, Roman, Christian, Euro-pean, Islamic, Hindu, Taoist);[2] but [he speculates] an equally large number no doubt occurring in preliterate times and among unknown people whose writings never reached us.[3]

DOI: 10.4324/9781003215905-2

Philosopher George David Panisnick (1975) likewise states that the reason why the Stone's origin is so problematic is due to the supposition "that it seems to have evolved out of a pre-alchemical consciousness which was concerned with . . . lithic myths."[4] Mircea Eliade, the well-known historian of religion, identifies a number of these myths, some of which play an important role as background for the alchemical idea of the Philosophers' Stone. Two provocative mythologems include the idea that the Stone generates and ripens in the bowels of the earth and that men are born from stones.[5] Alan Cardew amplifies these myths noting the living qualities of what we now consider inorganic materials. In them he finds what "were like veins of blood in animal life. . . [and] were akin to stars."[6] The implications of such ideas point to a way of thinking in which man and nature were intrinsically co-implicated and what Cardew calls a "dark hermetic equivalence,"[7] a way of imagining that is implicit in the well-known alchemical idea "as above so below." For Cardew, "[d]escending into the black labyrinths of the earth and exploring caverns was a journey back to the archaic, which was still at work with a daemonic magical force."[8] In such a descent into our history one could learn to discover and read the "primal plant . . . primal animal . . . and the primal stone (or *Urstein*)" which, according to E.T.A. Hoffmann, mirror the "secrets which are hidden above the clouds."[9]

It is hard for our modern consciousness to enter into such archaic and mythical thinking, but for Eliade it is necessary to do so to gain some sense of the worldview that lies behind many alchemical ideas, including the Philosophers' Stone. For Eliade, entering into the archaic and mythic imagination gives us a glimpse of how early societies related to what we now call "matter." He writes that the purpose of his study was

> to gain an understanding of the behavior of primitive societies in relation to Matter and to follow the spiritual adventures in which they became involved when they found themselves aware of their power to change the mode of being of substances.[10]

Eliade points out that the idea of the modification and transformation of substances is a key element of the alchemists' *"raison d'être."* In the world of the alchemists, "nature" was animated by a natural *telos* and entelechy that moved it toward its destiny and completion. The role of the ancient metallurgists and smiths, like that of the alchemists, was to cooperate with nature and to assist in the acceleration of the birth process helping it to bring to fruition its implicit goal. For many alchemists, this goal was the Philosophers' Stone. In this view, nature was alive, animated, and the engagement with "matter" was a sacred work, intertwined with initiation rites and mysteries.

While Eliade does not claim an unbroken connection between the early miners and smiths and the alchemists, he does posit a common "magico-religious"[11] worldview in which subject and object, psyche and matter, philosophically overlap and are intrinsically interrelated. From Eliade's perspective, contrary to some historians of science, alchemy was not simply a rudimentary chemistry, but was a sacred discipline first. It only became rudimentary chemistry when, "for the majority of its practitioners, its mental world had lost its validity and its *raison d'être*."[12] So, for Eliade, "chemistry was born . . . from the disintegration of the ideology of alchemy."[13] But, we will see, this is a point of view denied by many contemporary historians of science. Historians of science typically distinguish a fundamental discontinuity between alchemy and chemistry. Eliade maintains the validity of his research into the origins of science and technology, but also states that "the perspective of the historian of chemistry is perfectly defensible" in the sense that alchemy and chemistry each "work on the same mineral substances, uses the same apparatus, and generally speaking applies itself to the same experiments."[14] In this sense, alchemy and chemistry share these functional similarities. However, if we view the relationship between these similar but different endeavors "from the standpoint of the history of the human spirit we see the matter quite differently."[15] Alchemy continued to be a sacred science and "chemistry came into its own when substances had shed their sacred attributes"[16] and the alchemists their ritual practices.

This divide in the way of understanding the relationship of alchemy and chemistry continues to this day, and the history of science and the history of religion constitute very different historiographic positions; there remains a split in our contemporary imagination reflecting different philosophical perspectives. While it is clear that both alchemists and chemists carried out physical experiments in their laboratories, how these operations were understood and experienced were considerably different. Eliade notes that the chemist

> carries out his exact observations of physico-chemical phenomena and performs systematic experiments in order to penetrate to the structure

of matter. The alchemist on the other hand, is concerned with the "passion," "the death," the "marriage" of substances in so far as they will tend to transmute matter and human life. His goals were the Philosophers' Stone and the Elixir Vitae.[17]

Eliade's main concern in and through his analysis of the "historico-cultural context . . . has been to pierce through to the mental world which lies behind them."[18] For Eliade, "[o]nly by looking at things from the standpoint of the alchemist will we succeed in gaining insight into his mental world and thereby appraise the extent of its originality."[19] It was this intention that opened Eliade to Jung's perspective, which was both a psychological and philosophical shift in worldview with implications for religious studies as well. He notes that "Jung's observations are of interest not only to depth psychology; they also indirectly confirm the soteriological [the study of religious doctrine of salvation] function which is one of the main constituents of alchemy."[20]

For Eliade, as for Jung, "soteriological" applies to the alchemists and to the perspective that alchemy was a philosophy of religion. For Eliade, "Without a shadow of doubt, the Alexandrian alchemists were from the beginning aware that in pursuing the perfection of metals they were pursuing their own perfection."[21] Eliade confirms the above position historically by noting the *Liber Platonis quartorum* (which in its original Arabic cannot be later than the tenth century), which "gives great importance to the parallelism between the *opus alchymicum* and the inner experience of the adept."[22] The alchemist's work to achieve the state of an illuminated philosopher is also stated by Gerhard Dorn – a sixteenth century physician, philosopher, and alchemist – in the form of a challenge: "Transform yourself from dead stones into living philosophic stones."[23] Here Dorn addresses man as a Stone with a potential for transformation.[24] Another example is taken from Morienus addressing himself to King Kallid: "For this substance [that is, the one which conceals the divine secret] is extracted from you and you are its ore."[25] In short, for Eliade and Jung, "the Western alchemist, in his laboratory . . . worked upon himself – upon his psycho-physiological and philosophical life as well as on his moral and spiritual experience."[26] The alchemist must be totally engaged in the opus.

Eliade describes the ethical values attributed to alchemical works noting that the alchemist "must be healthy, humble, patient, chaste; his mind must be free and in harmony with his work; he must be intelligent and scholarly, he must work, meditate, pray. . . "[27] While these ethical virtues guide the way for the alchemists' work, in themselves they cannot produce the goal the alchemists sought. Eliade is quick to point out that in addition to such virtues an initiatory process is necessary to produce philosophical illumination and the attainment of the Philosophers' Stone or elixir of life.

Jung and the study of alchemy

There are many renditions of the alchemical process both in original alchemical sources as well as in secondary descriptions and interpretations of it. The general alchemical literature is considerable; several thousand books were published between the sixteenth through eighteenth centuries. A somewhat smaller number are known to focus on the process of creating the Philosophers' Stone. The books focusing on the discovery and development of the Philosophers' Stone run through the literature. A few important ones include: *The Secret of the Golden Flower* (8th century), the *Artis auriferae, volumina duo* (1593), *Rosarium philosophorum* (1550), and the *Aurora consurgens* (15th century). In addition, other manuscripts of value include *Splendor Solis* (1532–35), the Twelve Keys of Basil Valentine (1599/1602), the Crowning of Nature (16th century), *Philosophia reformata* of J.D. Mylius (1622), the Ripley Scroll of Sir George Ripley (15th century), and finally the *Mutus liber*, or the wordless or mute book (1677). All of these texts are replete with alchemical illustrations depicting the transformative process mostly aiming at the presentation of the Philosophers' Stone.

Many of alchemy's original manuscripts were studied and interpreted by Jung.[28] The careful study of his work on alchemy is a demanding task and the study of the Philosophers' Stone, even "simply" in the context of the above work, is also demanding. In the index noted above, reference to the lapis/*Lapis Philosophorum* (Philosophers' Stone)[29] spans twelve of Jung's twenty volumes, including Collected Works 4, 5, 8, 9i, 9ii, 10, 11, 12, 13, 14, 16, and 18, to say nothing of the yet unpublished work on alchemy in process with the Philemon Foundation. In addition, a proper study of the Philosophers' Stone requires cross-references to other related topics including Jung's notion of the individuation process and the Self. In short, to have a comprehensive understanding of the Philosophers' Stone in Jung's work requires nearly an overall grasp of his complete corpus and a book-length study in its own right. Nevertheless, it is possible to get a general grasp of his understanding of the stone and its meaning in the context of his psychology of the unconscious which can serve as a ground for this study.

In addition, Jung's understanding of alchemy made a major if now controversial impact on the historiography of alchemy, both in the history of science and chemistry as well as in the history of esotericism. Jung's approach to alchemy is now part of these historiographical perspectives and might be said to exist at the crossroads between them. Historian of chemistry "Gerhard Heym wrote that no modern authority prior to Jung had been able to decipher the 'abstruse and obscure' vocabulary . . . of Paracelsus."[30]

Likewise, eminent scholar Walter Pagel noted that Jung's interpretation of alchemical symbolism "will be fundamental for all future studies on the subject."[31] He sums up Jung's contribution noting that:

[Jung] succeeds: (1) in placing alchemy into an entirely new perspective in the history of science, medicine, theology and general human culture, (2) in explaining alchemical symbolism, hitherto a complete puzzle, by utilizing modern psychological analysis for the elucidation of an historical problem and – vice versa – making use of the latter for the advancement of modern psychology; and all this is a scholarly, well documented and scientifically unimpeachable exposition. If not the *whole* story of alchemy, he has tackled its "mystery," its "Nachtseite," i.e., the problem most urgent and vexing to the historian.[32]

Criticisms of Jung and Eliade (Principe and Newman)

Not all historians of alchemy have a positive judgment about Jung or of a spiritual or psychological understanding of alchemy in general. Two such contemporary researchers who have had a significant impact on the field are Lawrence Principe and William R. Newman. Principe points to a wealth of recent historical studies that have changed our understanding of alchemy radically during the last forty years. These studies point to the fact that mistakes in the historiography of alchemy have been repeated over and over again and that a fundamental step in coming to understand alchemy is to clear away many taken-for-granted errors. Principe and Newman argue that a fundamental difficulty in the study of alchemy has been the lack of reliable, trustworthy, contextual scholarship into its history. They note that a common failing of many interpretations of alchemy is the tendency to see it "as a uniform and constant monolith"[33] that overlooks the differentiations among the many different alchemies. They criticize Jung's archetypal perspective largely on this basis and state that the aim of continuing research is to "elucidate the spectrum of notions, attitudes, and pursuits generally grouped under the wide umbrella of 'alchemy' and to portray it as a vastly more dynamic field than has hitherto been presumed."[34]

In a more recent publication, Principe makes the distinction between alchemy and "alchemies" to underline his point that "the diversity and dynamism within historical alchemy is sufficiently extensive that historians have now begun to group individual authors and practitioners within 'schools' and to see the differences among their practices and goals."[35] Principe's work on the historiography of alchemy has been valuable and has made an important impact on other researchers in alchemy, particularly historians of science and chemistry. While Principe champions the importance of careful differentiations in the field, he does not seem to be aware that his own point of view has a strong philosophical bias that is not universally accepted by other credible academic historians. Important aspects of his perspective have been challenged by Hereward Tilton (2003), Florin George Căliăn (2010), Wouter Hanegraaff (2012), Aaron Cheak, and others. These researchers, while appreciating and accepting a number of Principe's and Newman's contributions, also note their bias toward reducing alchemy to their own monolithic orientation of a "natural philosophy" and an exclusively "natural scientific" perspective, to the exclusion of the vital history of esotericism and other philosophical orientations.

I would consider this a brand of historical and scientific positivism, though Principe and Newman are uncomfortable with this designation, "because of the diffuseness of [the term's] common use."[36] They differentiate their position from the kind of "positivism" that imposes its current scientific notions on the field of alchemy without sufficient interest "in the historical and cultural context of those ideas."[37] They label the above variety of positivism as " 'presentist' or 'Whig' historiography," meaning projecting current views anachronistically back on the historical context of alchemy, "which assigns relative importance to historical ideas based upon their level of connection with or similarity to current scientific notions."[38] For them, such a position shows "insufficient interest in the historical and cultural context of those ideas."[39]

It is interesting, however, that Principe and Newman, while seemingly open to the historical and cultural context of alchemical ideas beyond a "presentist" scientific perspective, seem singularly hostile and closed-minded about spiritual and psychological interpretations of alchemy. Further, they appear to hold an unscholarly, undifferentiated, and monolithic view with regard to these aspects of alchemical historiography. In their criticisms, they cite Eliade and Jung, but also historian Hélène Metzger who, in her emphasis on vitalism, ended up supporting the symbolic vision of alchemy elaborated by Jung and Eliade. In addition, they discount Eliade and Jung for their tendency to view alchemy as a "chronological constant" and, in so doing, they also indict a host of earlier and current historiographers of alchemy who have adopted a spiritual and psychological dimension of alchemy "without being aware of . . . their 'unsuitability.'"[40] The aspects of alchemy that Eliade and Jung have seen as symbolic, psychological, and religious are described by Principe and Newman as alien, strange, "bizarre,"[41] and "outlandish."[42] Not surprisingly, these aspects do not fit into their natural scientific worldview as being credible expressions of the alchemical mind. For Principe and Newman, these "ostensibly bizarre texts"[43] and their symbols are in essence code-names (*Decknamen*) for the language of the laboratory and of natural philosophy and, therefore, there is no need to interpret them into spiritual, psychological terms. For them, such prosaic translations serve to show that there is no need to divide *chemia* from *alchemia* in early modern texts and they go as far as to recommend that in early modern texts we can eliminate the term alchemy altogether. In essence, with the elimination of *alchemia* they simply dismiss what for Eliade and Jung were fundamental aspects of alchemy, namely its status as a religious philosophy with its importance as an initiatory practice. In the reduction of *alchemia* to *chemia*, there is nothing for Principe and Newman to worry about outside their field of expertise as chemists and positive historians. The philosophical underpinnings of their worldview remain taken for granted. As noted above, there are still credible historians of science who do not agree with such reductions of the alchemical worldview, even if they accept some of the research and insight provided by some of the less prejudicial views of Principe and Newman.

Limitations of Principe's and Newman's Criticisms (Tilton, Căliăn, Hanegraaff, Cheak)

Hereward Tilton

Tilton's work on the historiography of alchemy is a far more balanced study, which includes more informed and scholarly accounts of Eliade,

Jung, and the history of esotericism. While appreciating the contributions of Principe and Newman, he is also critical of them. In the Introduction to his book *The Quest for the Phoenix* (2003), he affirms the importance of seeing alchemy as part of the history of esotericism as well as within the history of science, and in his study he enters into both of these arenas of discourse. He notes that the arguments of Principe and Newman are concerned "not only with questions of historiography and nomenclature," but also with "the very nature of laboratory alchemy in the sixteenth and seventeenth centuries and its relation to the esoteric traditions."[44] Tilton's study of alchemist Michael Maier links Maier's religious ideas to his laboratory work and points out that Maier's role in the history of Western esotericism in itself presents difficulties for the assertions of Principe and Newman.

For Tilton, as well as for Eliade and Jung, if the study of esotericism is taken seriously, then the term "alchemy" is indispensable. Within this context, Tilton reconsiders "the reception of Jung and his psychoanalytic approach amongst historians of alchemy,"[45] recalling Jung's idea "that alchemical symbolism expresses psychological processes of an essentially religious nature [which had] wide currency in the academic study of alchemy."[46] While it is often pointed out that Jung reduced alchemy to psychology, Tilton is aware that for Jung both chemistry and psychology have emerged from it. Tilton quotes Jung: "I had long been aware that alchemy is not only the mother of chemistry, but is also the forerunner of our modern psychology of the unconscious."[47]

Nevertheless, those critical of Jung's approach claim that he overly minimizes the scientific content of alchemy. This position was expressed even by those who otherwise valued Jung's contributions. This was true even for Pagel who was an opponent of positivism in the history of science and who had also felt that "Jung had revolutionized the academic study of alchemy."[48] Pagel felt that "Jung's theories were an antidote to the positivist view of science."[49] Following in the spirit of Pagel, John Read commented "that it had required 'the discernment of a master' to elucidate the intimate relationship of alchemy to psychology."[50] Tilton points to both the support and criticism of other historians including Eduard Farber, Maurice Crosland, and Betty Dobbs. Dobbs, though critical of

> Jung's ahistorical approach, . . . followed Jung's historiography . . . describing an "older" ancient and medieval alchemy in which

psychological processes remained largely unconscious to the adept, and a "newer" alchemy arising with the advent of the Reformation, in which divisions began to appear between a conscious alchemical mysticism and an experientially-based alchemy.[51]

Tilton points out, however, that though Dobbs followed Jung's "distinction between a 'scientific' and a 'spiritual' alchemy . . . she did not believe Jung's work supported the notion of a radical discontinuity in the evolution of chemistry."[52]

More critical of Jung's historiography was Barbara Obrist, a French historian of alchemy, who "lamented" that Jung's perspective had taken on "the status of a self-evident truth and was no longer questioned by historians of alchemy."[53] For her, Jung's mistakes were later reinforced by Eliade. The two major views of Jung and Eliade that she criticizes were the fundamental religiosity of the alchemists and their animistic vitalist worldviews. Her work, which preceded Principe's and Newman's, argues the same point: that there was no good evidence to presume that "laboratory workers of this time were engaged in a spiritual quest for selfhood."[54] For her, Jung "projected the Protestant myth of the solitary, interior search into the Middle Ages."[55] She also claims that both Eliade and Jung simply copied Hélène Metzger, who sought to distinguish alchemy from mechanistic chemistry and instead saw it as having a vitalistic and organic view of the cosmos.

Newman follows and develops this criticism citing both Obrist and Robert Halleux as "serious" historians of alchemy who reject Jung. Tilton takes issue with a number of methodological and factual errors of both Principe and Newman. For one, he notes that Halleux holds no overt anti-Jungian position. In fact, he points out that Halleux praises Jung for his "scrupulous adherence to the fruits of erudition concerning the dating and authorship of texts, and speaks of Jung's 'brilliant' exegeses of certain particularly 'mystical' texts such as the Hellenistic Egyptian *Visions of Zosimos*."[56] Tilton shows that Halleux – contrary to Principe and Newman, who use him to criticize Jung – is in fact more critical of Obrist.

Another problem with Principe's and Newman's characterization of Jung is that they slant their language in a way to defame both him and the esoteric tradition they dislike and apparently know little about. Demonstrating this point, Tilton quotes Newman's caricature of the Jungian interpretation of the work of Philalethes. Newman, apparently in the service of mocking Jung's position, states that Philalethes' work is not "'the product of a disordered mind' [i.e., projection of the unconscious] or the work of 'an irrational mystic unable to express himself in clear English.'"[57] Newman misunderstands Jung's notion of projection, contrasting it to his idealized version of clear and distinct ideas, a Cartesian bias. Tilton notes, "It matters little [to Newman] that 'irrational mystics' have given rise to some of the finest literature in the English language."[58] For Tilton, what is at stake here is the devaluation of the mystical and religious aspects of alchemy. Tilton sums up:

> if we follow Principe and Newman in counterposing a positively valued "correct chemical analysis" carried out by "serious historians of alchemy" with a negatively valued "analysis of unreason," we not only run the risk of committing a violence against the texts at hand, but we also perform a disservice to contemporary scholarship on the subject of alchemy by excluding certain voices (principally those of psychoanalysts) from the realms of valid discourse.[59]

Another charge against Jung is the common one that he completely dismissed laboratory alchemy. While clearly Jung's breakthrough and expertise were in psychology, he in no way indicated that the alchemists were not engaged with the "material" reality in their alembics. Tilton points to the way Principe and Newman misrepresent comments about this issue by replacing what Jung said about the alchemists as dealing "*not only* with chemical experiments" with their rendition which states "*not* with chemical experiments *as such*."[60] With such emphasis, Principe and Newman more easily accuse Jung of concluding that the alchemists discounted alchemical substances and simply projected psychological reality on them. What is not pointed out and perhaps not understood is that projection for Jung is an unconscious process that goes on all the time. For Jung, the majority of alchemists were not in any way aware that there was a psychological dimension to what they were seeing and experiencing. They were indeed focused on the literal "reality" of their substances without realizing that through projection there was an "admixture of unconscious psychic material"[61] that was part of the alchemist's experience whether he/she was conscious of it or not. Extracting these projections yielded an understanding of the psychology of the alchemical experience that until Jung's insight was simply seen as irrational. Even for those alchemists whom Jung considered conscious of the psychological dimensions of the work, there was no indication that he "wrote laboratory experimentation out of the picture" when considering such individuals. Thus Jung describes Paracelsus as "*both* the father of modern pharmacology *and* 'a pioneer of empirical psychology and psychotherapy.'"[62]

Tilton acknowledges that Jung's notion of alchemy as "a great timeless unit"[63] is problematic, but Principe and Newman criticize Jung for saying that any alchemical texts that could be decoded into modern chemical language is inferior alchemy. Tilton points out that there is no evidence for this, noting only that Jung's comments about good and bad alchemical authors referred merely to the fact that there were many charlatans in the field who mystified their work to delude others.[64] Jung was not unaware that some of the strangeness of alchemical images and symbols were utilized by alchemists as code names for chemical substances. But, as Tilton points out, this fact should not be used to suggest that this proves that the primary reality of natural philosophy or "chemistry" was the only truly "real" level of legitimate understanding. Tilton points out that the flaw in the explanation is Principe and Newman's "either-or logic – *either* the symbols of alchemy are products of the unconscious psyche, *or* they are secret code-names for chemical substances."[65] For psychoanalysts, as in alchemical thinking, "a symbol may possess more than one significance."[66] Tilton describes Julius Ruska, whom Jung cites, as stating that "certain symbols in the history of alchemy have borne explicit religious and mystical significance alongside their narrowly chemical meaning."[67]

As for those symbols that emerge spontaneously throughout the alchemical work, Principe and Newman simply state "that the physical appearance of chemicals in the vessel is sometimes 'evocative.'"[68] Tilton rightly notes this "'explanation' is not explanation at all."[69] Then he goes on to say:

> When Theobald de Hoghelande describes "the wonderful variety of figures that appear in the course of the [alchemical] work . . . just as we sometimes imagine in the clouds or in the fire strange shapes of animals, reptiles or trees," there can be no doubt that the "arbitrary" [spontaneous] symbols of alchemy are evoked from the psyche of the individual alchemist as much as from the physical processes in the vessel.[70]

Tilton recognizes that the so-called arbitrary symbolism is for the psycho-analyst anything but arbitrary. Rather, there is an underlying imaginative psycho-logical process at work in and through the chemical logic of the material.

While Tilton remains open and balanced about Jung's views, he still maintains with other historians (Pagel, Dobbs, Halleux, Obrist, Princ-ipe and Newman) a criticism of Jung's treatment of "its symbolism as a mythology of timeless origin in the collective psyche."[71] In holding this position, he states that "Jung failed to give an adequate account of the cultural matrix from which his own ideas emerged, and consequently failed to recognize the bewildering diversity of endeavors that – for bet-ter or worse – have been gathered together under the rubric of the term 'alchemy.'"[72]

The status and development of Jung's views of archetypes and the col-lective unconscious is another matter about which there is much to say, but this aside, Tilton makes an interesting connection between Jung and modern esotericism. He cites Antoine Faivre's "four fundamental charac-teristics of modern esotericism" and links them to the characteristics of Jung's psychology: the "doctrine of correspondences and sympathies; a belief in a living and revelatory Nature; an emphasis on imagination as the means of revelation; and the practical objective of personal 'transfor-mation' through such revelation."[73] Recognizing these characteristics sug-gests to Tilton "we are no longer dealing with a doctrine that stands in the realms of [natural] science as it is known today."[74] Jung was aware that his ideas and work had a connection with the Freemasonic and Rosicrucian traditions, but, if so, it also stood in relationship to the science of his day. Jung stood at a crossroads.

However, Jung's openness to the esoteric tradition led Principe and Newman to follow the writing of Richard Noll, a figure who certainly has been given little credence in Jungian psychology because of his extremist biases.[75] Tilton is aware of the poor historiography of Noll, an "ex-Jun-gian," in his attempt "to expose his former mentor as a dangerous right-wing cultist and charlatan."[76] It is interesting that though Principe and Newman emphasize a careful scholarly historiography of alchemy, when it comes to Jung, they choose an "authority" who has a "well-established predilection for sensationalism."[77] Tilton is also aware of the not-so-well-known fact that Noll "published a number of articles in which he garnered experiential evidence to support Jung's conceptions of the archetype, psychological projection, and a transpersonal and atemporal 'collective unconscious.'"[78] In his introduction to the *Encyclopedia of Schizophrenia and Psychotic Disorders*, Noll wrote of Jung with "adulation" as a "giant" on whose shoulders he had stood and he thanked "the deceased psychoanalyst, 'for the tremendous impact his life and work had on my life, both personally and professionally.'"[79]

Now, I don't think it reasonable to discount someone's judgments because he/she may have had a change of view. However, Noll's antagonism to Jung and Jungians seems to suggest an agenda. He writes in a hostile tone and with questionable scholarship, as already mentioned previously. It is surprising that sober researchers in the historiography of alchemy would rely so strongly on such a controversial figure whose attack on Jung has been addressed by an eminent scholar of Jungian history, Sonu Shamdasani, in his book *Cult Fictions: C.G. Jung and the Founding of Analytical Psychology.* As Tilton has noted, "Whatever genuinely religious foundations analytical psychology may possess, a comparison of Jungian psychotherapy to the millennialist cults in question was simply inaccurate and misleading from the perspective of the academic study of religion."[80]

Principe's and Newman's persistent efforts to discredit spiritual alchemy appear more like a campaign than an objective evaluation. Their unscholarly claim that the alchemy of the early modern period "worked on 'material substances toward material goals,'" for Tilton,

> merely begs the question as to the [philosophical] nature of matter itself in the early modern world view, and displays precisely the presentism and positivism Principe and Newman claim to disown, by which contemporary notions of matter are unconsciously elevated to the realm of the definitive.[81]

For Tilton, what is important then is to reflect on the nature of "matter" and "spirit" and not simply to counterpose "a narrowly 'chemical' hermeneutic with a psychological model such as that proposed by Jung."[82] In short, for Tilton a philosophical understanding of the meaning of "matter," "spirit," and "psyche" should not be taken for granted. Ultimately for Tilton, there remained a continuing importance and ideological congruence in the history of esotericism with regard to matters of alchemy and the Philosophers' Stone in the nineteenth century. This congruence "formed the basis for the alchemical hermeneutic proposed first by Silberer and then by Jung."[83] Tilton follows Jung's argument for a coherent "tradition," rooting and differentiating the historical contexts at their source, which was not new with Jung. Historiographic matters continue to evolve in the history of the alchemical tradition, but, as Tilton notes with regard to Jung, he

> placed his own work in the context of a lineage of *symbolic* import rather than a Tradition *per se*, as he argued that psychological or "spiritual" elements in alchemical practice prior to the sixteenth century "fission" of *physica* and *mystica* remained largely unconscious to the "adepts."[84]

Tilton sums up his criticism of Principe and Newman with the following statement:

> On this matter we might follow the good advice of the historian of alchemy E.J. Holmyard, who stated that "it must be left to the psychologists" to pronounce judgment on the "profound psychological study" put forward by Jung, rather than intruding into fields which are not our rightful domain. We should also keep in mind Holmyard's accurate depiction of Jung's view of medieval alchemy as a "chemical research worked into which there entered, by way of projection, an admixture of unconscious psychic material;" as we have shown, when Principe and Newman speak of "Jung's assertion that alchemy ceases to be alchemy when it becomes clear enough to be understood in chemical terms," they betray their fundamental misunderstanding of the psychology of the unconscious.[85]

While I agree with this assessment, it is also important to recognize the lack of philosophical clarification of the presupposed ideas that run through these debates.

Florin George Căliăn

Căliăn takes up and reviews a number of the controversies on the historiography of alchemy, noting what has become, as we have seen, a fundamental divide in the perspectives from which alchemy is understood. The general way of describing this divide is between the approach of the history of science, which sees alchemy as a proto-science and accentuates laboratory work, and what has been seen under the auspices of the history of religion and/or esotericism in which alchemy is seen as part of religious behavior and under the rubric of what has generally been called "spiritual alchemy." Caliăn further differentiates religious spiritual alchemy (Mircea Eliade), Western esotericism (Antoine Faivre), the hermetic tradition (Julian Evola and Titus Burckhardt), and also includes under this designation the hermeneutic practice of Umberto Eco as well as the psychological perspective of C.G. Jung.

Caliăn takes up the positions of Jung and Eliade as representing the spiritual tradition and critiques them on the basis of historians of science Principe and Newman. I will not reiterate these arguments since we have already referred to them previously. He rehearses this critique as a ground for his own evaluation, which arrives at the conclusion, like Tilton's, that studying "alchemy as only protoscience sets too narrow limitations."[86]

Caliăn describes Principe and Newman's thesis "as an attempt to introduce a kind of exclusivist position . . . into the field of scholarly research on alchemy."[87] A striking claim among others given the approaches named above is that "there is almost no connection between early modern alchemy and the Western esoteric tradition."[88] Noting as well Principe and Newman's criticism of Jung, he concludes that their critique of Jung "does not fully undermine Jungian research, taking into account that his purpose was almost totally different from that of a historian."[89]

Caliăn continues to articulate the limitations of the protoscience thesis and the unjustified aspects of Principe and Newman. He notes the dramatically inflexible rejection of "spiritual alchemy,"

> which is difficult to sustain in the case of many alchemical texts, as for example *Aurora consurgens*, The Ripley Scroll, or authors such as Michael Maier [studied by Tilton] or Jakob Böhme, to name only some works and authors that cannot fit into the thesis of those two historians of science.[90]

Caliăn also rightly criticizes Principe and Newman, as noted above, for asserting that "Jung was a kind of 'victim' of the occultism of the nineteenth century."[91] They appear to arrive at such a judgment by depending on "a bizarre book as their authority, that of Richard Noll, *The Jung Cult*, which rather comes from tabloid literature than from the academic world."[92] While Principe and Newman link Jung and Eliade to the esoteric school, they do not mention that Evola and Burckhardt respected Jung's psychological thesis which for them "somehow left alchemy without its metaphysical components and placed it in the psyche, as a product of it. Therefore, it is not esoteric knowledge that has its root in a transcendent reality."[93] Calian notes that "[f]or religious and esoteric temperaments Jung is too positivistic in approaching religion, and for the scientist he is too spiritual in approaching the history of science."[94] As noted earlier, Jung's "psychology" seems to stand at the crossroads between disciplines. Crossroads have traditionally been both dangerous and sacred places.

Calian notes that the efforts of Principe and Newman, the distinction between "spiritual" and "physical" alchemy is still prevalent in serious works on alchemy. He quotes historian of chemistry Bruce T. Moran whose thesis is much like Eliade's: through a change in its methods alchemy "gradually lost its spiritual or religious aspect and became chemistry at the time of the so-called scientific revolution."[95] What was lost in the transformation to the material science of chemistry was precisely alchemy's spiritual dimension, that is, that "[t]he successful alchemist gained control of life's forces and uncovered secret wisdom – the essence of all truths and religions."[96] While an exaggerated ideal, it is part of the fantasy of the Philosophers' Stone, an image that continues to haunt the religious esoteric as well as the psychological idea of alchemy's historical goal.

Calian also points to the fact that the divide between spiritual and laboratory alchemy can be found in medieval alchemy and not only in the nineteenth century as Principe and Newman suggested. Calian marshals evidence for his thesis, which "supports the idea that alchemy had a double character – it was a science (the mundane facet), but also a *donum Dei* (a supernatural facet). In this context," he notes, "Petrus connected *lapis* with Christ, which means a *lapis divinus*."[97] The divide advances in the Renaissance as the abundance of speculative alchemical works begins to lose connections with laboratory alchemy. However, to reduce the whole of speculative alchemy to only chemical research is patently wrong. There are, as Calian shows, many spiritual alchemists who are seekers of a *unio mystica*, including Villanova, Ripley, Fludd, Maier, and others; and, as Tilton has concluded, "there exists an ideological congruence in the history of esotericism pertaining to matters of alchemy."[98]

An important point made by Calian is that "there are differences in the perception of the spirituality of alchemy."[99] He points out that "for Maier alchemy is the ultimate speculative and spiritual discipline, for Böhme it is a tool to create analogies with his mystic theology, while Newton saw in alchemy the possibility of understanding the divine plan."[100] While spiritual alchemy does not present a single vision, "it is sure that, in the light of [the above differentiations] a pure empirical approach was insufficient."[101]

Caliăn concludes his article by criticizing Principe and Newman's labeling of alchemy as a primarily scientific and positivistic inquiry, and states that their criticism of Jung's and Eliade's spiritual views of alchemy relies on unscholarly sources and assumptions. While Principe and Newman totally reject spiritual alchemy and claim that Jung dismisses the scientific perspective, in fact, Jung affirms both the spiritual and scientific views of alchemy in their complexity. Rather, it is Principe and Newman's thesis which is one-sided and reductionistic.

The rejection of esotericism in the study of alchemy is untenable, and the "dual face" of alchemy remains a viable and necessary component of alchemical studies in the complexity of the field. While esoteric studies have been seen in a negative light by many academics, the field is in the process of academic revision.

Wouter Hanegraaff

The work of many recent scholars such as Wouter Hanegraaff has brought esoteric studies to a high scholarly standard. Hanegraaff's perspective on esoteric studies is succinctly described as follows:

> Academics tend to look on "esoteric," "occult," or "magical" beliefs with contempt, but are usually ignorant about the religious and philosophical traditions to which these terms refer, or their relevance to intellectual history. Wouter J. Hanegraaff tells the neglected story of how intellectuals since the Renaissance have tried to come to terms with a cluster of "pagan" ideas from late antiquity that challenged the foundations of biblical religion and Greek rationality. Expelled from the academy . . . these traditions have come to be perceived as the Other by which academics define their identity to the present day. Hanegraaff grounds his discussion in a meticulous study of primary and secondary sources . . . from the fifteenth century to the present day, and asking what implications the forgotten history of exclusion has for established textbook narratives of religion, philosophy, and science.[102]

Hanegraaff, like Tilton and Caliăn, takes issue with the positions and scholarship of Principe and Newman and, with regard to Jung, makes clarifying differentiations about laboratory and spiritual alchemy. He notes that in the heat of debate between critics and defenders of Jung, "both sides tend to underestimate the differences between Jung's original statements and what we find in translations and interpretations by later followers."[103] Hanegraaff calls critical attention to Principe and Newman as well as to Tilton. He notes that Principe's arguments against Jung are based on quotes from a 1940 English translation of Jung's work by Stanley Hall of an article that was originally published in the Eranos Yearbooks. On the basis of this translation, one can assume Jung's adherence to "spiritual alchemy." Hanegraaff notes Tilton's criticism of this interpretation by pointing to a more accurate passage from *Psychology and Alchemy* (1940), which reads: "In the alchemical work, we are dealing *for the greatest part not only* with chemical experiments, but *also* with something resembling psychic processes expressed in pseudo-chemical language."[104] Hanegraaff points out that "neither Tilton nor Principe/Newman seem to have looked at the original Eranos lecture, which undermines both their positions."[105] The Eranos lecture "begins with a statement that is remarkably *negative* about a purely 'spiritual' understanding of alchemical symbolism."[106] Hanegraaff quotes Jung as saying:

> Gradually during the course of the eighteenth century, alchemy fell victim to its own obscurity. . . . The inner decay of alchemy began more than a century earlier, already in the time of Jacob Böhme, when many alchemists left their retorts and crucibles and devoted themselves exclusively to the hermetic philosophy. At that time, the *chemist* separated himself from the *hermeticist*. Chemistry became natural science, but hermeticism lost the empirical ground under its feet and lost its way in allegories and speculations that were as bombastic as they were empty of content, and merely lived off the memories of a better time. This better time, however, was when the spirit of the alchemist still truly struggled with the problems of matter, when the investigating mind was facing the realm of the unknown and believed to perceive forms and laws in it.[107]

Such statements serve to show that Jung in no way affirmed a position of the spiritual alchemist over and against what the "chemist" was engaged with in the struggle with "matter." "In other words," for Hanegraaff "Jung calls purely 'spiritual' alchemy a degenerate phenomenon!"[108] For Hanegraaff, "the absurd idea . . . that for Jung alchemy as a historical phenomenon was essentially unconcerned with laboratory" practices was due to "defective" English translations of his work, which was then taken up by his English readers who were also unconcerned with the history of science.[109] "It would seem then that Principe's and Newman's criticism is applicable to the drift of popular Jungian (mis)interpretations of alchemy . . . rather than to Jung's own work."[110] Hanegraaff links the "spiritual alchemy" that was dismissed by Jung with the "spiritual alchemy" highlighted by Tilton, which for Jung was "bombastic" and "empty of content."[111] I remain uncertain and reserve judgment with regard to whether the spiritual alchemy Jung dismisses is in fact equivalent to what Tilton highlights. However, if Jung was critical of a disembodied spiritualization of alchemy, he was also critical of the reduction of the "substances" of the alchemists to a preconceived literalist understanding of the "material world." Jung's criticism raised the question of just what the natures of "spirit" and "matter" are, and challenged the presuppositions that are historically projected onto them. In any case, the divide in the alchemical imagination and in its historiography continues to struggle with this two-fold subject-object divide.

Aaron Cheak

Cheak attempts to avoid the divide, but notes that the tensions among differing orientations to alchemy was never easily resolved and that restrictive and reductive definitions and approaches to alchemy were, as we have seen, characteristic of its historiography, in their attempt to define alchemy as either/or material or spiritual in its authentic and primary nature. Cheak notes that alchemy has "always been two-fold: *chrysopoeia* and *apotheosis* (gold-making and god-making) – the perfection of metals and mortals."[112]

Cheak emphasizes that the earliest works of alchemy were not material and protoscientific, but ritualistic, and that alchemical practices were considered to have been given to humanity by the gods. Alchemy was thus "a *divine* art [and] a *hieratikē technē*."[113] Alluding to the earlier development of alchemical practices in China, Cheak cites the two basic traditions of internal *neidan* and external *waidan*. While these two traditions differ in approach, one emphasizing oratory and the other the laboratory, they were seen to be complementary and as ultimately having the same goal:

"the attainment of perfection through liberation from conditional existence."[114] Nevertheless, the differing orientations to alchemy were never
resolved either in China or in the West. Cheak notes "that the effort to
define alchemy to everyone's satisfaction may well be impossible."[115]
Likewise, the contemporary historian of alchemy Lawrence Principe has
noted that "Arriving at solid, satisfactory conclusions about alchemy can
seem as difficult as finding the Philosophers' Stone itself."[116]

Cheak struggles with differing approaches and issues, the opposing tensions between universal and particular, synchronic and diachronic, trying to find a "golden mean" between them, recognizing that finding the
elusive center of such opposing forces "is something of an alchemical act
in and of itself."[117] Cheak seeks to get a glimpse of this elusive center by
circumambulating what he calls an "alchemical *mysterium*."[118] From this
perspective, alchemy can be seen in terms of " 'nodal points of qualitative
change' . . . or in instances of 'qualitative exaltation' . . .'' a transformative point "where 'art' becomes science and 'science' art."[119] In this way,
Cheak hopes to avoid the "fixed parameters of disciplinal specificity" and
allow for a wider and richer perspective that he links to the German philosophical tradition of "actual understanding (*Verstehen*) rather than mere
explanation (*Erklären*)."[120] In this Cheak is influenced by Dilthey, Hus-
serl, and Heidegger.[121] At the same time, Cheak recognizes that there is
an inherent tension to this balance. This tension requires one to embrace a
Heraclitean "harmony of contrasts" between deeply opposed methodolo-
gies. In circumambulating a center, whether "essentialist" or "relativist,"
the ultimate nature of the center, indeed the substantial existence of the
center itself, must remain an open question.

Having begun with the recognition of alchemy and the Philosophers'
Stone as enigmas, I have described what appears as a fundamental split
in the alchemical imagination and in our approaches to understanding it.
I have examined a range of ways of seeing alchemy primarily in the contexts of a natural or spiritual science, the historiographic tradition of the
history of science, and the history of religion. In addition, I have briefly
examined the new discipline of esoteric studies as well as the approach of
Jung's psychoanalytic point of view, which made a major contribution to
the historiography of alchemy. His psychological interpretation penetrated
to the symbolic level of alchemical thought rendering aspects of it understandable, which up until then had remained enigmatic. Jung's psychoanalytic point of view which I have described as sitting at the crossroads

of these perspectives draws fire from both sides of the divide, the center of which Cheak calls an "alchemical *mysterium*."[122] I believe that Jung, like Cheak, seeks to bridge the divide and is not content to understand the enigmatic quality of alchemy or the Philosophers' Stone by reduction of them to either subject or object, inner or outer, material and real versus spiritual and esoteric.

Notes

1 Grossinger, *Alchemy*, 195.
2 His description does not include Jewish alchemy, which has a significant history. For more on that, see Patai, *The Jewish Alchemists*.
3 Grossinger, *Alchemy*, 177.
4 Panisnick, "The Philosophical Significance," 100.
5 Eliade, *Forge and Crucible*, 43.
6 Cardew, "The Archaic and the Sublimity of Origins," 111.
7 Ibid., 112.
8 Ibid., 111–112.
9 Ibid.
10 Eliade, *Forge and Crucible*, 7.
11 Ibid., 8.
12 Ibid., 9.
13 Ibid.
14 Ibid.
15 Ibid.
16 Ibid.
17 Ibid., 11.
18 Ibid., 8.
19 Ibid., 11.
20 Ibid.
21 Ibid., 158.
22 Ibid.
23 Ibid.
24 Dorn was a symbolically-oriented alchemist and was therefore important to Jung's interpretation of alchemy.
25 Eliade, *Forge and Crucible*, 159; brackets included in original.
26 Ibid.
27 Ibid.
28 The story of how Jung's interest in alchemy developed is described below in Chapter 2 and more fully elaborated in his autobiography, *Memories, Dreams, Reflections*.
29 Thanks to Kevin Padawer at the Kristine Mann Library in New York City for the massive task of copying relevant passages from Jung's *Collected Works*.
30 Tilton, *The Quest for the Phoenix*, 3; includes a phrase from Heym, "Review of Paracelsica, Zwei Vorlesungen über den Arzt und Philosophen Theophrastus," 64–67.
31 Pagel, "Jung's Views on Alchemy," 48; quoted by Tilton, *The Quest for the Phoenix*, 4.
32 Pagel, "Jung's Views on Alchemy," 48; Tilton, *The Quest for the Phoenix*, 5.
33 Principe and Newman, "Some Problems," 419.
34 Ibid., 420.
35 Principe, "Alchemy I," 13.
36 Principe and Newman, "Some Problems," 415.

37 Ibid., 415–416.
38 Ibid., 415.
39 Ibid., 415–416.
40 Ibid., 417.
41 Ibid., 418.
42 Ibid., 417.
43 Ibid., 417–418.
44 Tilton, *The Quest for the Phoenix*, 2.
45 Ibid., 2.
46 Ibid., 2–3.
47 Ibid., 3.
48 Ibid., 5.
49 Ibid., 6.
50 Ibid.
51 Ibid., 7.
52 Ibid.
53 Ibid., 8.
54 Ibid., 9.
55 Ibid.
56 Ibid., 10.
57 Newman, "*Decknamen* or Pseudochemical Language?," 165, 188; quoted by Tilton, *The Quest for the Phoenix*, 11.
58 Tilton, *The Quest for the Phoenix*, 11.
59 Ibid.
60 Ibid., 12.
61 Holmyard, *Alchemy*, 160; quoted by Tilton, *The Quest for the Phoenix*, 255.
62 Tilton, *The Quest for the Phoenix*, 13.
63 Ibid., 13.
64 See Tilton, *The Quest for the Phoenix*, 13, footnote 55.
65 Tilton, *The Quest for the Phoenix*, 14.
66 Ibid.
67 Ibid.
68 Tilton, *The Quest for the Phoenix*, 14; includes a word quoted from Principe and Newman, "Some Problems," 407.
69 Tilton, *The Quest for the Phoenix*, 15.
70 Ibid.
71 Ibid., 16.
72 Ibid.
73 Ibid., 17.
74 Ibid., 17–18.
75 Richard Noll has written two controversial books about Jung, *The Jung Cult* and *The Aryan Christ*, both of which vilify Jung and have been strongly rejected by other scholars, including Sonu Shamdasani who in his book *Cult Fictions* points to Noll's lack of critical scholarship.
76 Tilton, *The Quest for the Phoenix*, 19.
77 Ibid., 20.
78 Ibid.
79 Ibid., 21, footnote 87.
80 Ibid., 20.
81 Ibid., 34.
82 Ibid.
83 Ibid., 254.

84 Ibid., 255.
85 Ibid.
86 Caliăn, *Alkimia Operativa*, 170.
87 Ibid.
88 Ibid., 171.
89 Ibid., 173.
90 Ibid., 174–175.
91 Ibid., 175.
92 Ibid.
93 Ibid., 175–176. See Caliăn's excellent summary of these issues, 176–177.
94 Ibid., 176.
95 Ibid., 177.
96 Ibid.
97 Ibid., 178.
98 Ibid., 253.
99 Ibid., 187.
100 Ibid.
101 Ibid.
102 Hanegraaff, *Esotericism and the Academy*, book jacket.
103 Ibid., 290.
104 Ibid. Italics added by Hanegraaff.
105 Ibid.
106 Ibid.
107 Ibid., 291.
108 Ibid.
109 Ibid.
110 Ibid.
111 Ibid.
112 Cheak, "Introduction," 18.
113 Ibid., 19.
114 Ibid.
115 Ibid.
116 Principe, *The Secrets of Alchemy*, 2.
117 Cheak, "Introduction," 19.
118 Ibid., 20.
119 Ibid., 19.
120 Ibid., 20.
121 Ibid., footnote 5.
122 Ibid.

Chapter 2

The eye of the winged serpent

Mercurius and overcoming the split in the alchemical imagination[1]

For Jung, alchemical images and graphics were of great value in attempting to overcome our modern divide between the alchemical binaries and to approach a center point. In *Psychology and Alchemy*, Jung published an alchemical image taken from the frontispiece of Michael Maier's *Tripus aureus*.[2] It is an image of what Jung called the "double face of alchemy."[3]

The image is divided into two parts. On the right is a representation of an alchemical laboratory with many alembics and laboratory instruments hanging on the wall. Just below we can see a distilling apparatus, a table, a shelf, and in the foreground a man partially clad in a short wrap, kneeling on one knee. He appears to be tending the fire inside a circular athanor or furnace. In his right hand is a hammer or ax-like instrument. There appears to be chopped wood, perhaps kindling, and leaning against the furnace is a pair of tongs and a bellows on its base, as well as instruments of the laboratory.

On the left is what appears to be a library with walls lined with books. In the foreground are three figures. Jung, following Maier, identified the men as the abbot John Cremer, the monk Basilius Valentinus (a legendary figure, possibly fictitious), and a layman, Thomas Norton. One of the men appears to be pointing to the laboratory and possibly to what is going on in the long-necked flask on a tripod sitting on top of the round furnace that is central to the image. Inside the flask is the winged serpent or dragon that is the inspiration for this reflection and whose perspective we will consider shortly.

For the moment, let us notice a divide that has entered the contemporary alchemical imagination. As some of us look at this illustration we tend to identify with one side of the divide or the other. Some of us retreat to

DOI: 10.4324/9781003215905-3

Figure 2.1 The dual face of alchemy. From Michael Maier, *Tripus aureus*, frontispiece, 1618.

Source: Public domain.

our libraries, studies, or consulting rooms and others to our labs and spy-
geric and chemical experiments. We come like the two serpents, perhaps
instinctively emerging from one side or another, ontologizing spirit or
matter, from library or laboratory, sometimes hissing at one another about
who is the real alchemist and what constitutes real alchemy.

From the point of view of what is now called "spiritual alchemy,"
those who work on the practical level are often seen as retro-chemists or
proto-pharmacists, hopelessly trying to practice the art, often without a
clue about its subtle nature and without spiritual insight, while from the
point of view of the practical laboratory alchemist, spiritual alchemists are
merely abstract thinkers who reduce the real engagement with nature to
facile ideas. They are seen as disembodied spirits projecting psychological
principles back onto the real work of engaging and transforming matter. It
is nothing new for alchemists to both berate and undermine one another.
Jung cites the examples of Bernard of Treviso, a famous alchemist, as calling the great Gerber (Jabir) "an obscurantist and a Proteus who promises
kernels and gives husks."[4]

From a Jungian point of view, one might imagine both the spiritual and laboratory alchemists as projecting the shadow onto each other. For the spiritual alchemist, who is not deeply grounded in the substance of the work, he or she disparages and/or secretly idealizes the practical alchemist, who appears to literally be engaged with what is absent in his or her own work. On the other hand, the practical alchemist may be defended against spiritual transformation, avoiding it by focusing on literal matter to the exclusion of its deep mystery. He or she disparages and/or idealizes the spiritual alchemist who appears to have a real inner knowledge of transformation. In both cases, a lack precedes the shadow projection. There is no sense of Mercurius duplex – and the hermetic complexity s/he embodies.

Figure 2.2 Sun and Moon, Rebis. From Heinrich Nollius, *Theoria Philosophiae Hermeticae*, 1617.

Source: Public domain.

The dual face of alchemy is literalized and split into spiritual versus material, and there is no insight into the one body of alchemy, which appears with two heads.

Returning to our image of the dual face of alchemy, let's notice how the athanor or furnace stands between the two rooms, library and laboratory, as if to link them. As the flask is heated up, an odd creature appears, a winged serpent or dragon within it. I imagine this creature as what the alchemists called a *monstrum*, a premature conjunction on the way toward a *coniunctio* of spirit and matter. The wings indicate the spiritual aspect that raises up the instinctual, material dimension illustrated by the serpent; the material, instinctual serpent grounds the winged energies. This circular and ouroboric play is a hint that we are approaching the subtle body of Mercurius duplex. It signals a more primary unified field. The image of Mercurius sits on a tripod and is as well a third possibility sitting in the flask between the split world, cooking and awaiting realization.

Mercurius duplex

Abraham describes Mercurius as "the central symbol in alchemy," who is

> also known by the equivalent Greek name Hermes, symbolizing the universal agent of transmutation. . . . Mercurius is a symbol for the alchemists' magical Arcanum, the transformative substance without which the opus cannot be performed. . . . Mercurius . . . is also the name of the divine spirit hidden in the depths of matter, the light of nature, anima mundi, the very spirit of life which must be released in order to make the philosophers' stone.[5]

For Jung, the dragon combines "the chthonic principle of the serpent and the aeriel principle of the bird."[6] The dragon is "a variant of Mercurius" as "the divine winged Hermes manifest in matter."[7]

In metallic terms, Mercury or "'living silver,' quicksilver . . . perfectly expressed" is the dual reality of Mercurius, outwardly metal, inwardly "the world-creating spirit."[8] Jung notes that "[t]he dragon is probably the oldest pictorial symbol in alchemy of which we have documentary evidence. It appears as the [*Ouroboros*], the tail-eater, in the *Codex Marcianus*, which dates from the tenth or eleventh century, together with the legend."[9]

Figure 2.3 Mercurius as a uniting symbol. From Valentinus, "Duodecim clavis," 16th century.

Source: Public domain.

Figure 2.4 Ouroboros, the tail-eater. From the "The Chrysopoeia of Cleopatra," preserved in *Codex Marcianus*, 10th-11th century.

Source: Public domain.

"Time and again the alchemists reiterate that the *opus* proceeds from the one and leads back to the one, that it is a sort of circle like a dragon biting its own tail."[10]

In a footnote, Jung quotes the *Rosarium* from the *Artis auriferae:*

> Therefore you must be single-minded in the work of nature. . . . For however much its names may differ, yet it is ever one thing alone, and from the *same* thing. . . . One is the stone, one the medicine, one the vessel, one the method and one the disposition.[11]

And again: "This magistery proceeds first from one root, which [root] then expands into more things, and then reverts to the one."[12] "For this reason," Jung states, "the *opus* was often called *circulare* (circular) or else *rota* (the wheel)."[13]

Here we see Mercurius turning the wheel symbolizing the alchemical process. Mercurius "is metallic yet liquid, matter yet spirit, cold yet fiery, poison yet healing draught,"[14] a pharmakon, as Plato and French philosopher Jacques Derrida would contend.

Figure 2.5 Mercurius turning the wheel which symbolizes the alchemical process. "Speculum veritatis," 17th century.

Source: Public domain.

In the earlier image entitled the "dual face of alchemy," two serpents representing forces from opposite sides of the alchemical divide were seen as crawling toward one another and in the flask above them was an image of the Mercurial dragon representing an early and/or premature stage of integration, what the alchemists call a *monstrum*. In the following image, the serpents can now be seen to be interlocking, linking Sun and Moon, King and Queen, representing a further integration of paired opposites, a moving toward the greater *coniunctio*, a deeper level of integration. In this circular process, what were the hissing serpents unite in a healing image symbolized by Mercurius and the caduceus, uniting pairs of opposites.

If, for Cheak, the center between opposites is an alchemical mysterium and must remain open, Jung attempts to give us a graphic and symbolic

Figure 2.6 Mercurius as caduceus unifying the opposites. From "Figurarum Aegyptiorum secretarum," 18th century.

Source: Public domain.

view of this open center, looking into it to see what goes on between the so-called opposites of the dual face of alchemy. The conjunction of opposites, as a *mysterium coniunctionis*, has been expressed through alchemical images of Mercurius duplex, the *ouroboros*, the *rota* or ever-moving wheel of the alchemical process. These images of the conjunction of opposites as an ever-revealing process give us a glimpse of what has been called the Philosophers' Stone. In the alchemical text, the *Aurora consurgens*, the Philosophers' Stone speaks:

> I am the mediatrix of the elements, making one to agree with another; that which is warm I make cold, and the reverse; that which is dry I make moist, and the reverse; that which is hard I soften, and the reverse. I am the end and my beloved is the beginning. I am the whole work and all science is hidden in me.[15]

In this odd statement, the Philosophers' Stone speaks, leaving the reader with the ambiguity of whether the Stone reflects some human reality or describes a vision of a natural cosmic process. This ambiguity captures what we have been describing as the tension in the alchemical imagination. The question itself reflects a taken-for-granted conviction, mainly a divide between the human and natural world. It is precisely this supposition which is challenged by the idea of a Philosophers' Stone. As we have seen for the alchemists, the "Philosophers' Stone" is itself seen as a union of opposites. "Philosophy, love of wisdom, is" identified as a deeply human and sentient activity, while "a stone is a crude, hard, material reality."[16] Somehow, the Philosophers' Stone attempts to bring these two realms of reality together as the goal of the alchemical process. For Jung, the Philosophers' Stone was a forerunner of the modern discovery of what he called the reality of the psyche and the Self, which also cannot be reduced to a preconceived model based on a complete separation of psyche from world.

For Jung, the literal reality of matter through "projection" created an "admixture" of psyche and substance recognized by the alchemists as a living symbolic reality such that for them it is not so strange to imagine the Philosophers' Stone as speaking and having a voice. For Jung,

> [w]hat the alchemists called "matter" was in reality the [unconscious] self. The "soul of the world," the *anima mundi*, which was identified with the *spiritus mercurius*, was imprisoned in matter. It is for this

reason that alchemists believed in the *truth* of "matter," because "matter" was actually their own psychic life. But it was a question of freeing this "matter," of saving it – in a word, of finding the philosophers' stone, the *corpus glorificationis*.[17]

Jung goes on to say that "The alchemical operations were real, only this reality was not physical but psychological. Alchemy represents the projection of a drama both cosmic and spiritual in laboratory terms. The *opus magnum* had two aims: the rescue of the human soul and the salvation of the cosmos."[18] The move brought alchemy into the realm of Jung's psychology, but it remains to be clarified just what "a psychology of alchemy" implies. On the one hand, Jung states,

> I am and remain a psychologist. I am not interested in anything that transcends the psychological content of human experience. I do not even ask myself whether such transcendence is possible, because in any case the trans-psychological is no longer the concern of the psychologist.[19]

In such statements, Jung appears to retreat to a "psychological reality" separated from the world. However, just what he meant by "psychological" never quite fit the category of an ego subject against an object world. When he was at times accused of being a reductionist for translating his experience into psychology, he would often counter that his critics act as if they knew what the "psyche" and "matter" really are. If Jung was right that the alchemists did indeed project "psyche" into matter, I think it is important to see that for Jung "psyche" was not simply subjective, not simply in us, and is ultimately for him an unknown, a mystery, as is the "matter" upon which so-called psyche is projected. "Matter" for Jung was not simply out there, totally independent of psyche. Projection, then, was movement from a mystery (psyche) to a mystery (matter), and this mystery is one "thing" and yet differentiated into a multiplicity at the same time.

The pre-alchemy Jung: initiation and the descent into the unconscious

If the work of alchemy and the production of the Philosophers' Stone required a *coniunctio oppositorum* that attempted to overcome the dualistic divides between spirit and matter, psyche and substance, self and world, alchemy and chemistry, it also required alchemical transformation to bring this about. From the point of view of Eliade and Jung, alchemy required an initiatory process or descent into the depth of death, renewal, leading to a change in the adept's mode of seeing and being. These initiatory rites are preserved in the descriptions of the transformation of "matter" as living substances from which Jung extracted his descriptions of what he was to call the individuation process. Jung ultimately saw this process as a precursor to his psychology of the unconscious.

Jung developed his way of understanding alchemy in and through such a process of personal initiation. The process was described in his autobiography *Memories, Dreams, Reflections*. In a chapter entitled "Confrontation with the Unconscious," Jung describes a powerful series of visions that brought him to the brink of psychosis.

> From the beginning I had conceived my voluntary confrontation with the unconscious as a scientific experiment which I myself was conducting and in whose outcome I was vitally interested. . . .
>
> . . . I was sitting at my desk once more, thinking over my fears. Then I let myself drop. Suddenly it was as though the ground literally gave way beneath my feet, and I plunged down into dark depths. I could not fend off a feeling of panic. But then, abruptly, at not too great a depth, I landed on my feet in a soft, sticky mass. I felt great relief, although I was apparently in complete darkness. After a while my eyes grew accustomed to the gloom, which was rather like a deep twilight. Before me was the entrance to a dark cave, in which stood a dwarf with a leathery skin, as if he were mummified. I squeezed past him through the narrow entrance and waded knee deep through icy water to the other end the cave where, on a projecting rock, I saw a glowing red crystal. I grasped the stone, lifted it, and discovered a hollow underneath. At first I could make out nothing, but then I saw at there was running water. In it a corpse floated by, a youth with blond hair and a wound in the head. He was followed by a gigantic black scarab and then by a red, newborn sun, rising up out of the depths of the water. Dazzled by the light, I wanted to replace the stone upon the opening, but then a fluid welled out. It was blood. A thick jet of it leaped up, and I felt nauseated. It seemed to me that the blood continued to spurt for an unendurably long time. At last it ceased, and the vision came to an end.

I was stunned by this vision. I realized, of course, that it was a hero and solar myth, a drama of death and renewal, the rebirth symbolized by the Egyptian scarab. At the end, the dawn of the new day should have followed, but instead came that intolerable outpouring of blood – an altogether abnormal phenomenon, so seemed to me. But then I recalled the vision of blood that I had had in the autumn of that same year, and I abandoned all further attempt to understand.[20]

Jung writes of his loneliness. He felt he could not speak to anyone about these experiences for fear they would be misunderstood. He notes: "I felt the gulf between the external world and the interior world of images in its most painful form. I could not yet see that interaction of both worlds which I now understand. I saw only an irreconcilable contradiction between 'inner' and 'outer.'"[21]

It was a long time before Jung felt he began to emerge from the darkness. One of the things that had helped him come to terms with his nearly overwhelming experiences was that he began to draw small circular drawings in a notebook every morning. He recognized such drawings as mandalas, which seemed to correspond to his inner situation at the time. Jung notes: "With the help of these drawings I could observe my psychic transformations from day to day."[22] Only gradually did Jung feel that he began to understand what these mandalas were. For Jung, these circular drawings came to be understood as representing "the self, the wholeness of the personality."[23] Jung writes:

My mandalas were cryptograms concerning the state of self which were presented to me anew each day. In them I saw the self – that is, my whole being – actively at work. To be sure at first I could only dimly understand them; but they seemed to me highly significant, and I guarded them like precious pearls. I had the distinct feeling that they were something central, and in time I acquired through them a living conception of the self. The self, I thought, was like the monad which I am, and which is my world. The mandala represents this monad, and corresponds to the microcosmic nature of the psyche.[24]

In his autobiography, Jung was aware that he was producing a great many such drawings and at one point he asks himself "What is this process leading to? Where is its goal?"[25] Jung realized he could not choose a goal which gave the ego too much control. He felt he had to let himself "be carried along by the current, without a notion of where it would lead [him]."[26] When he was drawing the mandalas, he could determine all the paths he had been following and they seemed to lead "back to a single point – namely, to the mid-point."[27] It became clear to Jung that the mandala "is the path to the center, to individuation."[28] He writes that during the "years between 1918 and 1920, I began to understand that the goal of psychic development is the self. There is no linear evolution; there is only a circumambulation of the self."[29] For Jung:

> Uniform development exists, at most, only at the beginning; later, everything points toward the center. This insight gave me stability, and gradually my inner peace returned. I knew that in finding the mandala as an expression of the self I had attained what was for me the ultimate. Perhaps someone else knows more, but not I.[30]

This process described in *Memories, Dreams, Reflections*, a late-life autobiography, was originally documented in his "Black Books," the private journals in which he recorded his fantasies and his "Confrontation with the Unconscious."[31] He then added these revised reflections and drawings to them, and transcribed them into what was known as *The Red Book*. This book was kept under wraps so to speak and only recently translated and published with an Introduction and scholarly notes by Sonu Shamdasani. In his Introduction, Shamdasani in a section entitled "The Way to the Self" refers to Jung as saying that "all of us stood between two worlds: the world of external perception and the world of perception of the unconscious."[32] The distinction depicted his world at the time of his writing a paper entitled "On the unconscious" in 1918. For Jung, "[t]he union of rational and irrational truth is to be found . . . in the symbol. . . [which contains] both the rational and irrational."[33] In and through his experiences documented in *The Red Book*, Jung continually worked on the issue of "how the problem of the opposites could be resolved through the production of the uniting or reconciling symbol."[34] In his work *Psychological Types*, Jung continued to struggle with how the opposites could be resolved studying this in "Hinduism, Taoism, Meister Eckhart, and . . . in the work of Carl Spitteler."[35] Out of these studies, the idea of the "self" emerged as a psychological concept.

> But inasmuch as the ego is only the center of my field of consciousness, it is not identical with the totality of my psyche, being merely one

complex among other complexes. I therefore distinguish between the ego and the *self*, since the ego is only the subject of my consciousness, while the self is the subject of my total psyche, which also includes the unconscious. In this sense the self would be an ideal entity which embraces the ego. In unconscious *fantasies* the self often appears as supraordinate or ideal personality, having somewhat the relationship of Faust to Goethe or Zarathustra to Nietzsche.[36]

Jung also linked the Self with the Hindu notion of Brahman/Atman. In this view, it is relevant to note that the Atman reflects the microcosmic self while Brahman its macrocosmic counterpart. From the perspective of the macrocosmic level of understanding in Hinduism, the Brahman is seen to have two aspects: Brahman with qualities (*saguna*) as "he" appears in the time and space and Brahman without qualities (*nirguna*) as "he" appears from the perspective of eternity. Ultimately from the Hindu perspective, there is a "oneness" between these two aspects – a linking of *nirguna* and *saguna* Brahman. This linking is described as having the qualities of *sat chit ananda* (truth, consciousness, bliss) and to represent the ultimate perspective of the ontological reading of the Self, a term also widely used in the Upanishads. The Hindu model is useful for recognizing that in Jung's understanding of the Self both personal and archetypal universal perspective make up a fuller understanding of the "self." In another place, Jung writes that the Self is also the goal of life because it is the most expressive "of that fateful combination we call individuality." With the experiencing of the Self as something irrational, "as an indefinable" being "to which the ego is neither opposed nor subjected," but is nevertheless in a relation of dependence, and around which it rotates, much like the earth orbits the sun – then the goal of individuation has been reached.[37]

In spite of what appears like confident statements about the Self, Jung remained somewhat uncertain about his discovery. It was very personal and emerged out of a deep struggle with his nearly overwhelming confrontation with the unconscious. The notion of the Self helped Jung feel stabilized, through the experience of this superordinate center. Jung came to feel that his notion of the Self was a "compensation for the conflict between inside and outside"[38] and that the circular mandalas he was drawing were symbolic expressions of the dynamic quality of the Self. Jung wrote some years later, around 1927, that he "obtained confirmation of [his] ideas about the center and the self by way of a dream," and he referenced its essence in a mandala which he called "Window on Eternity."[39]

A year later, he painted another mandala "with a golden castle in the center."[40] Jung believed the image to be Chinese in character, although it is not apparent why he thought this. Strangely, not long after Jung painted this image, he received a letter from Sineologist Richard Wilhelm along with a Taoist alchemical manuscript called *The Secret of the Golden Flower*, "with a request that [he] write a commentary on it."[41] This was an important turning point for Jung. He notes that this book gave him an "undreamed-of confirmation of my ideas about the mandala and the circumambulation of the center."[42] This sense of a parallel between Jung's understanding of the Self and the mandala with Chinese alchemy gave him a sense of affinity with others who had experienced something similar and broke through his feeling of isolation. At this point, Jung was "stirred by the desire to become more closely acquainted with the alchemical texts."[43] He soon acquired a copy of the *Rosarium Philosophorum*, a sixteenth century alchemical text, but it was a long time before he "found [his] way about in the labyrinth of alchemical thought processes."[44] It was in this text that he noticed a number of strange phrases, including the *lapis* (the Philosophers' Stone), and he gradually felt that it was as if he "were trying to solve the riddle of an unknown language. . . [that] gradually yielded up its meaning."[45] Jung recognized that his psychology "coincided in a most curious way with alchemy" and that he "had stumbled upon the historical counterpart of [his] psychology of the unconscious."[46] Once Jung discovered the symbolic meaning of alchemy he understood his confrontation with the unconscious in a new context and no longer needed *The Red Book* as a "container" for his discoveries. Instead, alchemy provided a new field of study that remained his passion for the rest of his life. With the help of alchemy, Jung felt he could finally absorb and arrange "the overpowering force of [his] original experiences."[47] Sanford Drob (2012) elaborates on this:

> As alchemy treated the symbols of chaos, the soul, evil, and the merging of opposites, Jung found a ready container for his *Red Book* experience and ideas. The alchemist's efforts to bring about a union of opposites in the laboratory and to perform what they spoke of as a "chymical wedding" were understood by Jung as antecedents to his

own "innovation" of merging the opposites and his attempt to distinguish, but at the same time forge a unity, e.g., between the masculine and feminine, and the good and evil aspects of the psyche. We might say that for Jung this "unity in difference" was *The Red Book*'s major theoretical and personal achievement.[48]

The *Rosarium philosophorum*

This theme is carried further in the *Rosarium philosophorum*, which contains a series of iconic images central to both alchemy and Jungian psychology, beginning with the initiatory death and separation, and ending

Figure 2.7 Male/female *coniunctio*. From the *Rosarium philosophorum*, Figure 5, 16th century.

Source: Public domain.

with the *coniunctio*, the goal of the work. This process requires a defeat of the ego, a going under, a death and descent into hell, and ultimately a spiritual renewal, all of which Jung and Eliade see as essential to the alchemical process. This is illustrated by twenty images from the *Rosarium*, only ten of which Jung refers to in his study of this text in "The Psychology of the Transference." The *Rosarium* portrays this process as progressive as well as circular. An example of the unification or *coniunctio* of masculine and feminine is graphically represented in the following image by a couple in connubial union.

Jung wrote about this image that "The sea has closed over the king and queen, and they have gone back to the chaotic beginnings, the *massa confusa*."[49] The union early on in the process takes place in an unconscious identity which he describes as a primitive initial state of chaos "where heterogeneous factors merge in an unconscious relationship."[50] As such, it is a

Figure 2.8 The death-like state of the soul standing on the black sun, a condition lacking differentiation. From J.D. Mylius, *Philosophia reformata*, 1622.

Source: Public domain.

premature union, a state of unconsciousness. Such an undifferentiated Absolute union was described by Hegel in his implicit critique of Schelling "as the night in which, as the saying goes, all cows are black."[51] In alchemical texts, this undifferentiated condition is illustrated graphically as a stage in the development of consciousness where "[t]he stone of solar and lunar conjunction [is] turned into the black sun of death."[52] The following two images illustrate alchemical variations of the undifferentiated state of the *nigredo:*

The second image likewise illustrates the dark phase of the alchemical work. In this image, the landscape has suffered a drought or been burned, dried up, and is flat or empty. Henderson and Sherwood note that the image depicts a "state of incubation . . . a need for change" in a pivotal yet temporal moment.[53]

Figure 2.9 Sol niger. The dark phase of the alchemical work. From *Splendor solis*, 16th century.

Source: Public domain.

Hegel's idea of the Absolute surpasses these undifferentiated conditions and, like the notion of the Philosophers' Stone, requires a more differentiated view. Jung, like Hegel, indicates the importance of going beyond the stage of a simple undifferentiated conjunction. He suggests, however, that even in the stage of undifferentiated darkness something is going on that sets the stage for further development. For Jung, the *Rosarium* illustrates a differentiating process in its images. One can discern such a movement throughout the ten figures Jung discusses. For example, in Figure 6 the "[k]ing and queen are dead and have melted into a single being with two heads,"[54] an undifferentiated state of the *prima materia*, an alchemical version of Hegel's "all cows are black."

Figure 2.10 King and Queen's return to the *prima materia*. From the *Rosarium philosophorum*, Figure 6, 16th century.

Source: Photo courtesy of the author.

Jung writes that when opposites unite at this stage "all energy ceases. . . [or] So at least it appears, looked at from the outside. . . ."[55] "Nuptial joy" gives way to a "stagnant pool . . . No new life can arise, says the alchemists [sic], without the death of the old."[56] This death, the blackness of the *nigredo*, is also implicitly the ground of a genesis – putrefaction, corruption are also fertility. Jung points out that the corpse left over from the connubial union is already in a new body. Half of the body is male and the other half female. For Jung, this hermaphrodite prefigures the long-sought goal of the *lapis* or Philosophers' Stone, symbolizing a "mysterious being yet to be begotten, for whose sake the *opus* is undertaken. But the *opus* has not yet reached its goal, because the *lapis* has not come alive."[57] Its differentiated quality is not yet conscious.

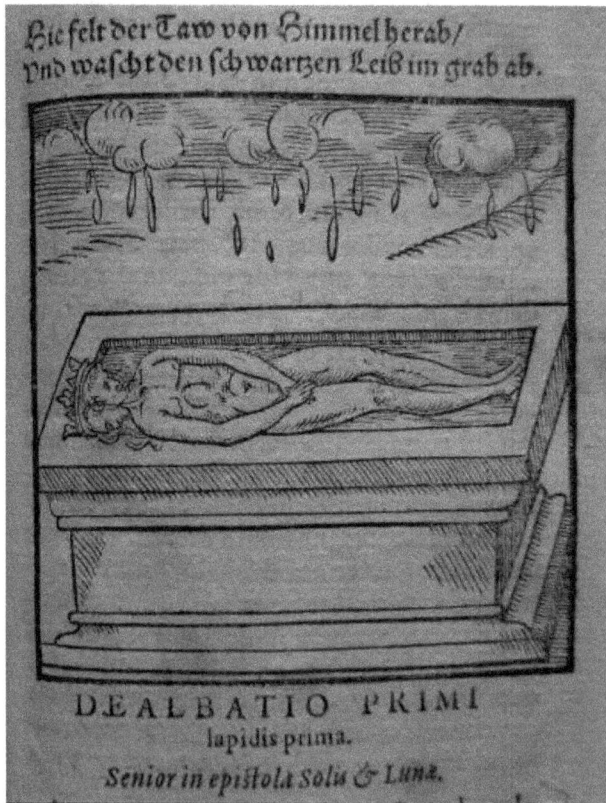

Figure 2.11 Energizing moisture. From the *Rosarium philosophorum*, Figure 8, 16th century.

Source: Photo courtesy of the author.

In Figure 8 of the *Rosarium*, there is a provocative, perhaps parallel, image entitled "Purification," in which an energizing moisture emerges from a cloud and activates psychic potential, setting in motion the catalyzing energy for a more differentiated state of existence. Jung asserts that "[t]he falling dew is a portent of the divine birth now at hand."[58] He notes that "(Gideon's dew) is a synonym for the *aqua permanens*, hence for Mercurius."[59]

An interesting variation on these *Rosarium* images was presented by an analysand in these two drawings.

Just as in alchemy, so in the analytic process, the activation of the soul can be seen in images. The first mirrors a variation on image 6 of the

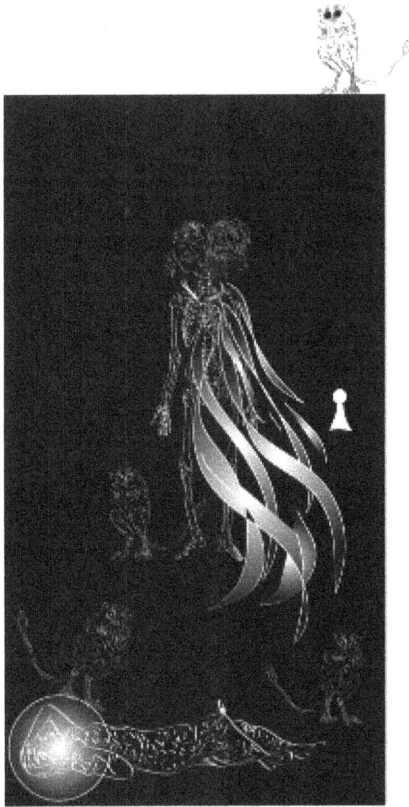

Figure 2.12 Return to the *prima materia*. Artwork by analysand.

Source: Used by permission.

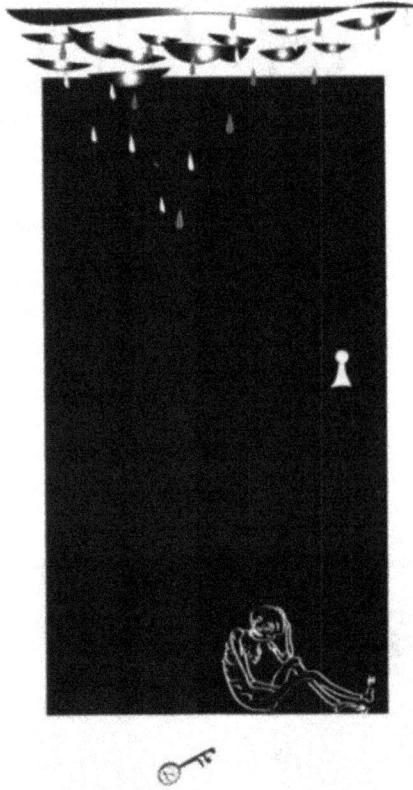

Figure 2.13 Energizing moisture. Artwork by analysand.
Source: Used by permission.

Rosarium. In it, one can see two heads attached to a single skeletal body whose garments have been shredded, again an image of the prima materia or of the undifferentiated state. However, the animal energies surrounding the figure anticipate the vitalizing moisture that does not emerge until image 8 of the *Rosarium*. This moisture becomes explicit in her second image in which a death-like skeletal figure sits in darkness, but the potentiality of further development can also be seen in the images of a doorway and a key.

This moisture, like the divine dew of alchemy, serves to energize the life force that Jung relates to the spirit of Mercurius which "descends . . . to

purify the blackness."[60] For Jung, the "divine" dew is a gift of "illumination and wisdom"[61] and is linked to the anticipation of the Philosophers'
Stone. About the Stone, Jung states "the acquisition of the stone is better
than the fruits of purest gold and silver."[62]

For Jung, the stage of movement beyond the darkness of non-differ-
entiation requires something more than abstract intellectual realization.
It requires the recognition of the importance of feeling. Jung states that
feelings open up a whole new perspective, even a whole new world. The
moisture signifies a freshness and animation of the deadness. "The black
or unconscious state that resulted from the union of opposites reaches the
nadir and a change sets in. The falling [moisture] signals resuscitation and
new light."[63] Alchemy is filled with such images that link death and new
life. The following image from the alchemical text *The Hermetic Museum*
illustrates this process, showing how grain grows from the grave symbolizing resurrection and new birth:

Figure 2.14 Grain growing from the grave. From D. Stolcius de Stolcenberg,
    Viridarium chymicum, 1624.

Source: Public domain.

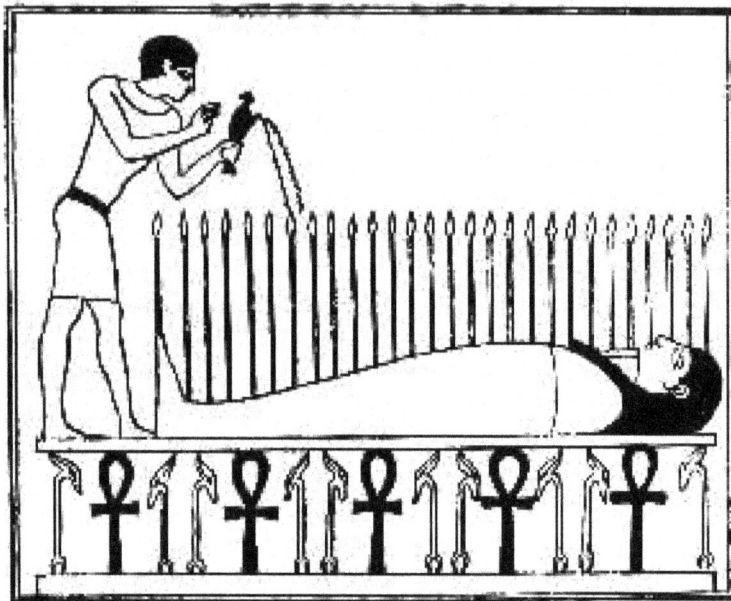

Figure 2.15 Grain growing from the corpse of Osiris. E. A Wallis Budge, *Egyptian Ideas of the Future Life*, 1900.

Source: Public domain.

A similar image is found in the Egyptian mysteries showing grain grow-ing from the corpse of Osiris:

The experience of new life emerging from an experience of death is not uncommon in analytic work. The following image was presented by a woman analysand upon coming out of a death-like depression:

The image of a tree and the movement of birds reflected a growing sense of vitality in the midst of darkness.

For Jung, the emergence of new life from death-like states suggests that the deepening descent into the unconscious does not mean that the soul was lost or destroyed, but rather that in that other world, it was form-ing a "living counterpole to the state of death in this world."[64] The dew in Figure 8 of the Rosarium indicates this counterpole in the form of the activation of feeling and new life. But, for Jung, this is not the final stage. The emergence of the vitality points the way to another kind of experience

Figure 2.16 A growing sense of vitality in the midst of darkness. Artwork by analysand.

Source: Used by permission.

Figure 2.17 The monstrous hermaphrodite. From the *Rosarium philosophorum*, Figure 10, 16th century.

Source: Public domain.

that anticipates the *lapis* as an "imaginative activity . . . intuition, without which no realization is complete."[65] For Jung, the imaginative activity opens a new range of psychological possibilities for insight and the way we see the world. Imagination "revels in the garden of magical possibilities as if they were real"[66] and nothing is more charged with such possibilities for the alchemist than the intuition of the *lapis philosophorum*, the Philosophers' Stone, which "rounds off the work into an experience of the totality of the individual."[67]

It is not possible here to go through every stage depicted by the *Rosarium philosophorum*, but I would like to skip ahead to the last image Jung describes in this process entitled "The New Birth." This is the last picture, number 10, of the series Jung discusses, and is a first image of the goal of the process.

It is a complex image described in many ways: as the alchemical *filius philosophorum*, as the Rebis, as a Christ figure, and as a hermaphrodite (a bisexual first man/woman, the Anthropos), and as the *lapis* or Philosophers' Stone. The image represents "the culminating point of the work beyond which it is impossible to go except by means of the *multiplicatio*."[68] It is a figure that Jung identifies as "a higher state of unity," a unity that is not a unity but a complex unity hard to understand and describe.[69] The *lapis* as the "cosmogonic First Man" is called *radix ipsius* (root of itself) and according to the *Rosarium* "everything has grown from this One and through this One. It is the Ouroboros, the serpent that fertilizes and gives birth to itself, by definition an *increatum* . . . ."[70] For Jung, the creation *increatum* is an impenetrable paradox. In his view, anything unknowable can best be described in terms of opposites, what Nicholas of Cusa regarded as antinomial thought.[71]

Jung states that it is not surprising that the alchemical *opus* ends with the idea of a highly paradoxical being that defies rational analysis. The work could hardly end in any other way since the *complexio oppositorum* cannot possibly lead to anything but a baffling paradox. Psychologically, this means that human wholeness can only be described in antimonies, which is always the case when dealing with a transcendental idea.[72] Jung, however, states that this paradoxical image of the goal holds out

the possibility of an *intuitive* and *emotional* experience, because the unity of the self, unknowable and incomprehensible, irradiates even the sphere of our discriminating, and hence divided, consciousness, and, like all unconscious contents, does so with very powerful effects. This inner unity, or experience of unity, is expressed most forcibly by the mystics in the idea of the *unio mystica*, and above all in the philosophies and religions of India, in Chinese Taoism, and in the Zen Buddhism of Japan.[73]

From Jung's psychological point of view, language does not seem to be intrinsically related to the reality of what is being described: "A rose by any other name would smell as sweet." For him, "the names we give to the self are quite irrelevant."[74] So, whatever we call the Self or the "goal" or the Philosophers' Stone remains a psychological reality independent of the metaphysical "truth" of the "thing-in-itself."

With the idea of the "psychic reality" in mind, Jung returns to the complex image of the goal of the *Rosarium* process in all its symbolic details. This image is filled with contrasting and complex imagery that, Jung notes, requires a study in its own regard. Jung suggests that the image of the hermaphrodite shows an apotheosis of the Rebis, an elevation of the image to a divine level. The image contains opposites such as male and female, the sun and moon, in the vessel that the alchemists called the *vas hermeticum*. The wings on the image suggest to Jung the qualities of both vitality and spirituality, and the serpents and the raven point to the problem of evil and its containment. The Mercurial and numerical play between three and four is seen in terms of number symbolism both in its religious Trinitarian aspects of the three serpents in one vessel and a fourth in another. The additional serpent stands outside the Trinity and yet must be included to complete the goal of the *opus*. The whole process is then reflected in what Jung calls the philosophical tree, or *arbor philosophica*, with sun and moon images depicting the coming to consciousness of the unconscious process represented in the work of the unification of opposites. What Jung finds most remarkable about the image is that "the fervently desired goal of the alchemist's endeavors should be conceived under so monstrous and horrific an image."[75]

In this chapter, I have attempted to show that alchemical and psychological work endeavor to overcome opposites and splits in the alchemical imagination. It has become clear that efforts to move beyond the dual face of alchemy cannot rest in a simple unification, that is, a unification without differentiation. Such a unity is not a simple unity, but a complex one bringing together contraries that appear from an ordinary everyday view as impossible to join together: life and death, male and female, good and evil. As such, this unification was called by Jung a *mysterium coniunctionis*, a designation expressed in the image of the Philosophers' Stone. For the alchemists, such a goal was not simply a rational process, but required the adept to see through the eye of the winged serpent Mercurius who unified unity *and* differences in a single vision. Murray Stein has noted:

> It is the genius of Mercurius that the many do not disappear into a singularity but rather retain their unique aspects and facets, diamondlike, while joining the wholeness structure of the mandala. Thus, room for diversity is preserved while unity is attained.

This is the answer to the dilemma of "the One or the Many." It has often been discussed among Jungian authors: Is the personality multiple and many, or is it one? Polytheism or monotheism? The answer is: "both" – diversity in unity; unity in diversity. This is the only realistic and sustainable goal for individuation given the complexity of the human personality. And this is the net implication of the [*Mysterium*] *Coniunctionis* in the title of the text: it is "unity" but it does not deny or eliminate diversity and differentiation.[76]

From an ordinary point of view, such a complexity can appear monstrous. Philosophically, Hegel's idea of the Absolute as a unity linking unity and difference approaches such complexity and may well be a parallel to the alchemical Mercurius. It offers a philosophical description of such a complexity and is useful in trying to understand what the alchemists had in mind by the goal of their *opus*.

Notes

1 This chapter is a modified version of a talk entitled "Archetypal Alchemy," which was originally given at the International Alchemy Conference, Las Vegas, NV, October 6, 2007.
2 Jung, *Psychology and Alchemy (CW12)*, 278.
3 Ibid., §404.
4 Ibid., §402.
5 Abraham, *A Dictionary of Alchemical Imagery*, 124–125.
6 Jung, *Psychology and Alchemy (CW12)*, §404.
7 Ibid.
8 Ibid.
9 Ibid.
10 Ibid.
11 Ibid., footnote 12(a).
12 Ibid., footnote 12(b); brackets included in original.
13 Ibid.
14 Ibid.
15 Von Franz, *Aurora Consurgens*, 143.
16 Edinger, *Anatomy*, 216.
17 Jung, *C.G. Jung Speaking*, 228.
18 Ibid.
19 Ibid., 229.
20 Jung, *Memories*, 178–179.
21 Ibid., 194.
22 Ibid., 195.
23 Ibid., 196.
24 Ibid.

25 Ibid.
26 Ibid.
27 Ibid.
28 Ibid.
29 Ibid.
30 Ibid., 197.
31 Ibid., 170–199.
32 Shamdasani, Introduction to *The Red Book*, 210.
33 Jung, *Civilization in Transition (CW10)*, §24; quoted by Shamdasani, Introduction to *The Red Book*, 210.
34 Shamdasani, Introduction to *The Red Book*, 210.
35 Ibid., 211.
36 Jung, *Psychological Types (CW6)*, §706.
37 Jung, *Two Essays on Analytical Psychology (CW7)*, §405.
38 Ibid., §404.
39 Jung, *Memories*, 197.
40 Ibid.
41 Ibid.
42 Ibid.
43 Ibid., 204.
44 Ibid., 205.
45 Ibid.
46 Ibid.
47 Jung, *The Red Book*, 360.
48 Drob, *Reading the Red Book*, 257. The issue of "the unity of unity and difference" in the work of Hegel is a related theme to be addressed in a later chapter and, like Hegel's *Phenomenology of Spirit*, Jung's *Red Book* was called an "impossible book." (Giegerich, "Liber Novus," 362).
49 Jung, *The Practice of Psychotherapy (CW16)*, §457.
50 Ibid., §462.
51 Hegel, *Phenomenology*, 9, §16. "Hegel is only making a claim about Schelling's cognitive claim in his view of the so-called indifference point, but not about the origins of nature, alchemy and so on." (Rockmore, personal communication).
52 Fabricius, *Alchemy*, 103.
53 Henderson and Sherwood, *Transformation of the Psyche*, 162.
54 Jung, *The Practice of Psychotherapy (CW16)*, §467.
55 Ibid.
56 Ibid.
57 Ibid., §468.
58 Ibid., §483.
59 Ibid.
60 Ibid., §484.
61 Ibid.
62 Ibid.
63 Ibid., §493.
64 Ibid.
65 Ibid., §492.
66 Ibid.
67 Ibid.
68 Ibid., §526.
69 Ibid.
70 Ibid., §527.

71 Ibid., footnote 9.
72 Here Jung reveals the influencer of Kant's idea of the antimonies. For a full account of Jung's relationship to Kant, see Brent, "Jung's Debt to Kant."
73 Jung, *The Practice of Psychotherapy (CW16)*, §532.
74 Ibid.
75 Ibid., §533.
76 Stein, "Mysterium Coniunctionis."

Chapter 3

Benign and monstrous conjunctions[1]

In alchemy, as in analysis, there are simple and complex, rational and mystical, benign and monstrous conjunctions representative of the Self's expression. Jung's "confrontation with the unconscious" was at the source of his struggle to bring the alien aspects of his psychic life into an integrated whole that he was to call the Self, and he saw this as a modern-day experience of the Philosophers' Stone. Jung's engagement with the depths of his psychic life was recorded in *The Red Book*, a book that has been compared to many of the major classics of Western literature, including Nietzsche's *Zarathustra*, St. Augustine's *Confessions*, Dante's *Divine Comedy*, Goethe's *Faust*, and Blake's illuminated manuscripts.

The Red Book has been called an "impossible book," a "book that is not a book," because of both its highly personal nature and its internal contradictions.[2] On the other hand, there are others who have positively imagined that these so-called contradictions are not necessarily opposed. Hillman, for instance, has described the book as a poetic text that embraces psyche and life in our age of scientific rationalism,[3] an important example of the vision that Jung has said is yet to come.

A difficulty for readers of *The Red Book* is its challenge to our modern intellect and imagination. What the nascently alchemical Jung called the "melting together of sense and non-sense"[4] is nearly impossible to understand from within our taken-for-granted categories. These early struggles with the otherness of the unconscious were at the root of Jung's idea of the transcendent function that sought some kind of accommodation between opposites. However, even Jung's own continuing attempt to describe his experience of the seemingly contradictory aspects of the psyche, using phrases such as *complexio oppositorum* and *mysterium coniunctionis*, can

DOI: 10.4324/9781003215905-4

become too easily assimilated and intellectualized, thus becoming benign clichés for the darkness, complexity, and profundity of the numinous unknown that Jung called the unconscious. What is important in reading *The Red Book* is to have an appreciation of its radical vision, a vision that points beyond any conventional sense of meaning. In *The Red Book*, Jung tries to convey this radicality by using the neologism *Übersinn*, which can be translated as "supreme meaning." The difficulty of understanding Jung's intent is noted by Wolfgang Giegerich who points out that *Übersinn* implies a meaning that is "over," "beyond," in "excess of meaning," even "counter-meaning."[5] He states that what Jung has in mind in *The Red Book* is "outrageous."[6] For James Hillman, Jung's vision jars even the most knowledgeable readers. It shocks and pushes us to the very limits and moves psyche and life beyond our understanding.[7]

In a review of *The Red Book* entitled "Carl Jung's Red Book," John Tarrant compares Jung's book to "the late Buddhist sutras," in which we are confronted "with thousand-armed deities and paradoxes and impossible statements that nonetheless make you feel changed after connecting with them."[8] It is not an uncommon experience to feel somehow changed after reading *The Red Book*. We might imagine such a change as the result of an encounter with the numinous, a quality of fear and awe in the face of a *tremendum* hard to define or understand and that challenges the fundamental beliefs and ideas of those who read it. In such a case, understanding is not only standing above or "overmeaning," but also a standing "under" which requires a descent and a decentering, a "going under" that results in a defeat for and relativization of the ego. The idea that a defeat for the ego is a victory for the Self, for the larger personality, is one of Jung's ways of speaking about the meaning of the Self. In essence, such a going under is an initiatory experience and a movement toward the goal of the alchemical and psychological process.

Such an encounter and experience with the unconscious brought Jung to the edge of his sanity, but his psychic strength and integrity allowed him to use his experience to forward a new vision of psychology. During Jung's time, he was not the only one to react to the perception that something had been left out of our notion of the psyche and soul. For him, beneath the surface of our historical, cultural, and philosophical attitude, was a seething irrationalism. Many creative artists, writers, philosophers, poets, and painters were, like Jung, experimenting with ways to access this unacknowledged depth. Tarrant noted, "Jung (in common with other prominent figures like Kandinsky) had terrible dreams of destruction overwhelming the land. We know now that Europe was heading toward a century of war."[9] In response, creative thinkers were turning away from traditional ways of understanding and seeking a deeper meaning of life.

> Rilke was writing sonnets – which he received more or less as dictation – to Orpheus, Yeats was studying automatic writing, and Eliot was trying to educate his unconscious creative processes by immersing himself in great literature. Picasso was experimenting with Cubism. The Dada movement was for a while closely linked to the Jungians. The idea that something had to come from the depths was important.[10]

The Red Book was ultimately Jung's reaction to the creative urgings of his imagination in response to personal and collective crises. He noted in *The Red Book*:

> I have learned that in addition to the spirit of this time there is still another spirit at work, namely that which rules the depths of everything contemporary. The spirit of this time would like to hear of use and value. I also thought this way, and my humanity still thinks this way. But that other spirit forces me to speak beyond justification, use, and meaning. . . . The spirit of the depths took my understanding and all my knowledge and placed them in the service of the inexplicable and the paradoxical.[11]

The "inexplicable and paradoxical" that Jung speaks of here remained with him throughout his life and in his works, from *The Red Book* to the *Mysterium Coniunctionis*. From its nascent beginnings to its mature form, Jung's work forges a vision of the unity of opposites, of wholeness, and the Self that is almost unbearable for the ego to tolerate.

The hermaphrodite

British Jungian analyst Neil Micklem has noted that there is still a tendency in reading Jung to pass over the shock and radicality of his vision.[12] Micklem emphasizes the importance of paradox rather than unity and notes that paradox usually gets glossed over as our attention moves toward the more attractive idea of the vision of the unity of the opposites. Micklem points

Figure 3.1 Extraction of the monster Mercurius and the raising of the feminine image of Mary into the hierarchy. "Speculum Trinitatis," from Hieronymus Reusner, *Pandora*, Emblem 14, 16th century.

Source: Public domain.

to the image of the hermaphrodite discussed in the previous chapter (see Figure 2.7) and notes that most people see it as a symbol representing an integrated wholeness without letting themselves experience its grotesque and monstrous character. Edinger gives another example of the monstrous in the image of the "Extraction of Mercurius and the coronation of the Virgin" from Reusner's *Pandora* (1582).

In this image, Edinger discusses the issue of monstrosity and the Christian psyche. Like Jung, he considers what issues might have been left out of Christian symbolism as it developed over the past two thousand years. He believes Reusner's picture of Pandora contains the essence of alchemy, and was for Jung the carrier of those psychological elements elided by Christianity, serving as a counterbalance to it. In this figure, we see the assumption of Mary into heaven and her coronation. In the lower part of the picture one can see what Edinger calls the birth of a monster. What is so shocking for Edinger is the juxtaposition of the spiritual image of the assumption with "the image of the birth of the monster out of the lump of matter."[13] The whole image reflects the struggle to integrate both the feminine and the principle of materiality into the Christian vision.

The image is monstrous to the Christian eye and for Edinger the lower image of birth from matter is humorously portrayed in the context of the Christian Weltanschauung as analogous to "a cuckoo's egg that's been laid in somebody else's nest" and from which "something unexpected is going to hatch." French philosopher Jacques Derrida has likewise linked the monstrous with the future. For Derrida, "The future is necessarily monstrous: The figure of the future, that is, that which can only be surprisingly, that for which we are not prepared, you see, is heralded by a species of monsters."[14]

Abraxas

Perhaps one of the most potent of such monsters appears in Jung's *Seven Sermons of the Dead* (1916). These Sermons have been considered to be an expression of "what Jung went through in the years [of confronting the unconscious] 1913–1917" and reflect "what he was trying to bring to birth."[15] The Sermons contain "hints or anticipations of ideas that were to figure later in his scientific writings, more particularly concerning the polaristic nature of the psyche, of life in general, and of all psychological statements."[16]

In Sermon I, Jung sets up the Gnostic distinction between the non-distinctive pleroma and the essence of man as distinctiveness. Jung says: "When we distinguish qualities of the pleroma, we are speaking from the ground of our own distinctiveness and concerning our own distinctiveness. But still we have said nothing concerning the pleroma."[17] The distinctions we *must* make are about us; Jung calls this the "principium individuationis."[18] All we can do is attribute our polar categories to the larger "reality." Jung mentions:

The Effective and the Ineffective.
Fullness and Emptiness.

Living and Dead.
Difference and Sameness.
Light and Darkness.
The Hot and the Cold.
Force and Matter.
Time and Space.
Good and Evil.
Beauty and Ugliness.
The One and the Many, etc.[19]

While Jung clearly notes that man, due to his nature, distinguishes qualities of the pleroma that are his own, he also speaks of these qualities as belonging to the pleroma which, paradoxically, in reality, has no qualities. But since he is also part of the pleroma and distinguishes qualities, one could also say that the pleroma expresses these qualities as well. In this arcane way, Jung links the finite with the infinite and the human with the divine. In essence, he writes, "we have said nothing concerning the pleroma. . . . However, it is needful to speak"[20] and we must be true to this need. If we do not make such distinctions, Jung says, we "get beyond our own nature" and "fall into indistinctiveness" and give ourselves over to dissolution into nothingness.[21] This is death to our human essence and so we fight against this "perilous sameness."[22] While Jung goes to some lengths to distinguish man from the pleroma, he also links them, noting "As we *are* the pleroma itself, we also have all these qualities in us."[23] Jung distinguishes how these qualities are different as they exist in us and in the pleroma, noting that in us these qualities "are not balanced and void, but effective. Thus are we the victims of the pairs of opposites. The pleroma is rent in us."[24]

In the pleroma, the opposites are balanced and void, but in us they are not. What this means for man is that as we attempt to attain the good and the beautiful, the evil and ugly are likewise implicitly a part of our human experience. One side cannot be completely separated from the other. While the pleroma in itself has no qualities, we create these opposites necessarily by our thinking. Two fundamental opposites are God and the devil, what Jung calls first manifestations of nothingness. In man, God and the devil do not extinguish themselves, but stand against one another as effective opposites. "God and the devil are distinguished by the qualities of fullness and emptiness, generation and destruction," and effectiveness (the generative principle of the opposites) stands above both, in essence, "is a god above god, since in its effect it uniteth fullness and emptiness."[25] For Jung, the radical and primeval living of the opposites as a demonic force is a monstrous and divine reality he calls by the Gnostic name Abraxas.

Jung reasons if Abraxas is effectiveness, nothing stands opposed to it, but the ineffective, so its effective nature freely unfolds itself. The ineffective is not. Therefore, it does not resist it, so one might imagine it as a primal theory of action. Jung continues, calling Abraxas an "improbable probability, unreal reality"[26] noting that if the pleroma had "a being, Abraxas would be its manifestation. It is the effective itself, not any particular effect, but effect in general."[27] Abraxas is thus force and duration, "the sun and at the same time the eternally sucking gorge of the void, the belittling and dismembering devil. . . . What the god-sun speaketh is life. What the devil speaketh is death. But Abraxas speaketh that hallowed and accursed word which is life and death at the same time."[28] This strange confluence and interpenetration of what we think of as opposites renders Abraxas "terrible" and a "monster."[29] Jung writes that Abraxas is "a monster of the underworld, a thousand-armed polyp, coiled knot of winged serpents, frenzy."[30] It is like the hermaphrodite we have seen above and

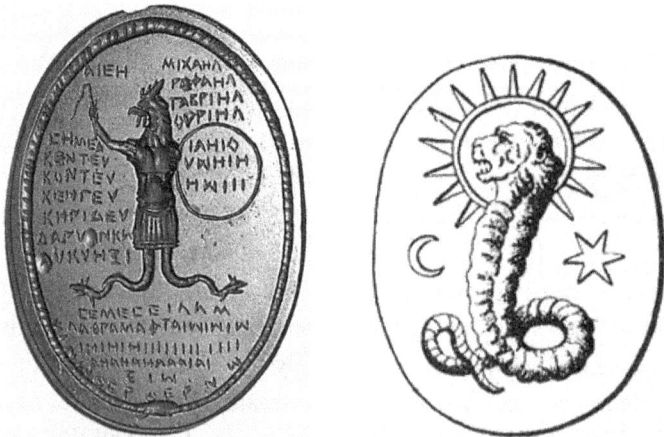

Figure 3.2 These images of Abraxas show its strange composite and monstrous form. (1) Magical amulet, green jasper, KM 2.6054. (Courtesy of the Kelsey Museum of Archaeology. University of Michigan, Ann Arbor.) (2) From Bernard de Montfaucon, *L'antiquité expliquée et représentée en figures*, 1722.

Source: Public domain.

"of the earliest beginning. It is the lord of the toads and frogs, which live in the water and go up on the land, whose chorus ascendeth at noon and at midnight. It is abundance that seeketh union with emptiness. It is holy begetting."[31]

It is hard to come to terms with the implications of such a deity with what Shamdasani describes as "the uniting of the Christian God with Satan."[32] "Abraxas himself is *LIFE*."[33] Such a characterization for Drob "invokes comparison not only with the unconscious, but with the broad conception of the . . . unforeseeable future."[34] Drob notes "Abraxas can be understood as the awesome future that can neither be anticipated nor circumscribed by words: 'Before him there is no question and no reply.'"[35] "Abraxas is the 'chaos,' the 'utterly boundless,' 'eternally incomprehensible . . . cruel contradictoriness of nature.'"[36] "'Abraxas,' we are told, 'is the world, its becoming and its passing.'"[37]

Mercurius

In the frontispiece to Jung's *Alchemical Studies*, the spirit of Mercurius is likewise represented as a monster.

For Jung, this image is one of the primal unconscious whose three extra heads represent Luna, Sol, and a *coniunctio* of Sol and Luna on the far right. The unity of the three is symbolized by Hermes, who represents the quaternity "in which the fourth is at the same time the unity of the three." This image captures the quality of paradox and monstrosity stressed by Jung, Micklem, and Edinger. It is a symbolic unification, but one not easily assimilable by the ego. This image may well be considered an example of a transformation going on in the God image of the Western psyche by virtue of the alchemical process that has been inserted into it, a process that gives birth to new possibilities. The new God image heralds the importance not only of incorporating the feminine and matter into our vision of spirit, but also of "the discovery of the unconscious and the process of individuation."[38]

On a personal level, it also signifies all of the struggles of incarnated existence, "[e]very hard disagreeable fact" of ordinary life.[39] Edinger uses the eloquence of Shakespeare to describe the painful facts:

> The slings and arrows of outrageous fortune, . . .
> . . . the whips and scorns of time,

Figure 3.3 An image of the Mercurial monster. From G.B. Nazari, *Della tramuta-tione metallica sogni tre*, 16th century.
Source: Public domain.

The oppressor's wrong, the proud man's contumely,
The pangs of dispriz'd love, the law's delay,
The insolence of office, and the spurns
That patient merit of the unworthy takes, . . .
To grunt and sweat under a weary life. . . .[40]

If one is honest, these insults of life cannot simply be passed over in any idealized transcendence. Such experiences hurt, sting, enrage, and sometimes depress and kill us, and yet they must be acknowledged, negotiated, and made conscious if any real awareness of the Self is to take place. Edinger notes, as Jung and Micklem have, that "[t]he living experience of the Self is a monstrosity. It's a coming together of opposites that appalls the ego and exposes it to anguish, demoralization and violation of all reasonable considerations."[41] It is a violation of everything we have come to expect as natural, reasonable, and normal. Edinger gives us a feeling for this in the following images of the unity of opposites. In alchemy, the monstrous aspect of the conjunction is particularly emphasized when the opposites that are brought together are not at first well differentiated. This situation is referred to as a *monstrum*, or premature unity, that is, any unity which does not differentiate itself into distinct realities.[42] The image of premature unity is sometimes expressed by images of incest and premature conjunction as in this image.

Figure 3.4 Union of opposites as monstrosity. From *Hexastichon Sebastiani Brant*, 1502.

Source: Public domain.

Figure 3.5 An alchemical image of two birds illustrating the spirit of antagonistic opposition. From *Theosophie alchimie*, 1678.

Source: Public domain.

Such an incestuous unification of opposites must be first broken apart so that the opposite can be more clearly differentiated. In such a process, considerable aggression and enmity is a result, as illustrated in the conflict between animals.

The confrontation of beastly forces anticipates a "higher" transformation of conflicting energies indicated by both the crowns and the wings of the lion figures. Jung speculates in *The Psychology of the Transference* that

> Had the alchemists understood the psychological aspects of their work, they would have been in a position to free their "unity symbol"

Figure 3.6 Two traditional images of the conflict between winged and unwinged lions – spirit and body. (1) From Michael Maier, *Atalanta Fugiens*, Emblem 16, 1617. (Public domain.) (2) From J.D. Mylius, *Philosophia reformata*, 1622.

Source: Public domain.

from the grip of instructive sexuality [and aggression] where, for better or worse, mere nature, unsupported by the critical intellect, was bound to leave it. Nature could say no more than that the contribution of supreme opposites was a hybrid thing.[43]

Jung speculates that the thing-like nature of the alchemists "unity symbol" was due to the fact that the alchemists were not yet in a position to see the implicit nature of consciousness in the midst of their images. The question remained: "how is the profound cleavage in man and world to be understood, how are we to respond to it and, if possible, abolish it?"[44] Jung notes that in the long course of the dialectical process the unconscious has continued to produce images of the goal of the work.

In *Psychology and Alchemy*, Jung describes this process as it existed in the work with a long series of dreams. These images were "mostly concerned with ideas of the mandala type, that is, the circle and the quaternity"[45] which represented images of the goal of the unity of opposites. The cross, circle, and sphere, as well as the less frequent images of "the luminous character of the center" or the image of a "superior type of personality,"[46] the enlightened or illuminate adept, represented the idea of unity and wholeness, the overcoming of warring opposites.

The linking of the opposites by the alchemist was imagined both as a chemical procedure as well as a mental and geometric one. One classic example of the benign conjunction is the image of the alchemist as a divine geometer.

In the example above, this task is depicted in an image of the alchemist as a divine geometer who brings opposites together into a grand design representing the Philosophers' Stone. The motto beneath the image states: "Make a circle out of a man and a woman, out of this a square, out of this a triangle. Make a circle and you will have the Philosopher's Stone."[47] The Stone is created by harmonizing and containing masculine and feminine energies representing a wide range of binary pairings, e.g., light and dark, spirit and matter, sulfur and mercury. These "opposites," expressed by the male and female images, are contained in the diagram's inner circle, which "represents the Hermetic vessel, the cosmic egg in which the Stone is prepared."[48] The square surrounded by the inner circle stands for the four elements and suggests the ancient enigmatic idea of squaring the circle: an impossible task in terms of modern mathematics, but an essential condition for the preparation of the Stone. This "impossible" conjunction is then imagined to be contained in a triangle representing the dynamic force of "the third," the mystery of generative possibilities. Finally,

Figure 3.7 The alchemist and the *lumen naturae*. Frontispiece from C.F.
Sabor, *Practica naturae vera*, 1721.

Source: Public domain.

the entire process is enclosed within a larger macrocosmic circle. The importance of man's contribution to the process is illustrated by the alchemist holding a giant compass with one point touching the inner circle and the other
resting on the outer sphere, thus linking the microcosmic unity of inner life
with the outer wholeness of the macrocosmic world and exemplifying the
famous adage, "as above so below." The work of linking above and below
was a classic alchemical theme represented in numerous forms in alchemical
literature and in the images which illustrated it.

The variety of images of the conjunction and the Philosophers' Stone
range from the very simple and benign to the very complex and monstrous.

Figure 3.8 The squaring of the circle as image of the Philosophers' Stone. From Michael Maier, *Atalanta Fugiens*, Emblem 21, 1687.

Source: Public domain.

Some images portray a simple process or moment in the work while others give us an image of the overall alchemical process.

For Jung, such grand images are attempts to express the complexity of the Self and the individuation process. They aim to represent psyche's attempt to achieve order and wholeness and, like the "self," to contain and organize the wholeness of psychic reality. As such, they attempt to grapple with what Edinger has called "a wild and luxuriant, tangled mass of overlapping images that is maddening to the order-seeking conscious mind."[49] In short, they maintain a sense of the monstrous which, for Jung, in principle is "always just beyond our reach."[50]

Figure 3.9 Four alchemical images depicting the linking of above and below. (1) From J.D. Mylius, *Philosophia reformata*, 1622. (Public domain.) (2) Maria the Jewess, famous alchemist of the 1st-2nd century A.D. From Michael Maier, *Symbola aurea mensae*, 1617. (Public domain.) (3) Hermes Trismegistos. From D. Stolcius de Stolcenberg, *Viridarium chymicum* (1624). (Public domain.) (4) Engraving by Nicolas Bonnart. From Nicolas de Locques, *Les Rudiments de la Philosophie Naturelle*, frontispiece, 1665. (Public domain.)

Mysterium Coniunctionis

Jung continued to reflect on the problem of opposites throughout his life and work. The fullest treatment of this issue was taken up in his final work entitled *Mysterium Coniunctionis: An Inquiry into the Separation and Synthesis of Psychic Opposites in Alchemy*. In this work, he followed his original

Figure 3.10 Two images of the benign conjunction, in which we see the unification of opposites in terms of the marriage of Sol and Luna. (1) From Johann Conrad Barchusen, *Elementa chemiae*, Plate 503, Figure 9, 1718. (Public domain.) (2) From J.D. Mylius, *Philosophia reformata*, Engraving 19, 1622. (Public domain.)

intention of representing the whole range of alchemy as a kind of "psychology of alchemy," and "as an alchemical basis for depth psychology."[51]

In *C. G. Jung Speaking*, Jung offered a synopsis of the alchemical process:

This work is difficult and strewn with obstacles; the alchemical opus is dangerous. Right at the beginning you meet the "dragon," the chthonic

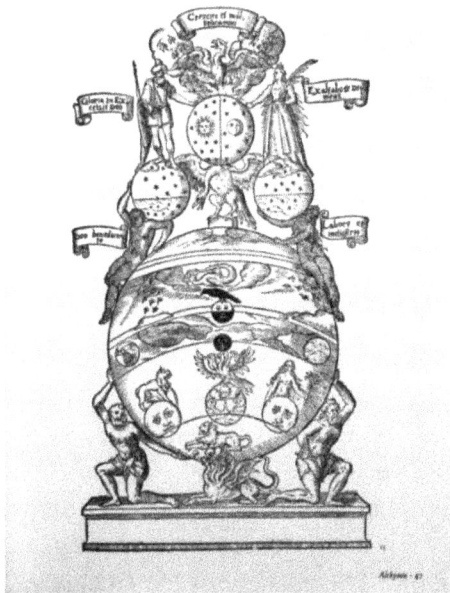

Figure 3.11 Two images of the complexity of alchemical stages. (1) Stephan Michelspacher, *Cabala*, Engraving 3, 1615. (Public domain.) (2) Woodcut from Andreas Libavius, *Commentariorum alchymiae*, 1606. (Public domain.)

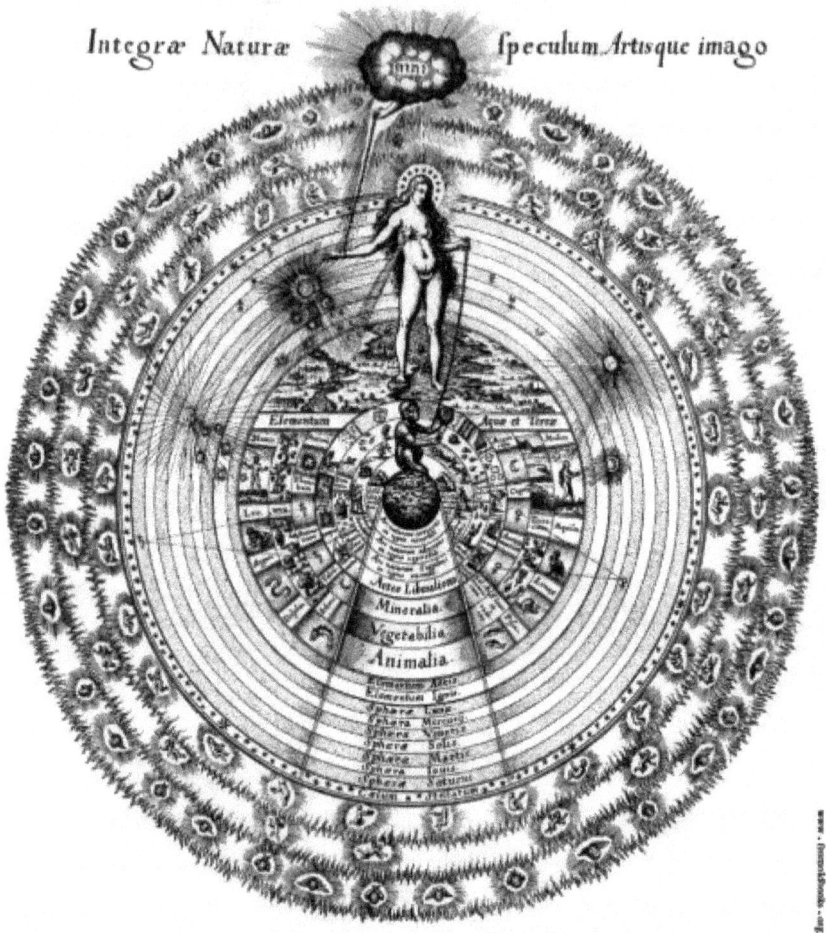

Figure 3.12 Grand image of the alchemical process. Engraving by J.T. de Bry, from Robert Fludd, *Utriusque cosmi*, 1618.

Source: Public domain.

spirit, the "devil" or, as the alchemists called it, the "blackness," the *nigredo,* and this encounter produces suffering. "Matter" suffers right up to the final disappearance of the blackness; in psychological terms, the soul finds itself in the throes of melancholy, locked in a struggle with the "shadow." The mystery of the *coniunctio,* the central mystery of alchemy, aims precisely at the synthesis of the opposites, the assimilation of the blackness, the integration of the devil. . . .

Figure 3.13 Cosmological vision of the achievement of the Philosophers' Stone. "Macrocosm and microcosm." From J.D. Mylius, Opus Medico-Chymicum, 1618.

Source: Public domain.

In the language of the alchemists, matter suffers until the *nigredo* disappears, when the "dawn" (*aurora*) will be announced by the "peacock's tail" (*cauda pavonis*) and a new day will break, the *leukosis* or *albedo*. But in this state of "whiteness" one does not *live* in the true sense of the word, it is a sort of abstract, ideal state. In order to make it come alive it must have "blood," it must have what the alchemists call the *rubedo*, the "redness" of life. Only the total experience of being can transform this ideal state of the *albedo* into a fully human mode of existence. Blood alone can reanimate a glorious state of consciousness in which the last trace of blackness is dissolved, in which the devil no longer has an autonomous existence but rejoins the profound unity of the psyche. Then the *opus magnum* is finished: the human soul is completed [sic] integrated.[52]

At the conclusion of his work, Jung's imagination was captured by the ideas and metaphors of alchemy, with its dragons, suffering matter, peacock's tail, alembics and athanors; its red and green lions, kings and queens, fishes' eyes and inverted philosophical trees, salamanders and hermaphrodites; its black suns and white earth, and its metals – lead, silver and gold; its colors – black, white, yellow and red; and its distillations and coagulations, and rich array of Latin terms. All of these became the best possible expressions of a psychic mystery as yet unknown, and enunciated and amplified his maturing vision of the parallels between alchemy and his own psychology of the unconscious. All this and far more, Jung saw as projected by the alchemists into matter. Their effort was to bring about unity from the disparate parts of the psyche, creating a *chymical* wedding. Jung saw this as the moral task of alchemy: to unify the disparate elements of the soul, both personal and ultimately cosmic, and thus to create the goal, the *lapis* or Philosophers' Stone. Likewise, Jung's psychology works with the conflicts and dissociations of psychic life and attempts to bring about the mysterious "unification" and a sense of wholeness. We have seen such images in the benign form of the geometric conjunction and in the monstrous forms of the hermaphrodite, Mercurius, and Abraxas. All of these are images of supreme meaning (*Übersinn*) and thus images that move toward what Jung saw as the notions of the Self and the Philosophers' Stone. With his *Mysterium Coniunctionis*, Jung noted that his psychology was at last "given its place in reality and established upon its historical foundations."[53]

Notes

1 Portions of this chapter were previously published as the "Foreword," in *Reading the Red Book*, ix–xv (Reused with the kind permission of Spring Journal, Inc).
2 Giegerich, "Liber Novus," 362.
3 Hillman, at "Carl Gustav Jung & the Red Book."
4 Giegerich, "Liber Novus," 384.
5 Ibid., 383–384.
6 Ibid., 383.
7 Hillman, at "Carl Gustav Jung & the Red Book."
8 Tarrant, "Carl Jung's Red Book." (Used by kind permission of the author).
9 Ibid.
10 Ibid.
11 Jung, *The Red Book*, 229.
12 Micklem, "I Am Not Myself."
13 Edinger, *Mysterium Lectures*, 134.
14 Derrida, "Passages," 386–387. For more about Derrida and his idea of the monstrous, see, for example, Derrida, "Deconstruction and the Other," 123; see also Derrida,

"Passages – from Traumatism to Promise"; Drob, *Reading the Red Book*, 289–290, footnote 19.

15 Aniela Jaffé. Introductory comments to Appendix V of C.G. Jung, *Memories*, 378.
16 Ibid.
17 Jung, *Memories*, 380.
18 Ibid.
19 Ibid., 380–381.
20 Ibid., 380.
21 Ibid.
22 Ibid.
23 Ibid., 381; emphasis mine.
24 Ibid.
25 Ibid., 383.
26 Ibid.
27 Ibid.
28 Ibid.
29 Ibid., 384.
30 Ibid.
31 Ibid.
32 Shamdasani, Introduction to *The Red Book*, 206.
33 Drob, *Reading the Red Book*, 236.
34 Ibid.
35 Ibid. Includes quote from Jung, *The Red Book*, 350b.
36 Ibid.
37 Ibid.
38 Edinger, *Mysterium Lectures*, 135.
39 Ibid.
40 Although Edinger does quote this passage from Shakespeare, *Hamlet*, Act 3, Scene 1, please note that this particular translation was retrieved from Project Gutenberg.
41 Edinger, *Mysterium Lectures*, 136.
42 Hillman, *Alchemical Psychology*, 193.
43 Jung, *The Practice of Psychotherapy (CW16)*, §533.
44 Ibid., §534.
45 Ibid., §535.
46 Ibid.
47 Coudert, *Alchemy*, 58.
48 Ibid.
49 Edinger, *Anatomy*, 14.
50 Jung, *The Practice of Psychotherapy (CW16)*, §536.
51 Jung, *Memories*, 221.
52 Jung, *C.G. Jung Speaking*, 228–229.
53 Jung, *Memories*, 221.

Chapter 4

Classical development of Jung's ideas of alchemy and the Philosophers' Stone in Von Franz and Edinger[1]

Jung's studies of alchemy strongly influenced his close followers, Marie-Louise von Franz (1915–1988) in Europe and Edward Edinger (1922–1998) in the United States. Both von Franz and Edinger held Jung's work to be fundamental and viewed themselves primarily as elaborators of his ideas, and as commentators who gave students easier access to the work of the master. These rather humble self-assessments do not adequately represent the extent to which their own contributions have extended and contributed to the field of analytical psychology and especially to our understanding of alchemy.

Marie-Louise von Franz

Von Franz has been considered the primary developer of Jung's alchemical legacy. She "became world renowned among followers of Jung and after his death was an eloquent spokesperson for his ideas."[2] Von Franz met Jung when she was 18 years old in 1933, just around the time Jung's interest in alchemy was catalyzing. He analyzed her in exchange for her work on translations of texts from Greek and Latin. She continued as a close collaborator and eventually published what was in essence the third part of *the Mysterium Coniunctionis* called the *Aurora consurgens* (1966). The *Aurora* is an account of and commentary on an alchemical text that dated roughly from the thirteenth century. The text has been ascribed to Thomas Aquinas, though its authorship is disputed. Jung chose this text as exemplary of medieval Christianity's attempt to come to terms with alchemical philosophy and as an instance of the alchemical problem of the opposites. Von Franz's (1966) commentary shows how Jung's analytical

DOI: 10.4324/9781003215905-5

psychology may be used as a key to unlock the meaning of this difficult and very psychological text, and how the traditional practice of alchemy is best understood as a symbolic process.

Von Franz extended her work on alchemy through lectures to students at the Jung Institute in Zurich in 1959. These lectures were transcribed by Una Thomas, a member of the seminar, and published in 1980 under the title *Alchemy: An Introduction to the Symbolism and the Psychology*. The book was designed to be an introduction to Jung's more difficult study and is a "practical account of what the alchemists were really looking for – emotional balance and wholeness."[3] The text contains lectures on old Greek and Arabic alchemy as well as on later European alchemy and the *Aurora consurgens*. In giving her course and publishing this book von Franz hoped to enable students to read Jung with more comprehension. She recognized how dark and difficult his alchemical writings were and that even many of his closest students could not follow his work in this area. Nevertheless, she stressed the importance of this work. Her lectures continued in Zurich in January and February of 1969, and her book *Alchemical Active Imagination* was published in 1979. In addition to a short history of alchemy, von Franz concentrated on Gerhard Dorn, an alchemist and physician who lived probably in the sixteenth century. Following his work as a whole, and staying close to the original, she showed the similarity between the alchemist's practice and Jung's technique of active imagination, both of which promote a dialogue with the unconscious.

Von Franz's last direct work on alchemy, a "Psychological Commentary" on the *Kitāb Ḥall ar-Rumūz* (or *Clearing of Enigmas*) is a historical introduction to this Arabic alchemical text. The author, Muhammad Ibn Umail ("Senior"), lived in the tenth century AD. This text among others represents the missing link within the mystical branch of alchemy, connecting Gnostic-Hermetic Greek alchemy to the mystical Latin alchemy of Europe.

Until her death, Von Franz acted as a collaborator, translator, and creative developer of Jung's alchemical work. She contributed to the history of alchemy, the dialogue of alchemy with Christianity, and the importance of a symbolic and psychological approach. She also furthered our thinking about the alchemical problem of the opposites and our understanding of the *unus mundus*, the unified field upon which the opposites rely. These themes are further elaborated in her book *Psyche and Matter* (1992). In it, she brings together reflections on number, time, synchronicity, and the relationship between depth psychology, contemporary physics, and quantum theory. She has also contributed to Jung's view of Christianity and an understanding of the importance of alchemy as a religious contribution to the Christian myth. In an interview, when asked what the main value was of Jung's and her own work on alchemy, she stated that:

> civilization needs a myth to live . . . And I think that the Christian myth, on which we have lived, has degenerated and become one-sided and insufficient. I think alchemy is the complete myth. If our Western civilization has a possibility of survival, it would be by accepting the alchemical myth, which is a richer completion and continuation of the Christian myth . . . The Christian myth is deficient in not including enough of the feminine. (Catholicism has the Virgin Mary, but it's only the purified feminine; it does not include the dark feminine). Christianity treats matter as dead and does not face the problem of the opposites – of evil. Alchemy faces the problem of the opposites, faces the problem of matter, and faces the problem of the feminine.[4]

Edward F. Edinger

If von Franz can be considered the pre-eminent follower of Jung's in Europe, few would argue against the same status for Edward Edinger in the United States. For more than forty years, "in lectures, books, tapes and videos, he masterfully presented and distilled the essence of Jung's work, illuminating its relevance for both collective and individual psychology."[5] Though Edinger wrote on a wide range of topics, including Moby Dick, Faust, Greek philosophy, the Bible, the Apocalypse, and the God image, like von Franz he had a special passion for alchemy. In the first issue of *Quadrant* (spring 1968), the New York Institute announced its final spring series of lectures by Edinger entitled "Psychotherapy and Alchemy," and the following issue contained a précis of Edinger's lectures, "Alchemy as a Psychological Process." These lectures, given in New York and Los Angeles in the late 1970s and early 1980s, were serially published in *Quadrant: Journal of the CG. Jung Foundation for Analytical Psychology* and later collected for his book *Anatomy of the Psyche: Alchemical Symbolism in Psychotherapy* (1985).

In these lectures and in his book, Edinger focused on seven selected images, which he used to organize the typical stages of the alchemical process: *calcinatio, solutio, coagulatio, sublimatio, mortficatio, separatio,* and *coniunctio.* By focusing on these images/operations, Edinger attempts to bring order to "the chaos of alchemy."[6] Each of these operations is found to be the center of an elaborate symbol system. "These central symbols of transformation . . . provide basic categories by which to understand the life of the psyche, and they illustrate almost the full range of experiences that constitute individuation."[7]

In his work, Edinger views Jung's discovery of the "reality of the psyche" as a new approach to understanding alchemy and other pre- or pseudo-sciences such as astrology. For Edinger, these systems of thought are expressions of a phenomenology that can serve to illustrate patterns and regularities of the objective psyche. As such they serve as archetypal images of transformation. What Edinger considers himself and Jung as presenting are psychic facts rather than "a theoretical construct [or] a philosophical speculation."[8]

Edinger was also concerned with the practical problems of psychotherapy. His goal was to become familiar enough with archetypal images and to have sufficient enough knowledge drawn from personal analysis that one can discover an anatomy of the psyche, as "objective as the anatomy of the body."[9] He contended that psychological theories are often too narrow and inadequate, and that when analysis goes deep, things are set in motion which are mysterious and profound. It is easy for both therapist and patient to lose their way. According to Edinger:

> What makes alchemy so valuable for psychotherapy is that its images concretize the experiences of transformation that one undergoes in psychotherapy. Taken as a whole, alchemy provides a kind of anatomy of individuation. Its images will be most meaningful . . . to those who have had a personal experience of the unconscious.[10]

For him, as for Jung, the work of alchemy can be equated with the individuation process, but the alchemical corpus exceeds any individual's process in richness and scope. In the end, for Edinger, alchemy was considered to be a sacred work, one that required a religious attitude; and like von Franz, he saw Jung's work in alchemy as a development of the Christian myth.

Edinger's examination of Jung's work on alchemy continued with a number of texts carefully devoted to explicating it. While *Anatomy of the Psyche* (1985) is an overall look at alchemical processes and the symbolism of the individuation process, Edinger's further reflections focus on particular works of Jung in order to give his readers access to and help in understanding them. In 1994, he published *The Mystery of Coniunctio: Alchemical Image of Individuation*. It contains both an introduction to Jung's *Mysterium Coniunctionis* and an essay on the psychological interpretation of the *Rosarium* pictures. These essays were first presented as lectures at the C.G. Jung Institute of San Francisco during 19–20 October 1984. In this work, Edinger takes a somewhat different stance from Jung, suggesting other ways to look at the pictures of the *Rosarium*. He does not oppose Jung's interpretations but suggests that the images have multiple facets, meanings, and contexts in which they can be seen.

In 1995, Edinger published *The Mysterium Lectures* based on a course he gave to members of the Jung Society of Los Angeles during 1986–1987. In this text he leads his readers through Jung's most difficult work. He follows his fundamental metaphor of the anatomy of the psyche, suggesting that this is a book of facts described in "images." He selects the major images throughout the *Mysterium* and elaborates them with amplificatory material and commentary. Edinger had the capacity to take difficult symbolic material and to translate it into clear, contemporary psychological statements, making it possible to integrate the material into our current psychological worldview.

In his work *The Aion Lectures: Exploring the Self in C.G. Jung's Aion*, Edinger elaborates a reading of Jung that emphasizes psychic reality as empirical facts described in images. Edinger's reading has a basis in Jung's thought. For instance, in *The Psychology of the Transference*, Jung writes "My business is merely the natural science of the psyche, and my main concern is to establish the facts. How these facts are named and what further interpretation is then placed upon them is of secondary importance. Natural science is not a science of words and ideas, but facts." Jung continues:

> I am no terminological rigorist – call the existing symbols "wholeness," "self," "consciousness," "higher ego," or what you will, it makes little difference. I for my part only try not to give any false or misleading names. All these terms are simply names for the facts that alone carry weight. The names I give do not imply a philosophy, although I cannot prevent people from barking at these terminological phantoms as if they were metaphysical postulates. The facts are

sufficient in themselves, and it is well to know about them. But their interpretation should be left to the individual's discretion.[11]

On the basis of such statements, one can read Jung as holding a position in which language and interpretation are separate from facts and, with such a conviction, one can see Jung as coming from a fundamentally natural scientific position. However, to emphasize such a position does not do justice to the complexity of his position. Jung's stance as a natural scientist was often expressed when he was concerned about justifying his research to a scientific community.

What Jung and Edinger called "facts" are both more and less than the term is commonly understood to mean in a natural scientific perspective. This ambiguity continues throughout the development of the Jungian tradition and in Edinger's work. The strange ambiguity in Edinger's description is that every time he used the words "fact" and "objective," he italicizes the words as if to set them apart from our common understanding of fact and objectivity. I believe he does this because, beyond the common and natural scientific use of these words, he recognizes as Jung did that approaching psychic reality is not well understood within the simple Cartesian binaries of subject and object. At the same time, however, he holds onto the pre-phenomenological scientific and medical framework in which he was trained as a physician and psychiatrist because he is still struggling with a methodology which can do justice to the complexity that psychic reality demands. In the spirit of science and the medical model, Edinger writes about "facts" which he claims "go to make up an *anatomy of the psyche*, which is at the same time an embryology, since we are dealing with a process of development and transformation."[12] For Edinger, as noted earlier, this *anatomy of the psyche* "is as objective as the anatomy of the body."

Edinger's medical analogies link psyche to a natural scientific view of reality, but he sees psychic reality as symbolic and expresses this side by side with his medical frame of reference. He speaks as well of a "*phenomenology* of the objective psyche" by which he seems to mean "to bring into visibility certain experiential modes or categories of the individuation process. . . [which] serve to illustrate patterns and regularities of the objective psyche."[13] He saw these phenomenological patterns and categories both as facts that can be put into an ordered and objective frame of scientific objectivities and, alternatively, as "facts" that can be put into a structured and ordered phenomenology of psyche itself. To amplify this idea, Edinger quotes an old alchemical saying, "Dissolve the matter in its own water."[14]

Alchemy provided a rich and complex network of images that Edinger considered phenomenological and it was these "presentational" images that he considered psyche's own waters. In *The Aion Lectures*, Edinger states that

> Jung writes about the psyche in what I call a presentational way, by which I mean he presents us with psychic facts rather than with theories about the facts. We are so used to living out of a conceptual context that we spare ourselves the encounter with the raw facts. And because we are not familiar with the psychic facts Jung presents, they seem alien and disconnected. Our task is to become familiar with the facts Jung gives us. As we gradually gain that familiarity, their inner connections and the whole presentational method become visible. This leads into a mode of thinking different from the usual.[15]

From Edinger's perspective, we are used to linear thinking whereas what he is proposing is an ordering and presentation of psychic facts following Jung's method of active imagination and amplification. I believe in this process. Edinger is aiming at something that goes beyond seeing psyche as a simple "object" of consciousness. Based on Jung's ideas of active imagination and amplification, Edinger develops what he calls a method of "cluster thinking," something that is more like a structural phenomenology of images that gives one a variegated, dynamic, and mosaic view of psyche. He describes "cluster thinking" as beginning with a "central image and. . . [finding] a cluster of related images connected to it."[16]

In *Anatomy of the Psyche*, Edinger gives examples of cluster thinking based on the operations of alchemy. As noted above, he organizes the alchemical process on the basis of seven operations: *calcinatio, solutio, coagulatio, sublimatio, mortficatio, separatio,* and *coniunctio*. He dedicates a chapter of his book to each operation, placing each of them at the center of its own elaborate symbol system, which then provides "the basic categories by which to understand the life of the psyche."[17] At the beginning of each chapter, Edinger depicts this complex symbol system imagistically, creating a map of psychic reality as it presents itself in the alchemical process. I include below two of the seven basic operations fundamental to the alchemical transformation process illustrated by Edinger: *mortificatio/putrefactio* and *coniunctio*:

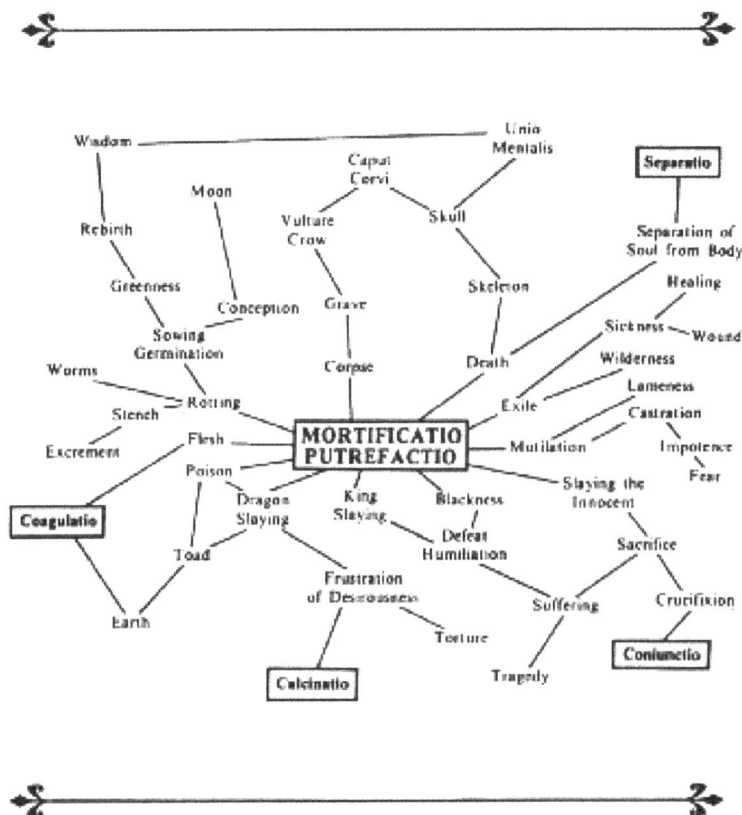

Figure 4.1 Mortificatio/Putrefactio. From Edward Edinger, Anatomy of the Psyche: Alchemical Symbolism in Psychotherapy, 146.

Source: Courtesy Open Court Books.

In these diagrams, Edinger surrounds each operational image with a web of related images, tracing the phenomenological and structural relations between them by connecting lines of relatedness. As the central image is changed, the connecting lines likewise change, resulting in a different con-stellation of psychic reality. On the basis of the diagrams themselves, it is not easy or even possible to adequately understand all of the relational aspects of the mosaic. However, when one reads the details of each of the opera-tions and then looks at the chart, one gets a structurally rich and variegated overview of the psychic reality Edinger is pointing to. I believe Edinger intends these maps of "psychic reality" to be seen as dynamic and changing processes, a moving and transformational view of the psyche rather than a static or fixed representation of it. In addition, if we imagine that all seven

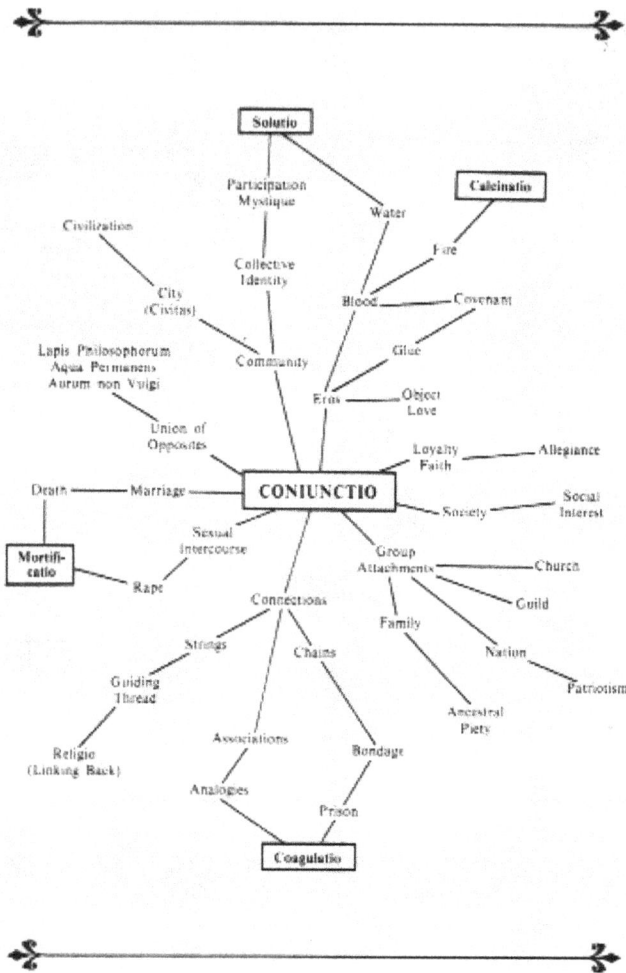

Figure 4.2 Coniunctio. From Edward Edinger, *Anatomy of the Psyche: Alchemical Symbolism in Psychotherapy*, 210.

Source: Courtesy Open Court Books.

diagrams are interrelated and that the constellations around the seven processes change along with the central image, the process view of psyche is richly enhanced. It is as if the psyche can be viewed in each moment through the eye of the central image or from any point in the dynamic process. Earlier we spoke of the eye of Mercurius in the clash between two serpents and here we might imagine the possibility of multiple and changing viewpoints, multiple eyes through which we might view psychic reality.

Each chapter of Edinger's book then might be seen not simply as a linear process that ends with the *coniunctio* and the Philosophers' Stone, but also as a circular, ongoing process with changing matrices showing an image of the psyche at each moment from a central but changing standpoint, with no Archimedean transcendental point outside psyche itself. Perhaps this dynamic view of psychic reality is itself a way of imaging the Philosophers' Stone and the Self. While Edinger does not elaborate this view, I believe it is implicit in his exegesis and that it sits side-by-side with his translation of alchemical images into a "scientific," medical, anatomical frame of reference and into the language of classical Jungian psychological categories. While this latter perspective seems to make alchemy more understandable to modern consciousness, it also runs the risk of oversimplification and static reification. When this occurs, the complexities of alchemy, the Philosophers' Stone, and "psychic reality" are translated into a "psychology of alchemy" and the unknown monstrosities of ideas like the Philosophers' Stone are translated into the Jungian notion of "the Self." Put in this way, and in spite of my positive regard for both Von Franz and Edinger, they at times too easily translate alchemy into a conceptual, taken-for-granted framework of Jung's psychology. Such a reductive reading invites alternative readings and thus sets the stage for the revisionist theories of James Hillman and Wolfgang Giegerich.

Notes

1 Sections of this chapter are a modified version of my entry Marlan, "Alchemy," 263–295.
2 Kirsch, *The Jungians*, 11.
3 Von Franz, *Alchemy*, 273.
4 Von Franz, in Wagner, "A Conversation," 15–16.
5 Sharp, "Tribute for E. Edinger," 18.
6 Edinger, *Anatomy*, 14.
7 Ibid., 15.
8 Ibid., Preface.
9 Ibid.
10 Ibid., 2.
11 Jung, *The Practice of Psychotherapy (CW16)*, §537.
12 Edinger, *Anatomy*, Preface.
13 Ibid.; emphasis mine.
14 Ibid., 1.
15 Edinger, *The Aion Lectures*, 11.
16 Ibid.
17 Edinger, *Anatomy*, 15.

Chapter 5

Innovations, criticisms, and developments: James Hillman and Wolfgang Giegerich

James Hillman and archetypal psychology: imagination is the cornerstone[1]

If von Franz and Edinger were major classical disciples of Jung's work, James Hillman is an important revisionist of Jungian theory. From one perspective, Hillman fundamentally revised Jung's – and by extension Von Franz's and Edinger's – thought, but from another he returns to its radical essence, carrying its implications to a new level.

Hillman accuses traditional psychology of being blindly rooted in the scientific paradigm and devoid of ideas, and complains that modern psychology has "replaced ideas with nominalistic allegorical and disembodied words. We count heads and make classifications, exchange information as if we were thinking."[2] Such bold and iconoclastic statements "turn upside down many ideas that people hold dear and unreflected."[3] Hillman's style is provocative and this can lead some to dismiss him, but as Moore notes "he seeks to engage and enjoy polemics, persuasion and controversy"[4] not for their own sake but for the sake of reactivating imagination.

The imagination is fundamental to Hillman's thought and "metapsychology itself is one of the ways of the imagination proper to psychology."[5] In Hillman's hands, psychoanalytic concepts and ideas have to be "deliteralized" and can be heard as expressions of the imagination. But his notion of the imagination is not the one we imagine. Hillman re-visions/re-envisions the imagination in a way that challenges the history of our Western traditions and renders it secondary to conceptual thinking. He reverses this pattern and reopens the question of the relationship of concept and metaphor. His methodological reversal reminds psychology that "it too is an activity of the soul"[6] and that it is unpsychological to proceed with concepts that have become hardened and unreflected. This hardening can too easily become the bedrock dogmas of philosophy and psychoanalysis.

DOI: 10.4324/9781003215905-6

Part of the work of archetypal psychology aims at "seeing through" to the originary images in our conceptual formulations. To see through our literal concepts in both psychology and psychoanalysis leads us to "envision the basic nature and structure of the soul in an imaginary way and to approach the basic questions of psychology first of all by means of imagination."[7] To take an archetypal perspective then means

> to envision archetypal structures as the deepest patterns of psychic functioning, the roots of the soul governing the perspectives we have of ourselves and our world. They are . . . the images to which psychic life and our theories about it ever return. All ways of speaking about archetypes are translations from one metaphor to another. Even sober operational definitions in the language of science and logic are no less metaphorical.[8]

Hillman uses the designation "archetypal" to refer to a perspective, "to a move one makes rather than a thing or a substance."[9] It is a move that places whatever is seen in a mythic perspective. For Hillman, psychoanalysts are "myth makers" and "myth preservers."[10] "What holds us to Freud, provoking countless retellings and commentaries, is not the science in the theory but the myth in the science."[11] Hillman quotes Freud's communication to Einstein in 1922:

> It may perhaps seem to you as though our theories are a kind of mythology and, in the present case, not even an agreeable one. But does not every science come in the end to a kind of mythology like this? Cannot the same be said today of your own physics?

The question for Hillman is not a question simply of myth versus science, but of the reification of single myths as opposed to a broad mythic awareness. For Hillman, when a living myth hardens and becomes literalized, we imagine it as fundamental and central, and we fall into a philosophically and psychologically monomythic mode.[12] For Hillman, the Oedipal tale has become such a central myth in psychoanalysis. As analysts,

> . . . we go on ritualizing the Oedipal Tale, go on affirming the cosmic power of the parents and child for discovering identity. By divining the parental world, each patient discovers a budding Oedipus in the

soul. We believe we are what we are because of our childhoods in family but this is only because the actual family is "really" Oedipal, that is, mythical. Even as actual sociological, statistical family life dissolves psychoanalysis retains the myth.[13]

He continues:

We emerge into life as creatures in a drama, . . . as budding Oedipus; . . . we immediately transpose the stock figures of mom and dad, or their stand-ins, into Jocasta and Laius enabling desire, early family scenes, early abandonments, abuses, and mutilations, little boy and little girl wishes, and endowing these small, preinitiatory events with salient inevitable determinacy.[14]

And, as Moore notes, "for Hillman, none of this is literally absolute, all these emotions and configurations are ways in which we are remythologized, and that is why they carry such importance."[15] Hillman states "they are doors to Sophocles and Sophocles, himself a door, their importance rising not from historical events but mythical happenings that as Sallustius said never happened but always are fictions."[16] Thus for Hillman "depth psychology believes in myth, practices myth, teaches myth"[17] and, I would add, that it is no different for an archetypal psychology, except insofar as being self-reflexive about its mythic practice it opens the door to a polymythic sensibility, to a broad range of archetypal perspectives.

Instead of making a norm of singleness of soul, Hillman portrays the psyche as "inherently multiple."[18] Hillman states that "we need a psychology that gives place to multiplicity, not demanding integration and other forms of unity, and at the same time offering a language adequate to a psyche that has many faces."[19] The psyche is not only multiple, "it is a communication of many persons each with specific needs, fears, longings, styles and language."[20] The many persons echo the many perspectives and mythic modes which archetypal psychology investigates.

A focus upon the many and different styles of thought provides archetypal psychology with a variety of ways of looking at the psyche. Mythical paradigms as well as analytic perspectives may suggest metaphoric insight. A Jungian might now find himself in a Freudian or Adlerian metaphor to differentiate a psychic phenomenon. Hillman used the metaphor of the *bricoleur* to describe this ready-to-hand activity and uses such an approach to tease out several perspectives on "pathologizing." He gives an example of depression, which may be understood,

> on the model of Christ and his suffering and resurrection; it may through Saturn gain the depth of melancholy and inspiration, or through Apollo serve to release the black bird of prophetic insight. From the perspective of Demeter depression may yield awareness of the mother-daughter mystery, or through Dionysus, we may find depression a refuge from the excessive demands of the ruling will.[21]

In Hillman's hands, this approach is far from a simple eclecticism or moral relativism, perspectives which he differentiates from his own. His "claim and contention" is that sensitivity to the variety of perspectives discovered in myth will prove to be more psychological, that is "to produce more insights into emotions, images and relationships and reflect more accurately the illusions and entanglements of the soul."[22]

Hillman's aim is "to restore psychology to the widest, richest, deepest volume so that it would resonate with the soul in its descriptions as unfathomable, multiple, prior, generative and necessary."[23] For Hillman, it is not necessary to "get it all together," to integrate it all, or to find "some ultimate blending of the many impulses and directions."[24] It is rather essential to find "vitality in tension, learn from paradox, getting wisdom by straddling ambivalence and gain confidence in trusting the confusion that naturally arises with multiplicity."[25]

Hillman's work ultimately leads out of the consulting room into the world. He attacks vigorously what has become the shadow narcissism of psychological and philosophical reductionism. In so doing, he broadens the scope of psychology. For example, in *A Blue Fire* he traces many themes: education, work, money, transportation, sex, war, terrorism, eros, and love; in short, the psychological aspects of everyday life or, perhaps better, everyday life insofar as it also transcends psychological subjectivity.

As the parameters, range, and implications of Hillman's thought have continued to emerge, his work has grown in influence, impacting a wide range of thinkers, cultural historians, philosophers, novelists, and a great number of poets and analysts. The quality and originality of Hillman's carefully crafted prose has led poet Robert Bly to consider Hillman "one of the most lively and original psychologists and thinkers we've had in America since William James."[26] Whether or not one agrees with such accolades, it is clear that Hillman's work is to be grappled with by any serious, intellectually-minded psychologist, psychoanalyst, or philosopher.

Hillman's work drives one to question and reexamine the fundamental beliefs of Jung and his followers as well as thinkers in the academic disciplines of psychology and philosophy. He is a gadfly and an iconoclast who challenges whatever has become hackneyed and complacent. He has pressed himself and others hard to become thinkers, to be more "literate and less literal, stuck in the case without a vision of soul."[27] His own vision is richly articulated, but true to his own critiques of unreflective ontologizing he is careful to include a statement in a deconstructive postmodern spirit titled a "professional exit."[28]

> Though this has been a groundwork of irreplaceable insights, they are to be taken neither as foundations for a systematic theory nor even a prolegomenon for any future archetypal psychology. Soul-making needs adequate ideational vessels, and it equally needs to let go of them. In this sense all that is written in the foregoing pages is confessed to with passionate conviction, to be defended as articles of faith, and at the same time disavowed, broken, and left behind. By holding to nothing, nothing holds back the movement of soul-making from its ongoing process, which now like a long Renaissance processional slips away from us into memory, off-stage and out of sight. They are leaving – even the Bricoleur and the Rogue Errant who put together the work and charted its course; . . . when the last image vanishes, all icons gone, the soul begins again to populate the stilled realms with figures and fantasies born of the imaginative heart.[29]

Hillman as an important revisionist of Jungian theory has nevertheless philosophically followed Jung closely with regard to the fundamental importance of images at the basis of psychic life. This is nowhere more evident than in his alchemical psychology.

Hillman's alchemical psychology[30]

His first organized attempts to present his alchemical reflections were in lectures given at the Zurich Institute in 1966. He stated that he had been drawn by alchemy's "obscure poetic language and strange images, and by its amazing insights especially in Jung's introduction to *The Secret of the Golden Flower* and [in Jung's essay on] 'The Philosophical Tree.'"[31] Later, in 1968, while at the University of Chicago, Hillman continued his lectures and "expanded [his] library research and collection of dreams with alchemical motifs."[32] These lectures were given in an old wooden chemistry hall and were entitled "Analytic work – Alchemical Opus."[33] His approach in these lectures was "to exhibit a background to analytical work that is metaphorical, even preposterous, and so, less encumbered by clinical literalism."[34] This theme runs through Hillman's alchemical papers beginning with his 1970 publication "On Senex Consciousness." In 1978 Hillman published "The Therapeutic Value of Alchemical Language" which set the stage for his continuing reflections.

Unlike Edinger, Hillman's approach to reading alchemy resists translating its images and language into the structures of any reductive rationalism that leaves the image behind. He gives these examples:

> White Queen and Red King have become [for Jung, Von Franz, and Edinger] feminine and masculine principles; their incestuous sexual intercourse has become the union of opposites; the freakish hermaphrodite and uniped, the golden head . . . have all become paradoxical representations of the goal, examples of androgyny, symbols of the Self.[35]

For him, these are a move from "precision to generality."[36] Hillman challenges us to imagine the process of reading alchemy differently. For him, sticking to the image recovers the point of Plutarch's ancient maxim "save the phenomena,"[37] and allows us to speak imaginatively and to dream the dream onward. Hillman is not simply suggesting that we replace our concepts with "the archaic neologisms of alchemy" or take alchemical language literally as substitutions for our own concepts. It is not the literal return to alchemy that he proposes, but rather a "restoration of the alchemical mode of imagining." For Hillman, this means the move from a psychology of alchemy to an alchemical psychology rooted in the fundamental principle of the imagination and not in reified, fixed structures of theoretical abstractions.

One might imagine Hillman here as making a revolutionary psychological and philosophical move beyond Jung and the classical Jungians, or perhaps just emphasizing the fundamental importance of the primacy of images and imagination, and resisting the further movement into what he calls "conceptual rationalism."[38] In either case, Hillman's emphasis has evolved into what has now been called archetypal psychology, a discipline of thought in which images speak more directly when their metaphysical covering "can be peeled away, so that the material may speak more phenomenally. Then pagan images stand out: metals, planets, minerals, stars, plants, charms, animals, vessels, fires, and specific locales."[39]

For Hillman these alchemical images have been obscured by both Jung's psychology and its association with Christian metaphysics. He explained this awareness to the International Congress of the International Association of Analytical Psychologists in Rome in 1977, noting that "[w]hile Jung reclaimed alchemy for the psyche, he also claimed it for his psychology" and that its "liberation of alchemy from the former traps (mysticism, charlatanism, and pre- or pseudo-science) entangled it in his system of opposites and Christian symbols and thought."[40] Jung's metapsychology and his reliance on Christian imagery led Hillman to make the distinction not only between a *psychology of alchemy* and an *alchemical psychology*, but also between "an alchemy of spirit and an alchemy of soul."[41] He further noted that the transformation of the psyche can be distinguished from the Christian idea of redemption. He stated that when we make this distinction, then

> the subtle changes in color, heat, bodily forms, and other qualities refer to the psyche's processes, useful to the practice of therapy for reflecting the changes going on in the psyche without linking these changes to a progressive program or redemptive vision.[42]

In short, alchemy's curious images and sayings are valuable not so much because alchemy is a grand narrative of the stages of individuation and its conjunction of opposites, nor for its reflection on the Christian process of redemption, "but rather because of alchemy's myriad, cryptic, arcane, paradoxical, and mainly conflicting texts [which] reveal the psyche phenomenally."[43]

For Hillman, alchemy needs to be encountered with "the least possible intrusion of metaphysics."[44] He saw Jung, von Franz, and Edinger as informed consciously or unconsciously by a metaphysical attitude, and thus attempting to examine alchemy in a scholarly manner in order to find objective meaning. He, on the other hand, saw himself as emphasizing the "matters" of alchemy as metaphorical substances and archetypal principles. He sought to activate alchemical language and images in order to find those qualities of human life which act on the very substance of personality.

> The work of soul-making requires corrosive acids, heavy earth, ascending birds; there are sweating kings, dogs, and bitches, stenches, urine, and blood . . . I know that I am not composed of sulfur and salt, buried in horse dung, putrefying or congealing, turning white or green or yellow, encircled by a tail-biting serpent, rising on wings. And yet I am! I cannot take any of this literally, even if it is all accurate, descriptively true.[45]

In contrast to Jung and Edinger, for Hillman, language is fundamental and his thinking about language both resists reducing alchemical metaphors to generalized abstractions while also wanting to re-materialize our concepts, "giving them body, sense, and weight."[46] It is not absolutely clear to what extent Hillman's references to body, sticking to images, and saving the phenomena parallel Edinger's idea of "presentational" images. What is clear is that Hillman rejects any medicalized, factualized, or objective, literalized notion of the body as a model. For him, conceptual rationalization of any sort obscures the richness and complexity of images and imagistic language.

While Edinger used alchemical operations to organize his exposition of the alchemical process, Hillman aesthetically organized the majority of his study of alchemical psychology around a rainbow of colors: black, blue, silver/white, yellow, and red, all intrinsic to the azure vault, which is an image of the "final" realization of the alchemical opus. For Hillman, color imagery indicates both the stages of alchemical work as well as independent states of soul. His analysis leans away from developmental and progressivist interpretations of individuation and toward a co-presence of aesthetic fields. In the traditional view of alchemical stages, blackness is often thought of as an early phase of the work. In blackness, the soul of the alchemist finds itself in a dark place. In Hillman's reflection on "The Seduction of Black" (Chapter 4 in *Alchemical Psychology*), however, there is far more to be appreciated about blackness. For the alchemist, blackness is also an accomplishment. In it, Hillman finds an intentionality, a deepening of the soul, a suffering that teaches endurance, and a halting of the exaggerated passions that Hillman called the "fervor of salt."[47] Perhaps most importantly, the experience of blackness serves to deconstruct positivities and paradigms, and to overcome the fundamentalisms of "hopefully-colored illusions."[48] The blacker-than-black aspect of this condition brings with it the dread of nonbeing, but it also is the "unbounded ground of possibility."[49] As black despair moves toward reflection, black turns to blue and imagination penetrates the darkness. Psyche ponders and considers as it moves toward the *albedo*, a silvery white condition of the soul characterized by lunafication and lustration, a gleaming white condition, the white earth as the archetypal basis of psychic life and what Hillman calls the poetic basis of mind. In this silvery white light, Hillman aims to reframe and reform our language. He calls for a poetic speech that "speaks to clinical conditions in their own tongue."[50] This whiteness of the *albedo* was the first goal of the alchemists, but, as Hillman notes, Jung said: "in this state of 'whiteness' one does not *live*."[51] "The sure optimism of solar clarity is the blind spot itself" – something more is required, and "Sol dissolves in the darkness of its own light."[52] The purity of whiteness has to spoil and this leads to what the alchemists called the yellowing of the work necessary to a later reddening into a fuller life.

In "The Yellowing of the Work" (Chapter 7 in *Alchemical Psychology*), Hillman describes this important transitional process of putrefaction, decay, and rot. Yellowing saves us from the whiteness and abstractions of psychological insight, what Hillman saw as the continuing translation of experience into bloodless concepts. For the work to approach the highest level, it must reach the world, deconstruct and spoil itself, develop a "jaundiced eye"[53] to the whiteness of psychology. Yellowing moves us toward these potentialities and brings both the decay and illumination that are found together. Movement from white to yellow brings the goal of alchemy into further relief and anticipates the reddening that brings life to the abstractions of whiteness and living fullness to the intellectual soul. The reddening signifies the animation of the vital reality of psyche, the goal of the alchemists, the Philosophers' Stone, the gold of the alchemists.

Hillman then takes up the issue of the goal of the alchemical process in his reflection "Concerning the Stone: Alchemical Images of the Goal" (Chapter 8 in *Alchemical Psychology*). In this reflection, Hillman notes that the grand images of alchemy – the gold, the elixir, the Philosophers' Stone, and others – are not meant to be understood as literal achievements at the end of a process, but rather as ideas intended to impel the adept into the long work of the opus of life. As such, the goal is the work itself with no static fixed end. Psychologically, this alters the heroic desire for ever-continuing improvement – rather, the soul circles around itself in an ongoing process, a ouroboric *rotatio* where beginning and end meet. Put another way, Hillman states that

[t]he goal images correlate precisely with this motion of circularity, since the *iteratio* (repetition, or as the maxim goes, "one operation does not make an artist"), *circulatio*, and *rotatio* are often considered among the last operations of the *opus*.

The *rotatio*, like a turning wheel, announces that no position can remain fixed, no statement finally true, no end place achieved. Development makes little sense when no place is better or worse, higher or lower. As the wheel rotates what was up is now down, what was inferior, now superior and will become again inferior. What rises, falls, repeatedly: "Only the fool, fixed in his folly, may think he can turn the wheel on which he turns." Linear motion as a line of development from any point of the rotation only goes off at a tangent. Developmental process actually moves away from the soul's goal which is turning in circles. As Figulus says: "What we seek is here or nowhere."[54]

He goes on to say:

The *rotatio* also returns *telos* itself to its root meaning. *Telos* does not simply mean end, goal, purpose, finis. "Instead," says Onians, "I would suggest that with this root notion of 'turning around' [*telos*] meant 'circling' or 'circle.'" The goal itself circles, because it is a psychic goal; or, the goal is psyche itself obeying the laws of its own motion, a motion that is not going somewhere else; no journey, no process, no improvement. And so the images of the goal put to final rest the subjective urge that has impelled the entire work from the start. We awaken to the fact that the goal of the work is nothing else than *the objectification of the very urge that propels it*.[55]

A dream experience illustrates a concrete example of such a moment. The dreamer was obsessed with the idea of entering a Tibetan monastery, but he was in conflict because his life demands made it nearly impossible to do so – the sacrifices were too great – yet he was on the brink of making such a sacrifice. While walking down the street, he suddenly remembered hearing a voice from an earlier dream that said directly to him: "You are already in a Tibetan monastery." Remembering this dream had a dramatic effect on his thought process. The idea that the dreamer was already where he wanted to be was more than a rationalization. It, in effect, opened him to the recognition that what he valued in his study of the Tibetan Buddhist tradition was the idea of the fullness of the present moment. The idea was well known to him, but not deeply experienced. With the recollection of this dream, the conflict began to subside since what was psychologically intrinsic about going to the monastery was the desire to live more fully in the moment. In such a dream, the fantasy of the future returns to the present and the dreamer experienced a feeling of greater completion. In a sense, the *telos* of going forward returned to itself. The goal of his intention was not simply out there in some "actuality" to be realized in the future, but rather in the existential structure of the "moment." In such transformative moments, the psyche's conception of temporality changes from linear extension to a circular deepening – one might say, from an "ego psychology" of a being-in-time to a "self psychology" whose being-in-time is grounded in a larger sense of temporality. Put another way: "By imagining the goal as *feelings already familiar*, we are . . . deliteralising the goal by removing it from a temporal presence and activating it as an idea already present in the human condition and intermittently available to our feelings, spurring the desire for supreme values."[56] Hillman refers to philosopher Edward Casey, noting that Casey has set forth "the idea that imagination is so closely related to time, both psychologically and ontologically, that actual image-work not only takes time into soul or makes temporal events soul events but also makes time in soul."[57]

What is important for Hillman is that alchemical goals must be de-literalized and that "alchemy's images of [the goals], the hermaphrodite, the gold, or the red stone" are not to be taken "as actualized events" in time or even symbolic representations.[58] It is this idea that motivates psyche into the long process of the alchemical work. For Hillman, the motivation for both work and life requires attractive goals that promise healing, redemption, fantasies, possibilities, and even beauty. In short, "*An inflated vision of supreme beauty is a necessary fiction for the soul-making opus we call our lifetime.*"[59]

For Hillman, "[t]*he purpose of the work is purposiveness itself*, not this or that formulated purpose, which quickly degenerates into an ideology and just as quickly loses effectiveness as motive power."[60] It is not what can be attained that moves us toward our ends, but what is unattainable. Hillman elaborates the difference between what he earlier called a spiritual approach and the soul approach noting that the spirit approach takes alchemical fictions "as metaphysical realities, and measures progress toward them in literal stages. The soul approach maintains the images as supreme values but takes them always as fictions."[61]

To hold fictions as a supreme value is a strange idea. In modern times, there seems to be a tendency to devalue fiction, opposing it to truth, and to value "reality" over what is called "fantasy" or "imagination." However, for Hillman, imagination is raised to the highest value. Hillman notes:

> We must start, as [the alchemist] Benedictus Figulus says, in the *caelum*, the sky-blue firmament over our heads, the mind already in the blue of heaven, imagination opened. The blue *caelum* of imagination gives to the *opus* a rock-hard standpoint from above downward, just as firm and solid as literal physical reality. A sapphire stone already at the beginning. The sophic activity of the mind. . . .[62]

For Hillman, archetypal psychology is fundamentally an imaginal psychology. It "*axiomatically* assumes imagistic universals" which Hillman compares "to the *universali fantastici* of Vico."[63] For him this means that imaginal realities are at the core of human thought and constitute a poetic basis of human consciousness. He notes: "By means of the archetypal image, natural phenomena present faces that speak to the imagining soul rather than only conceal hidden laws and probabilities and manifest their objectification."[64] For Hillman, it is important to remain open to imagination and its ongoing imagery, to the "openings of the heart and mind and senses."[65] It is a method rich in "texture, images, language, emotion, and sudden mysterious arrivals."[66]

Hillman links his style to a rhetorical device *peitho*, which the Greeks sometimes called Aphrodite. It is sophistical in the sense that its intent is "to invite, seduce, charm, enhance, and convince by rhetorical, even poetic, means."[67] It is a method that was earlier rejected in the history of philosophy, which sought absolute truths, perhaps most notable in Plato and Aristotle, but one that returns as a contemporary style in rhetoric and in some postmodern philosophy. It is a method that includes anima sensibilities at its core, to a greater extent than does the rational logos of Greek philosophical thought. It was also an approach that Jung rejected when an anima voice told him that his work was art.[68] Hillman has noted that had Jung entertained this anima voice more openly, the direction of his psychology may have been very different. One way to imagine this difference is to recognize that Hillman's work has not only taken up this call to the aesthetic and art, but also made it central to his own psychology, which he so forcefully demonstrates in his alchemical psychology.

Jung's and Hillman's ideas are in turn criticized by another important revisionist, Wolfgang Giegerich, whose philosophical orientation, strongly influenced by the work of Hegel, challenges the fundamental place of image in psychic life.

Wolfgang Giegerich and the soul's logical life

If James Hillman has been the champion of the imagination and of Jung's idea that images are at the non-reductive basis of psychic life, Wolfgang Giegerich raises the most challenging criticism of this point of view from within the Jungian tradition. Giegerich, originally a close collaborator of Hillman's, was part of a small archetypally oriented group helping to develop an archetypal perspective. Since the publication of his ground-breaking book *The Soul's Logical Life* (1998), he has been the foremost critic of both Jung and Hillman from within the Jungian tradition, including their views of alchemy and the Philosophers' Stone. In all, Giegerich has about 200 publications in several languages and his scholarship has inspired the development of the International Society for Psychology as the Discipline of Interiority.

Giegerich has been seen as extending both Jung's and Hillman's work and has been thought of as representing a third wave in Jungian scholarship. Both praise and criticism are woven together in his work. In the preface to *The Soul's Logical Life*, Giegerich praises and criticizes both Jung and Hillman noting "why it has to be, more or less exclusively, JUNG from among the many important psychologists of this century and all the various psychological schools that must be the base and starting point for our search for a rigorous notion of psychology."[69] He then offers

> a critical assessment of first JUNG's, then conventional Jungianism's and finally archetypal psychology's relevance for a strict notion of psychology. . . . [T]he state-of-affairs of conventional Jungianism seems to be a regression far behind the achievement of JUNG, while

archetypal psychology is again a great advance, but is nonetheless in need of a radical criticism (with respect to its *imaginal* bias). To arrive at a rigorous concept of psychology we have to go beyond the imaginal.[70]

Giegerich is one of the most philosophically oriented Jungian analysts and he has been heavily influenced by Hegel and Heidegger. His criticism of the imaginal basis of Jung's and Hillman's psychologies is largely based on his reading of Hegel's phenomenological and logical works. Giegerich acknowledges his Hegelian influence though he claims not to be a Hegelian:

> I find that often people try to make me a Hegelian, simply because I refer to Hegel and have learned a few things from him. But neither do I propagate Hegel's philosophy, nor do I claim that what I say is such that Hegel would have been of one mind with me. I do not even claim to understand Hegel properly. My work is in psychology and about our modern situation, and is not an attempt to propound Hegel's philosophy. Our purpose in our time cannot be to inscribe our modern psychological interests and needs into the ready-made form of Hegel's system and to rely on him as an authority that validates our own work. We have to think from within our own historical situation and on our own responsibility. However, I think that in trying to do so there is no way around Hegel. It is the most advanced, comprehensive, and differentiated thinking and supersedes everything that came afterwards. . . .[71]

In short, Giegerich applies many of Hegel's fundamental concepts to his critical work, including sublation, dialectics, absolute knowing, absolute negativity, and spirit as the fundamental philosophical idea that goes beyond the limits of the Kantian-based epistemology which he attributes to Jung.[72] Following Hegel's lead, Giegerich's perspective sets the stage for moving from imagination to "thought."

In *The Soul's Logical Life*, Giegerich makes the case for the importance of thought as fundamental to an understanding of psychological life, and he contends that "[t]he time of . . . logical innocence, where truth could still *really* happen in the *form* of symbols, images or rituals, have long been passé."[73] Giegerich remarks on the complexity of modern life and notes that we must move "beyond natural pictorial thinking and move on to the abstract level of thought proper."[74] Contrasting imaginal imagination with thought proper, Giegerich states:

> Image is a form in which what is actually (that is, "in itself," but not "for itself") a thought or Notion initially appears in consciousness. As long as it appears in the form of a symbol or image, the thought cannot yet be consciously *thought* (past participle); it can only be "beheld" or "contemplated," as if it were an object or a scene and not a thought. Because it is a thought "in visible [*anschaulicher*] form," the form of a pictorial representation, its thought character remains "invisible" [*unanschaulich*] or unconscious, implicit.[75]

For Giegerich, the movement beyond picture thinking which is

> *immersed* in the medium of an emotional of an envisioned image has to be transposed into the form of explicit (or consciously thought) thought . . . in JUNG's case in the form of a psychological theory. One might say with FREUD, what at first had the status of "It" would be transposed into the status of "I-ness." Expressed in HEGEL's language, what at first was grasped and expressed only as *Substance* [a perceived or envisioned imaginal content, which, as perceived or envisioned, was so-to-speak vis-à-vis the perceiving person] would also be grasped and expressed as *Subject*, namely as one's own thinking, one's own actual and living thought. As such it could turn into what HEGEL terms the Notion (*der Begriff*).[76]

By using an example from Jung, Giegerich helps us to see what he means by the movement from emotion to thought, from image to the soul's logical life. He recalls Jung's later-life statement that he no longer needed to dialogue with his autonomous images of his soul (anima). He quotes Jung as saying, "To-day I am directly conscious of the anima's ideas," and then goes on, "that is, they now are his own thoughts that he is consciously thinking."[77] Giegerich, using Hegel's philosophical insights, suggests a way of understanding the relationship between emotion/image and thought/notion.

> A psychosomatic symptom is "in itself" or, as it were, unbeknownst to itself, emotion (or, it is implicit, latent emotion); it is not "for itself"

emotion, not explicitly or manifestly so (it is *ansichseiend*, not *fürsi-chseiend*, emotion). And emotion is *ansichseiend* (or latent) image; image is *ansichseiend* (or latent) Notion. Conversely, Notion is *sublated* (*aufgehoben*) image; image is *sublated* emotion; emotion is *sublated* (interiorized, psychologized) behavior or physical condition.[78]

Giegerich points out that in Jung's autobiography he speaks about how important it was for him "to translate the emotions into images – that is to say, to find the images which were concealed in the emotions."[79] For Giegerich, another move is essential – the move from image to thought – which he feels is underrepresented in Jung's thought, and it is this move which he feels is necessary to go beyond and complete Jung's and Hillman's psychologies and move them toward a more rigorous philosophical psychology. Giegerich states that this move is an "even more far-reaching consequence to be drawn from the cited idea of JUNG's that the practical work of psychology has to make the initially latent thought 'complete' . . . ."[80]

> In the last analysis, *soul is Notion, is logical life*. This corresponds to the gold or philosopher's stone of the alchemists. Logically, even though not temporally, it is not primarily emotion, affect, feeling, drive, desire, not even image or fantasy (which all correspond to impure forms of the prime matter in alchemy, the *massa confusa*, etc.). To be sure, soul is *also* emotion and desire and especially, as JUNG often insisted, image. Indeed, it is even physical behavior and psychosomatic, even somatic, symptom. But it is symptom, emotion and desire only because, as again JUNG taught us to realize, each of those phenomena contains an image or idea hidden within itself or *is* one guise in which an image or idea may first appear when it is deeply immersed in (psychological or alchemical) matter. And the image is one guise in which a thought or notion presents itself under the conditions, or in the medium, of a consciousness that is in the spell of sensory intuition (*Anschauung*), imagination, pictorial representation (*Vorstellung*).[81]

Importantly, Giegerich develops his idea of sublation and the Notion by pointing out that

> Being *sublated* psychosomatic symptom, emotion, and image, the Notion is not their simple (undialectical) opposite. It is not the abstract,

"nothing but" type of notion, merely intellectual, cut off from living experience. Rather, it is the concrete Notion which, due to its genesis from emotion and image, is still satiated with them, but now with them in their form as sublated moments *within* thought. The sensual, emotional and imaginal qualities have not been lost altogether. They have been alchemically distilled and brought home from their alienation in the initial crude, literal state in which they first were manifested.[82]

In this important paragraph, Giegerich clearly makes explicit that the Notion is not something abstractly separate from image and emotion. In fact, the Notion or Idea is "satiated" with the sensate imagination; at least these sensual "qualities have *not been lost altogether*."[83] Yet, in spite of this recognition, it is also clear that for Giegerich the idea of "sublation," the movement to thought proper, is seen as a higher level psychological and philosophical position from which image and emotion can be seen as distilled, brought home from their crude, alienated state.[84] The image is thus assimilated into a higher-level process and is relieved of its monstrous alterity. Ultimately Giegerich (via Hegel) will claim to have surpassed, gone beyond, and completed what was underdeveloped in the work of Jung and Hillman.

Giegerich, following his move to the soul's logical life, states:

This holding on to the visible, spatial and ontological as a firm ground is really inexcusable for a field that wants to be true psychology beyond the ego-stance. It just will not do to subjectively free psychology from the standpoint of the ego while receiving one's object of study, the life of the soul, from the hands of the ego with its positivizing modes of relating to phenomena (perception, sensory intuition, pictorial thinking) and in the form of "people's psychologies."

More than a re-visioning: a real sublation of psychology is needed: a fundamental self-negation, self-putrefaction of an imagination-based psychology in favor of a logic of the soul. I stated before that psychology is sublated science, sublated religion, sublated medicine, and further that psychology proper *exists* only to the extent that it is also *sublated* immediate psychology. With this self-sublation, psychology does not collapse and give way to some Other, as was the case with alchemy. Its self-sublation is psychology's *beginning*, the process of its foundation.[85]

Giegerich's alchemy[86]

Just as Jung and Hillman found alchemy important for their psychology, Giegerich likewise takes up alchemy as an important touchstone. His major reflections on alchemy are found in his *The Soul's Logical Life*, particularly in the section entitled "Excursus: Alchemy's Opus Contra Imagination." In addition, there are two papers dedicated to alchemy, one entitled "Closure and Setting Free or the Bottled Spirit of Alchemy and Psychology" and another entitled "Once More 'the Stone which is Not a Stone.' Further Reflections on the 'Not.'" In addition, Giegerich has also made a number of comments about alchemy by personal communication to this author and I have included some of these in my chapter entitled "Alchemy" in *The Handbook of Jungian Psychology*.

In Giegerich's personal comments to the author, he notes that alchemy entered Jung's psychology only as a topic or content. Giegerich objects that Jung's scientific/modernist metapsychology seems to remain the same, maintaining a subject/object split, while at the same time making an object of alchemical ideas that do not fit into these categories. Giegerich believes that Jung reduces alchemical processes to events "in" the unconscious or the interior of the personality. He notes that: "the individual, the personality, the inner, and 'the unconscious' are our names for the 'bottle' in which the mercurial 'substance' had to stay firmly enclosed for Jung."[87]

Giegerich continues his reflection by noting that "because Mercurius remained enclosed in the above way 'it' had to stay a substance, an object, and entity" and could not be true to its own nature as a spirit (something intangible and unrepresentable). This interpretation sets the stage for the fundamental thrust of Giegerich's emphasis in *The Soul's Logical Life*. According to Giegerich, when Jung, and Hillman for that matter, stick to "images" as fundamental, they are in fact objectifying the spirit of alchemy. The image itself becomes objectified, while the true spirit of alchemy aims at realizing the logical life of the soul, which is conceptual, subtle, non-positive, intangible. Throughout Giegerich's critique, he juxtaposes images and a "pictorial form of thinking" which valorizes perception and imagination against what he considers to be the true aim of alchemy, which is to achieve the level of dialectical thought and logical expression that he describes in *The Soul's Logical Life*. For Giegerich, when Jung opts to hold the image as fundamental, he steps over the goal of alchemy to release the spirit from its container and ignores the "self-sublation" or death that the alchemical process requires. In doing so he skips "over the successive psychological development of several centuries."[88]

> Jung pronounced his psychology of the unconscious to be the immediate successor and redemptor of alchemy. In this way he could declare the previous image-oriented (pictorial) mode of thinking, long overcome by the history of the soul, to still be "the" psychological mode and decry the later development into which alchemy had dissolved as a mere rationalism, intellectualization, i.e., mere "ego." Jung excluded from his psychological reception of alchemy the fact that the telos of alchemy had been the overcoming of itself. He froze it, and psychology along with it, in an earlier phase.[89]

For Giegerich, the task of alchemy was to deconstruct itself, or at least, in his terms, to surpass itself as a movement of the historical expression of the soul. Here a Hegelian dialectical understanding of history influences Giegerich. For him, Jung and the classical analysts did not give enough emphasis to the active dimensions of consciousness as constituting the reality of the psyche. That is, alchemy was an active human project, which meant that the observer of the alchemical process was not passive. He notes that even in the activity of "registering, recording, maybe painting, the dream or fantasy images received and in thinking *about* them as a text," there was still the tendency to relate to this text as a finished "product."[90] "But consciousness had to refrain from entering the process of the production of images themselves."[91] Giegerich qualifies this statement to note the "exception" of active imagination, though even in this instance "what is to become active and enter the production process is not the reflecting mind, but the empirical ego."[92] In short, the mythos of Jungian work, both psychological and alchemical, is that the "natural process of the production of images was not to be interfered with."[93] For Giegerich, this was the vestige of fundamental naturalism left in Jung's psychology, which in the end "was contrary to the spirit of alchemy."[94] He notes that in Jung: "we have the curious spectacle . . . of a singular dedication to and propagation of alchemy 'and' its simultaneous repression. His advancement of alchemy as a psychological paradigm was 'in itself' the substance of what it was intrinsically about."[95]

Hillman's and Giegerich's ideas on psychology, alchemy, and the Philosophers' Stone express both a mutual appreciation and important differences in perspective. I have identified these approaches as being grounded respectively in the notions of soul (Hillman) and spirit (Giegerich). In the next chapter, the similarities and differences between these revisionist thinkers will be explored.

Notes

1 The following section was previously published as Marlan, "A Blue Fire."
2 Hillman, quoted by Marlan in "A Blue Fire," 5.
3 Ibid.
4 Moore, quoted by Marlan in "A Blue Fire: The Work of James Hillman," 5.
5 Hillman, quoted by Marlan in "A Blue Fire: The Work of James Hillman," 5.
6 Ibid.
7 Ibid., 6.
8 Ibid.
9 Ibid.
10 Ibid.
11 Ibid.
12 Ibid.
13 Ibid.
14 Ibid.
15 Ibid.
16 Ibid.
17 Ibid.
18 Ibid.
19 Ibid.
20 Ibid.
21 Ibid.
22 Ibid.
23 Ibid.
24 Ibid.
25 Ibid.
26 Ibid., 7.
27 Ibid.
28 Ibid.
29 Hillman, *Revisioning*, 229.
30 Portions of this section were previously published in my entry Marlan, "Alchemy," 263–295.
31 Hillman, "A Note for Stanton Marlan," 101.
32 Ibid.
33 Ibid., 102.
34 Ibid.
35 Hillman, *Alchemical Psychology*, 15.
36 Ibid.
37 Plutarch, *On the Face in the Orb of the Moon*, line 923A.
38 Ibid., 18.
39 Hillman, "A Note for Stanton Marlan," 102.
40 Ibid.
41 Ibid.
42 Ibid., 103.

43 Ibid.
44 Ibid.
45 Hillman, "The Therapeutic Value of Alchemical Language," 37, 39.
46 Ibid.
47 Hillman, "Salt," 173.
48 Hillman, *Alchemical Psychology*, 96.
49 Ibid., 94; quoted in Marlan, "Colors of the Soul," 73.
50 Hillman, *Alchemical Psychology*, 203; quoted in Marlan, "Colors of the Soul," 74.
51 Hillman, *Alchemical Psychology*, 215; quoted in Marlan, "Colors of the Soul," 74.
52 Hillman, *Alchemical Psychology*, 217; quoted in Marlan, "Colors of the Soul," 74.
53 Hillman, *Alchemical Psychology*, 224; quoted in Marlan, "Colors of the Soul," 74.
54 Hillman, *Alchemical Psychology*, 256.
55 Ibid.
56 Ibid., 238.
57 Hillman, *Archetypal Psychology*, 27.
58 Hillman, *Alchemical Psychology*, 232. It would be interesting to explore Heidegger's notion of temporalizing and his "not yet" view of the future as amplifying Hillman's notion of telos returning to itself, but I cannot develop this theme here.
59 Ibid., 233.
60 Ibid.
61 Ibid., 238.
62 Ibid., 239.
63 Hillman, *Archetypal Psychology*, 23 (From Giambattista Vico. Scienza Nuova. Napoli, 1744 [in translation: The New Science. Ithaca: Cornell University Press, 1968]).
64 Ibid.
65 Hillman, *Alchemical Psychology*, 330.
66 Ibid., 329.
67 Ibid.
68 See Jung, *Memories*, 185–187, for the full story. In brief: at one point during his confrontation with the unconscious, as Jung was writing down some of his fantasies, he heard a voice telling him that his work was "art." (185) At first, he dismissed this as an interference from "a woman . . . within," "the 'soul,' in the primitive sense." (186) Eventually, he came to believe that it was essential to interact with this inner figure in order "to differentiate oneself from these unconscious contents by personifying them, and at the same time to bring them into relationship with consciousness. That is the technique for stripping them of their power." (187) However, he also was convinced that, in general, the anima was "full of a deep cunning" and if he had trusted her and accepted that his work was "art," he would have been "seduced . . . into believing that [he] was a misunderstood artist" and that this could have destroyed him. (187) For Jung, what was important was the question of philosophical objectivity and scientific validity. He wanted to be seen as a serious thinker and to make a contribution to the science of psychology.
69 Giegerich, *The Soul's Logical Life*, 11.
70 Ibid.
71 Giegerich, "Conflict/Resolution," 8–9.
72 In light of this congruence with Hegelian thought, it would be interesting to ask in what ways Giegerich's ideas actually differ from Hegel's in any significant way, but I will not pursue this theme here.
73 Giegerich, *The Soul's Logical Life*, 23–24.
74 Ibid., 29.
75 Ibid., 47.
76 Ibid.
77 Ibid., 48.

78 Ibid.
79 Jung, *Memories*, 177; quoted by Giegerich, *The Soul's Logical Life*, 48.
80 Giegerich, *The Soul's Logical Life*, 49.
81 Ibid.
82 Ibid.
83 Ibid.; emphasis mine. The importance of the intrinsic connection between Notion and Idea, image and emotion, needs further elaboration, but is beyond the scope of this work.
84 Ibid.; emphasis mine.
85 Ibid., 191–192.
86 Portions of this section were previously published in my chapter Marlan, "Alchemy."
87 Giegerich, personal communication, 2000.
88 Ibid.
89 Ibid.
90 Ibid.
91 Ibid.
92 Ibid.
93 Ibid.
94 Ibid.
95 Ibid. Yasuhiro Tanaka, a Japanese analyst, picks up on Giegerich's critique of "images" and the limitations of an "imaginal psychology." For him, if we remain one-sidedly dependent on such a perspective "then we fall into the trap of remaining on the horizon of surface-psychology rather than depth psychology" (Tanaka, personal communication, 2000). For Tanaka, as for Giegerich, "we psychologists living after Jung, have to address the alchemical logic in analytical psychology." His assessment of Jung is that while Jung on a personal level perceived the logical, paradoxical, and dialectic dimension of alchemy, he could not "interiorize it enough" or adequately apply it to his psychology as a theory. Thus, for Tanaka, our work now is "not to fashion the bridge between alchemy and our clinical practice" but to examine the theoretical limitations of Jung's psychology: "Alchemy was not only [Jung's] historical background but also his logical background in the sense that for Jung it was none other than the theoria for sublating his own experience into his psychology." This then means it was Jung's theory that could dispel the *massa confusa* and it is to this that we must now give our attention.

Chapter 6

James Hillman and Wolfgang Giegerich

Unification and divergence in their psychological and philosophical perspectives

The tension between recognizing that there is something about the monstrous complexity of alchemical images that remains essential (Hillman) and holding that thought rather than images are essential (Giegerich) has been seen as an important divide between Jung's and Hillman's versions of an image-based psychology and Giegerich's logical life of the soul. The struggle of coming to terms with the unconscious often has been understood as making the unconscious conscious, the unknown known, the alien familiar, the darkness light, and so on. It is a process familiar to nearly all forms of psychoanalysis and it has been seen as fundamental to the healing process. In making this move toward "consciousness," whether in Freud or Giegerich, albeit recognizing their considerable philosophical differences, both of these thinkers emphasize the translation from image to thought. Hillman, on the other hand, radically reverses this tide, claiming the resistance of the image to translation into what he calls conceptual rationalism. Using dream life as an example, Hillman notes that Freud called the dream

> the *via regia* to the unconscious. But because this *via regia* in most psychotherapy since his time, has become a straight one-way street of all morning traffic, moving out of the unconscious toward the ego's city, I have chosen to face the other way. Hence my title [*The Dream and the Underworld*], which is a directional signpost for a different one-way movement, let us say vesperal, into the dark.[1]

This is a "move backwards from logos to mythos, [a] move against the historical stream of our culture."[2] For Hillman, this move – similar to the

DOI: 10.4324/9781003215905-7

one he makes with regard to alchemy – is a criticism of translation from the phenomena of dreams or alchemical symbols into any conscious structure that leaves the image behind. Rather than seeking the light, interpreting dreams or alchemy, Hillman proposes, as Jung did, that we dream the dream onward, sticking with its images in a mythopoetic way, and resisting any translation into the categories of the soul's logical life.

The difference between the mythopoetic and the logical life of the soul is seen in the contrast between Giegerich's and Hillman's attitudes toward "the unconscious" (a notion Giegerich ultimately rejects) and their approach to the alchemical text *Aurora consurgens*. For Giegerich, alchemy works toward the *aurora*, bringing about a new sunrise, the new sun of a *"new* 'day,'"[3] whereas for Hillman, the work is not toward the "day world" but toward the underworld of night.

> Dreams are children of the Night, and we have to look at their brightest dayworld image also through our selfsame smoky glasses. So we work into the dream without forethoughts of *Aurora consurgens*, for Eos (Dawn) prefers heroes and takes them up. [sublates them?] Instead: the resurrection of Death. Instead of turning to the dream for a new start and for foresight . . . there will always be going downward, first with feelings of hopelessness, then, and the mind's eye dilates in the dark, with increasing surprise and joy.[4]

Here Hillman finds something in the dark that for Giegerich is an imprisonment in matter. For Giegerich, this is an old attitude while for Hillman this darkening of consciousness is on the verge of the monstrously new, "so utterly foreign and incomprehensible."[5] For Hillman, this turn toward the dark leaves Promethean consciousness behind, making consciousness less visual and more auditory, far removed from therapies that aim to bring things to light. The move toward the darkness is also a move toward sensing,

> from eye to ear and then through the senses of touch, taste, and scent so that we begin to perceive more and more in particulars, less and less overviews. We become more and more aware of an animal discrimination going on below our reflections and guiding them.[6]

For Hillman, "Sensual imagination restores to the image [and imagination] its primacy as *psychic basis of sensation*."[7] It is important here to note that for Hillman the "image" is not simply based on what we think of as natural sensations. Hillman writes:

> To take our senses only on the level of natural sensations is a natural-istic fallacy. It's like believing that we have to see an image to imagine or hear music to listen musically. The image makes possible the sens-ing of it.
>
> This turns upside down what psychology has been teaching ever since Aristotle: images result from sensations and soul is built of the bricks of sense experience (dayworld residues). Once we deliteralize sensation and take our senses too as metaphorical modes of perceiv-ing, we are finally across the bridge and can look back on the all-too-solid brick structure where we live our lives as manmade defenses against the soul, as an "anthropomorphism called reality."[8]

In this turn to the underworld, Hillman intentionally polarizes the day-world and the underworld, as is his tendency when he wants to reveal important contrasts. He works "The Dream Bridge" in a one-way direc-tion with a "singleness of intent."[9] The underworld becomes a paradox of extremity, a realm of radicality, of coldness, of the unconscious, and he differentiates the hero's night sea-journey from the *nekyia*, a descent "to a zone of utter coldness."[10] Further, there is a return from the journey, leav-ing the explorer "in better shape for the tasks of life," but from the *nekyia* there is no return.[11] It is a journey he likens to Dante's descent to the Ninth Circle of the Inferno, a "frozen *topos*," "deep, deep down," that is all ice.[12]

> Here we are numb, chilled. All our reactions are in cold storage. This is a psychic place of dread and of a terror so deep that it comes in uncanny experiences, such as voodoo death and the *totstell* reflex. A killer lives in the ice.[13]

For Hillman, the "glacial cold" of the underworld is likened to psychopa-thy, to figures such as Cain, Judas, and Lucifer, to the unredeemable; and yet such a place and such figures "serve a function in the soul" that cannot be reached by any religious or psychological humanism.[14] For Hillman, the icy coldness of the underworld is "beyond human warmth" and must be met homeopathically in kind. In the clinical realm, the warm-hearted desire to show sensitive feelings to a paranoid or borderline patient is like showing blood to a vampire or a shark; one will quickly be eaten alive. For Hillman, the urge to warm the cold and melt the ice "reflects a therapeutic effort that has not been able to meet the ice at its own level. The curative urge conceals the fear of the Ninth Circle, of going all the way down" into the cold.[15] Hillman notes that there is a part of our soul "that would live forever cast out from both human and heavenly company,"[16] and contact with this place is essential for any therapist who would truly work as a depth psychologist.

If we take Hillman's idea of the difference between the night sea-journey and the *nekyia* seriously – that it is only the hero who returns from the journey in better shape for the tasks of life – what conclusion can we draw within ourselves from those who have had the capacity to face such cold-blooded experiences? Are we not better off for doing so as therapists and human beings? Are we not able to engage life in a fuller way by connecting to our own psychopathic depths?

I would claim that we are, and I take Hillman's division between the night sea-journey and the *nekyia* to be a polemical strategy to reveal something about the profound depths of psychic life that ordinarily remain invisible or unconscious. His strategy is a one-way exploration, with "singleness of intent," "a vesperal, into the dark,"[17] as he calls it. It is a strategy he used in *The Dream and the Underworld* and, in addition, in his essay "Peaks and Vales." In that essay, he again draws apart the polarities of psychic life to reveal, by stark contrast in this case, the differences between spirit and soul, *puer* and psyche, heights and depths. For Hillman this is an act of violence, "urging strife, or *eris*, or *polemos*," an imaginal act of *separatio* (separation).[18] Hillman hopes to clarify both spirit and soul as separate ways of imagining. We recognize these ways of seeing by virtue of their imaginary styles and language. He describes spirit as abstract, unified, and concentrated, while soul is concrete, multiple, and imminent. I believe that their separation is in part artificial and that ultimately there is a need for accommodation between differences. In "Peaks and Vales," Hillman ultimately makes a move toward this accommodation in what he calls the *puer*-psyche marriage.

> The accommodation between the high-driving spirit on the one hand and the nymph, the valley, or the soul on the other can be imagined as the puer-psyche marriage. It has been recounted in many ways – for instance, in Jung's *Mysterium Coniunctionis* as an alchemical

conjunction of personified substances, or in Apuleius's tale of Eros and Psyche. In the same manner as these models, let us imagine in a personified style. Then we can feel the different needs within us as volitions of distinct persons, where puer is the Who in our spirit flight, and anima (or psyche) is the Who in our soul.[19]

The idea here is that the "opposites" of spirit and soul are in intimate embrace. For Hillman, the soul or anima – the archetype of life – reflects the endless mess of everyday life and its endless problems. Hillman speculates that perhaps "these very endless labyrinthine 'problems' *are* its depth. The anima [soul] embroils and twists and screws us to the breaking point."[20] For Hillman, bringing our spirit to the soul is a relationship of perplexity and it is perplexity that "consciousness needs to marry." Puer and psyche, spirit and soul, need each other. The fruits of this marriage transform the soul such that it

can regard its own needs in a new way. Then these needs are no longer attempts to adapt to Hera's civilizational requirements, or to Venus's insistence that love is God, or to Apollo's medical cures, or even Psyche's work of soul-making. Not for the sake of learning love only, or for community, or for better marriages and better families, or for independence does the psyche present its symptoms and neurotic claims. Rather these demands are asking also for inspiration, for long-distance vision, for ascending eros, for vivification and intensification (*not* relaxation), for radicality, transcendence, and meaning – in short, the psyche has spiritual needs, which the puer part of us can fulfill. Soul asks that its preoccupations be not dismissed as trivia but seen through in terms of higher and deeper perspectives, the verticalities of the spirit. When we realize that our psychic malaise points to a spiritual hunger beyond what psychology offers and that our spiritual dryness points to a need for psychic waters beyond what spiritual discipline offers, then we are beginning to move both therapy and discipline.[21]

For Hillman, the engagement between spirit and soul constructs a

walled space, the thalamus or bridal chamber, neither peak nor vale, but rather a place where both can be looked at through glass windows or be closed off with doors. This increased interiority means that each new puer inspiration, each hot idea, at whatever time of life in whomever, be given psychization. It will first be drawn through the labyrinthine ways of the soul, which wind it and slow it and nourish it from many sides (the "many" nurses and "many" maenads), developing the spirit from a one-way mania for "ups" to *polytropos*, the many-sidedness of the Hermetic old hero, Ulysses. The soul performs the service of indirection to the puer arrow, bringing to the sulphuric compulsions of the spirit the lasting salt of soul.[22]

Clearly then, Hillman points to the benefits of a *coniunctio* between spirit and soul, and aims to bring them together within his psychological vision. However, it is interesting to consider how or whether such a marriage is possible between the work of Hillman and that of Giegerich. While both Hillman's and Giegerich's works, within themselves, attempt an integration between spirit and soul, I think it is fair to say that each also leans in one direction more than the other. Hillman has clearly emphasized the soul or anima psychology, while Giegerich the spiritual or animus psychology. Contemporary Jungian theory continues to struggle with both of these directions.

In general, Hillman and Giegerich have much in common and have expressed an appreciation of each other's work in spite of their differences. Both use Jung's later work as a starting point and both criticize Jung. Neither is simply an imitator or disciple. Both criticize orthodoxy, literalizing, substantializing, personalizing, and ontologizing as well as the limits of ego psychology. Both want to go beyond literal notions of ego and unconscious and agree that psychology needs to be re-envisioned. While neither says the consulting room and long-term analysis are not valuable, both criticize the introverted style, which does not pay adequate attention to the importance of the larger psychological world beyond the clinic, and both emphasize the importance of going beyond the limits of the consulting room. Both value thinking and have a view of thinking that is not limited to Jung's conception of it in his typological works. Both emphasize the importance of the soul, though they have differing views of it. Both value history, but again have different conceptions of it. And, finally, both Hillman and Giegerich propose a rethinking of our notions of the ego, the Self, wholeness, balance, growth, individuation, dream interpretation, Christian metaphysics, and so on.

Giegerich sees archetypal psychology as a major step forward and as a real advance in psychological theory – not as a school beside other schools, but as an advancement that supersedes classical and developmental approaches; a new level of reflection that future developments must pass through, as opposed to avoiding or going around. It is state of the art. Archetypal psychology thus has the merit of having re-visioned psychology. It has accepted the root metaphor of the soul, a theoretical feat not found elsewhere. It has approached phenomena like psychopathology from internal reflection, from "within psyche's own waters" (as noted previously by Edinger) – a deepening from within that follows and advances Jung's thought. Giegerich feels there is something radical and free about Hillman's approach, and likes his way of responding to psychological phenomena, seeing it as characterized by what Jung called a subtler intelligence. For Giegerich, archetypal psychology has a logical fluidity by virtue of being in touch with a fiery liquid center of the psyche. It has a concern for the magnum opus of the soul, the great riddle of the human mind, and for our place in the real historically-formed world. For Giegerich, archetypal psychology does justice to the soul under the conditions of modernity and, as such, is more aware of the predicament of the Western soul than traditional approaches.

For these reasons, Giegerich believes that archetypal psychology deserves to be taken very seriously, and thus also deserves careful review and criticism. The re-visioning of psychology in Hillman's hands is not the creation of a total system; rather, it is a series of forays into and critiques of the issues of psychic life. It does not leave us with an intellectually-closed system or doctrine, but instead opens many doors through which we can perceive an enormous number of new possibilities.[23]

As we have seen, there are many points of agreement between Hillman and Giegerich. However, there are also many points of disagreement. Giegerich believes that just as Hillman has surpassed Jung, he himself has surpassed Hillman in that he has thought things through to the end and gone beyond image into thought proper. For Giegerich, archetypal psychology is stuck in the image, which is fixed and tender-minded. The problem with images and metaphors is that they lend themselves to a naturalistic reduction despite the effort to not read them literally. What is required is a real cut through the image to its logical basis, which rethinks the subjective, personalized, ontologized reality of "ego" and "the unconscious." Much of Giegerich's criticism of Hillman has to do with his perception that

Table 6.1 Fundamental differences between James Hillman and Wolfgang Giegerich.

JAMES HILLMAN		WOLFGANG GIEGERICH
1	Imaginal	VS	Logical
2	Images	VS	Dialectical thought/notion/concept
3	Semantics	VS	Syntax or logical form
4	Hesitancy	VS	Going all the way
5	Not making the cut	VS	Making the cut
			Paying the price
			Leave ego at the door
			Cross the threshold into the abyss
			No middle ground
6	Picture thinking.	VS	Logical thinking. Notion.
	Even though image is not something set before the eyes or even before the mind, it is something into which I enter and by which I am embraced. Images hold image sense.		Images are not reducible to sense impressions, but images are still reductive. Image has anima-like innocence.
7	Silvery image. Yellowing the image.	VS	Negativity of the image
8	Metaphorical holding of images.	VS	Vaporizing images. The liquification of images.
9	Image as imaginal psychic reality, metaphor, play, humor, aesthetic.	VS	Image must be worked through to the level of logical thought.
10	Sticking with the image	VS	Labor of concept
11	OK to hold different philosophical convictions	VS	Not OK to simply stop with different convictions—positions must be worked through. (At other points, Giegerich appears to agree that differences are based on irreducible philosophical convictions.)
12	Imaginal ego	VS	Logical subject
13	Thought opens to image	VS	Image gives rise to thought
14	Return to the gods and myth	VS	Ancient modes of myth and the gods have been surpassed.
15	Historicality The archetypal structure of man's existential condition, man's being as time. Circularity	VS	Historicity History seen as developmental, progressive, diachronic, Being-in-time. Linearity

Hillman's psychology retains vestiges of the literal and natural implicit in the image and the imagination. As ordinarily read, this leads to a number of complex binaries and juxtapositions, which I have schematized in the following chart. The chart briefly highlights the fundamental concepts, in a shorthand language, illustrating the fundamental differences in ideas between the two thinkers.

If we read the above differences as binaries, we might say that Giegerich, inspired by Hegel, pushes off from Jung and Hillman. He develops an alternative perspective based on a movement of the soul's attempting to go beyond its embeddedness in the imaginal life and the ego.

Notes

1 Hillman, *The Dream and the Underworld*, 1.
2 Ibid., 3.
3 Giegerich, *The Soul's Logical Life*, 140.
4 Hillman, *The Dream and the Underworld*, 191.
5 Ibid., 192.
6 Ibid.
7 Ibid.
8 Ibid., 192–193.
9 Ibid., 1.
10 Ibid., 168.
11 Ibid.
12 Ibid.
13 Ibid., 169.
14 Ibid.
15 Ibid., 170.
16 Ibid., 169.
17 Ibid., 1.
18 Hillman, *Blue Fire*, 114.
19 Hillman, "Peaks and Vales," 66.
20 Ibid.
21 Ibid., 68.
22 Ibid.
23 In personal communications to this author, Hillman many times told me that, in general, he did not respond to critics of his work because he felt that this would be a distraction from the work he still wanted to complete. Although he always tried to digest criticisms, he preferred "to avoid the challenges of combat" in favor of accepting the fact that he had a point of view that diverged from that of others, including his friend Giegerich (Hillman, "Divergences" 6).

Chapter 7

Exposition and criticism of Giegerich's philosophical view of psychology proper and the human-all-too-human[1]

We might imagine Giegerich's view of psychology proper as a philosophical paradigm shift that redefines psychology as syntactic rather than semantic, logical rather than ontological, thoughtful rather than imaginal, and so on.[2] What appears as a fundamental, ontological divide creates a new paradigm in which the human person is no longer presupposed as "the foundation or container of the life of the soul."[3]

Insofar as psychology has moved beyond the human person into the logical life of the soul and has fully separated itself from all vestiges of the ego, perhaps we can say that a radical cut has been made, the Rubicon has been crossed, and we have traveled to a place where no return is possible. We have entered an underworld of the soul's logical life, described by Giegerich as "cold, abstract, formal, irrepresentable" and "ghostly,"[4] totally removed from life, at least from its biological understanding. This radical cut is difficult because it injures our narcissism, wounds the "virginal innocence as 'natural' consciousness," and dissolves the *unio mentalis*.[5] For Giegerich, the work of alchemy is precisely aimed at such a dissolution, "[p]utrefaction, fermenting corruption, pulverization, dissolution, etc., are all aimed at violently decomposing the imaginal shape of the matter worked with."[6] For Giegerich, a psychology informed by alchemy has as its goal the task of totally liquefying and freeing the spirit of Mercurius – the thought that is imprisoned in matter, in nature, in the image, in emotion, and in the body.

On first reflection, it would appear that for Giegerich, philosophically, there is an unbridgeable divide between thought proper and the everyday life of the human person and, moreover, to do psychology seems to require keeping them apart. Real psychology, in Giegerich's sense, is not an ego

DOI: 10.4324/9781003215905-8

psychology and not even a psychology of the person or of people at all. If this characterization is correct, I find myself wondering to what extent or in what way such a psychology is really possible. To what extent is it possible to pass over to a strictly logical psychology in Giegerich's sense? Can one go over to the other side and not return? Philosophically, is there any such thing as a complete sublation, a complete cut or break that takes us beyond the human ego – beyond life, to a total liquification, even vaporization of alchemical Mercurius as the goal of the Philosophers' Stone? And does such a philosophical vision of psychology absolutize the cut in such a way that the cut becomes cutting – the violence of the kill literalized – and, in so doing, engage in semantic violence? "No admission for the unqualified. Only true scholars and seekers enter here. Pay the price. Leave your garments and your ego at the door. Cross the threshold and dive into the abyss you passive, stay-at-home, unscathed pop psychologist!"[7]

Now, perhaps, this is all just hyperbole and the vitriol of semantic one-sidedness in the passion to escape from ego psychology. Both Giegerich and Hillman exhibit such a passion and even a violence, urging separation and strife, *eris* or *polemos*, "which Heraclitus, the first [philosophical] ancestor of psychology, has said is the father of all."[8] One might ask: can such creative urges at times become insensitive to the virtues of passivity, to home, and to the important aspects of the feminine? Does it demean the mother-daughter archetype, nature, the sensitivities of the innocent soul? Does it cut right through them in a literal gesture of rape – Hades-like? Does the rage and grief of Demeter go unnoticed or ignored? Would she or Persephone be satisfied if Zeus were to tell them their concerns were only semantic? This would indeed be a cold, abstract, formal, and ghostly response more typical of Hades than of his brother Zeus with whom a bargain can be struck. But perhaps it is the case that Demeter's perspective, like ours, is too identified with the mother and Persephone, with innocent nature, that they and we see things too much through the eyes of Eros, human life, and love. We panic in the face of crisis, of going under, and we are repelled by the marriage of the innocent soul to Hades – to her becoming his wife. If this is the case, perhaps Giegerich's psychology sets the stage for such a wedding.

Perhaps the cool eye of Hecate's perspective, familiar with the underworld, knows more. Trained in both archetypal psychology and the logical life of the soul, she can see beyond the mother complex, beyond life and love, and has a calm wisdom that exceeds what Hillman derisively calls the "flap of Persephone."[9] Is it the case that both Hillman and Giegerich, in their appreciation of Hecate and the underworld, see psychology as a one-way trip to the shades or to dissolution? Hillman, like Giegerich, reacts against the limitations of ego psychology and to its one-way traffic out of the unconscious toward ego assimilation.[10] As we have discussed, Hillman proposes a reversal, another one-way movement into the underworld, "a vesperal into the dark,"[11] as he calls it, and Giegerich's alchemy articulates the cut that gets us there.

In this comparison, one can begin to see the limitations of strict opposi-tions. If it is fair to characterize (though it is too simple) Hillman's contri-bution as an anima psychology and Giegerich's as an animus one, can or should the two of them be joined in an alchemical marriage, a *circulatio*, with each moment leading in and out of one another? Logical psychology would go beyond all the literal residues of the imaginal, and imaginal psy-chology would continue to give flesh to the unseen and unseemly – *solve et coagula*, say the alchemists, a dynamic and fundamental syzygy. For me, the telos of Mercurius is not simply aimed at liquification or evapora-tion. Mercurius is an odd and creative duplex, living on the edge of a trem-bling ground of poetic undecidables, the site of a monstrous and unstable *coniunctio*, and, as Jung noted, he/she is "sometimes . . . a substance. . ., sometimes . . . a philosophy"[12] or thought. Panisnick, following Ficino, has commented, "*Eros* impels the spirit out of the corporeal and sensi-ble world, but *Eros* also projects the spirit into that realm and it thereby becomes a dynamic connective between the two worlds."[13]

Giegerich appears to favor one dimension of Mercurius, and one aim of alchemy, namely, the work of dissolution. When he cites the alchemical operations, he omits *coagulatio* and he follows a linear view of history, pointing out that alchemy properly undergoes dissolution. It remains a question if alchemy and history are so progressive. Alchemy also remains active and continues to die and be reborn in an eternal recurrence while still emerging in the present in differing historical forms. All of its opera-tions are archetypal, in an eternal play between *solve et coagula*.[14] The dialectic is more circular and requires an ongoing interplay between anima and animus, the positivity of the soul and its ongoing dissolution, a syzygy between anima and animus psychologies. However, to imagine a syzygy between archetypal psychology and the logical life of the soul in this way is also to do both an injustice. Each is more complex than I have as yet indicated. Interior to both theories is an intrinsic relationship between anima and animus, soul and spirit – though overall one might characterize each as leaning in one direction or another and as exhibiting an overarching archetypal pattern.

Giegerich further differentiates and characterizes these fundamentally different patterns, namely, the standpoints of the anima, animus, and syzygy. He observes that both the anima and animus points of view rely on mythical figures or concepts of forces imagined as brought into union by the syzygy above them. But, for Giegerich, psychology can and must rise to the level of the syzygy itself. For him, bringing anima and animus together is a Jungian fantasy based on mythological thinking, in which the anima imagines the syzygical relation in the naturalistic imagery of marriage. Anima and animus are seen from an outside view as images or forces, entities needing to be combined or reconciled. For him, such a relationship needs to be sublated to reveal the subtle structure of the syzygy itself, no longer seen as above or encompassing the anima and animus. As separate figures, they disappear and show themselves as sublated moments, the syzygy. They no longer need to be imagined as yoked together, no need for a yoga to connect them. They are already connected dialectically in the movement of thought as a unity of unity and difference, a notion we will return to in a later discussion of Hegel's philosophy.

In this analysis, Giegerich not only moves beyond an ego and anima psychology, but he pushes off from an animus psychology as well. In so doing, he appears to follow the phenomenology of spirit beyond the level of force and understanding to an even subtler level. From the logical standpoint of the form of the syzygy itself, there is no longer a concern with the intuition of contents. The work of sublation continues to cut away at the coagulations and remaining positivities of the soul, freeing the spirit for what appears to be a never-ending story, an endless march to Dionysian freedom – but to what extent is such freedom possible? To what extent and how should it be the goal of psychology?

If a true psychology in Giegerich's sense is to be identified with the radical philosophical discipline of interiority and with an ongoing sublation, is something left behind, unaccounted for – a residue surpassed, a shadow that lingers and requires our attention if psychology is to be adequate to its calling? Here I look into the margins of Giegerich's own reflections and into the development of his own concept of the soul. For Giegerich, the goal of his true psychology is virtually identical with his understanding of the alchemical philosopher's achievement of pure gold, which he interprets as the total liquification of Mercurius. But if this is the aim of both alchemical philosophy and his psychology, what should we make of his statement that he has actually never reached true gold in his work?[15] If the master of the discipline of interiority has himself not been able to achieve the radical cut leading to the syzygy itself, to pure thought or true gold, we might ask to what extent is such a goal possible? I suspect putting this issue this way is not quite fair because it assumes that the goal or gold is some kind of positivity that could be possessed in a moment of literal time and that the radical cut necessary for a true psychology is also a literal event done by the psychologist as a human being. I think such a conception misses the point.

Let's recall that, for Jung and Hillman, the goal is important only as an idea, and that this de-literalizes the idea of the goal right at the beginning. Goals are not actualized events or psychological accomplishments. They are necessary fictions of the soul-making opus. I think no one understands this better or has worked more diligently than Giegerich to think through and develop the idea implicit in this view. But it is perplexing that he seems to write about achieving true gold as if it were a literal possibility, rather than clarifying in that moment the misconception of the kind of achievement he indicates he has not attained. Is it the case that in such moments – and there are only a few of them – Giegerich, the human being, falls short of his radical view of psychology and steps into a semantic concern, a moment in which he shows himself to be a "civil man" and a private individual? Is there a moment of confusion between the practical man and the psychologist? Or, is what we are calling a confusion, an inevitable divide, a shadow that suggests the return of the repressed, of something that fell into a crack in the work of sublation? Does psychology have to remain an activity that leaves the human being behind and separates man from soul?

Near the end of Giegerich's book *What Is Soul?*, he addresses and complicates his position, noting that in clinical work with actual patients, something more may be required than "true psychology." He notes:

> As practicing *therapists*, we are not totally identical with the psychologist in ourselves. We must have one leg in psychology and one leg in practical reality, the sphere of the human, all-too-human. We must be able to display a true, unadulterated access to soul as well as a practical knowledge of the world (which includes a realistic insight into human nature) and understand the needs of the patient as human

being. And, this is most important, we have to *know when it is a question of one or the other*.[16]

This seems to me to be a significant departure from the true psychology Giegerich has been advocating to this point. He continues: "So while I do not wish to water down in any way the severe requirements presented above for doing psychology, a psychology *with* soul, I also do not want to absolutize psychology, as if in the consulting room nothing but psychology was permitted."[17]

At first glance, it does appear that Giegerich is precisely caught between absolutizing and watering down psychology, as opposed to liquefying it. All of his emphasis on the importance of the radical cut, of crossing the Rubicon to the point of no return, seems contradicted by the return of the man in the consulting room. Did the stay-at-home psychologist stay, or return home, unscathed? Is it a return of the repressed, of the practical person, the human being who was banished or degraded in the heroic march to a real psychology? Is this the psychology that until now Giegerich claimed is precisely not a psychology of the human person, but a psychology of the soul proper?

Is such a divide a regression, concession, and compensation, a semantic falling back into a side-by-side and undialectical view of the psychologist and psychology? Does a true psychology of the soul need the contribution of the common man to be complete or comprehensive, a magnum opus? Should we now view the psychologist as philosophically divided against him or herself, against the liberation of thought from its entanglements in the illusions of its ontic identity, or does this divide require a further labor of the concept and sublation to a more integrated view of psychology?

As I noted above, Giegerich is aware that this dual, side-by-side view considerably complicates his theory, and he makes an effort to see the divide conceptually in terms of the soul's dual intentionalities, namely, the soul's need for initiation as well as emancipation: on the one hand, the need for grounding, embeddedness in imagination, myth and metaphysics, and, on the other hand, for emancipation from all the above. For Giegerich, this contradiction needs to be understood in terms of the soul's inner dialectic and self-regulation. The purpose of emancipation from the soul (initiation) is itself a soul purpose, an *opus contra naturam*, a work by and in the spirit of the nature of the soul itself. Even more strongly, Giegerich states: "Emancipation from soul does not mean absolute defection from soul, because this emancipation from soul conversely occurs only within soul."[18]

From here, this apparent contradiction/conflict continues to gain complexity. Giegerich goes on to speak both about the individual soul and the condition of soul in modernity, the condition in which we find ourselves already thrown (perhaps in a Heideggerian sense) into the logical condition of psychologically-born man. For Giegerich, this is a condition in which myth, metaphysics, gods, and God have become impossible – since Modern Man is born out of the soul as an autonomous individual, a civil man, an ego. It would appear that the emancipatory intentionality of the soul has been successful in departing from its initiatory needs in the *participation mystique* and anima identification. In fact, the initiatory needs of the soul in modernity are now moving in harmony and support of its emancipatory desires, to be born out of itself and into the world as subjectivity, subjective mind, consciousness, and logical form.

The movement of initiation toward emancipation leads Giegerich to a recognition of the soul's need for historical development. Thus, for Giegerich, modern man's initiation now means the absolute negative interiorization of the phenomenon, deepening into itself and thus releasing itself into spirit and truth. It is in casting off his mythological garments that modern man finds his human dignity. And, so, for Giegerich freedom from soul today is irrevocable and total.

It would appear that the logical life of the soul has been a successful march to freedom and human dignity – but then comes a major caveat and exception – *neurosis*! For Giegerich, neurosis is the soul's stubborn insistence on somehow remaining linked to a mythic or metaphysical identity at a time when the soul knows that such an identity has been historically surpassed. Giegerich submits then that the soul itself "invented neurosis for itself both as an *incentive* and as a kind of *springboard* to push off from."[19] But such an emancipation does not come easily or naturally. It requires a struggle against the fascinating pull exerted by myth and metaphysics. Giegerich puts it this way: The soul

> has to actively, systematically, in detail and in full awareness *work off* its own fascination and infatuation with the metaphysical, the mythic, the numinous and suggestive power of the imaginal – *through* pulling itself out of its neurosis, *really* stepping out of it and leaving it behind as the nothing that it is.[20]

Only then has the *full price* been paid for the departure from a previous stage of consciousness, while it is the soul itself that "emancipates itself from itself" and then becomes "explicitly and *for itself* a born soul." It "is born *as* human consciousness and its infinite *interiority*."[21] This is all the work of the soul, but at the same time, Giegerich notes, it is only the human person who can push off from his or her neurosis and truly be freed of it, and one does go through the utilization of "strictly analytic, conceptual thought. . . [by] uncompromisingly seeing through and critiquing the neuroticness of the soul's pervers[ity] . . . in all its practical details."[22]

I'm not sure what to say about what the soul in itself is capable of, but it is hard for me to imagine any human person who has achieved, or could achieve, total freedom from neurosis, from all mythic and metaphysical fascinations, as if there is in fact some other hard core "truth" that can be known and that would set one totally free. Giegerich's definition of this freedom from neurosis is the achievement of infinite interiority, again paying the full price, crossing the Rubicon to the point of no return. But here I am reminded of Giegerich's comment about "true gold," and that he had not achieved it with his work! I wonder if he would claim anything different for the achievement of a total freedom from neurosis? It is for him to answer, but I imagine it would be reasonable for him to tell us that this is a semantic concern and as a "psychologist" he can think it all the way through. Here there is a problematic distinction between the ordinary human-all-too-human being and the psychologist. At the end of Chapter Three of his book *What Is Soul?*, Giegerich tells us that as a private individual, as a civil man, he does not confuse himself with the psychologist he "hopes" he is.[23] But what an odd divide this is from the point of view of his psychology. Why hope? Is this the concern of the psychologist who has not made the radical cut, worked this dialectic all the way through?

This hope cannot be the hope of the psychologist proper, but only the hope of the human-all-too-human being, and the idea of hoping signifies the divide between them. For Hillman, hope is a fantasy that distracts us from the present and, in this case, from our human reality, and for that reason he also sees it as the one last evil left in Pandora's box before the lid closes.[24]

So, does this mean that, as a private individual like the rest of us, Giegerich remains neurotic – attached to myth and metaphysics, and hoping to overcome them? Again, has he fallen back into semantics – or never left it? Either way, there appears to be a continuing and unresolved binary between the private individual and the psychologist – and it is this private man who is now invited into the consulting room so that by instinct and the feeling function he can help the psychologist discern the actual needs of the soul in each moment, while to the psychologist proper is left only the "caustic analytic work . . . necessary" to cauterize the patient.[25]

I personally would like to think of the psychologist as capable of the full range of clinical responsiveness, using his or her capabilities to discern whatever it is that the soul needs in the eachness of the moment. I would imagine such a therapist as an analyst who is not totally identified with being a psychologist or with any method, and remembers his or her humanity while offering what is possible in the clinical and human encounter. With regard to this encounter, Giegerich has given the analyst a refined understanding of dialectical and syntactic awareness. The shadow of this contribution is that when it is absolutized and removed from the human all-too-human, the never-ending quest for liberation, and the continuing need to push off from every initiatory connection that is not the dialectic itself, it can be as neurotic as the attachment it tries to cure.

In Buddhism, the caustic work of *sunyata*, of the Vajra or diamond cutter, reduces all attachment to nothingness, but nothingness itself needs to logically void itself, which returns the soul to the world in an ever-recurring circle of life. Thus, liberation is not beyond or transcendent to the world of *samsara* image and illusion. It is one with it or, as the Buddhists say, there is not a hair's-breadth difference between them (i.e., between *samsara* and *nirvana*). Seen alchemically, this is a hermetic circle embodying the dual aspect of Mercurius, which to my mind is not only the liquefying solvent, but the coagulatory agent as well. The liquification of Mercurius is also not a liquification in any literal sense, and the caustic work of analysis need not be literally caustic. As it turns out, the psychologist is also not a psychologist. Another turn of the dialectic reveals the psychologist as human, all-too-human. Perhaps this is the case for Giegerich as well, as he hopes to be a good psychologist, and, in so doing, reveals himself as a psychologist who is not a psychologist and as a human being, human-all-too-human. Is this the failure of the dialectic, its success, or both? In his work on soul, Giegerich discovers what for me has been a missing remainder in his work, the human being and his feeling function, and it is this that for me exceeds, goes beyond, and complicates his work. In so doing, it returns the debt to human feeling, the enigma of the unconscious, and the mystery that is not vanquished by the spirit.

In my criticism of Giegerich, I have pointed to what appears to be a philosophical contradiction or, at least, a tendency to divide a "true psychology" from the human-all-too-human ego psychology which remains embedded in emotion and images. Yet, for Giegerich, the human person returns into the consulting room as a return of the repressed (that is, as the human-all-too-human) and as a necessary aspect of clinical work. Hence Giegerich's "true psychology" must include what he has earlier defined as not psychological at all. Thus, the humanistic subject comes back into play side-by-side with the psychologist, as an Other to all that Giegerich has developed. I have called this "human subject" an unassimilable remnant left out of Giegerich's dialectic proper. But if this is so, it is only one instance of what resists assimilation to the logical life of the soul. It is an instance in which there appears to remain a polarity or, at least, a polar tendency to catapult "idea" beyond "image," in which case something does not fully get taken up into his dialectical process, remaining outside as a remainder. I discuss this aspect more fully in the next chapter.

Notes

1   This chapter is modified from a paper entitled "The Psychologist Who's Not a Psychologist: A Deconstructive Reading of Wolfgang Giegerich's Idea of Psychology Proper," presented at the International Society for Psychology as the Discipline of Interiority Conference, Berlin, Germany, July 24, 2012, and later published in "The Psychologist Who's Not a Psychologist," 223–238.
2   Giegerich, "Psychology," 251.
3   Ibid.
4   Ibid., 254.
5   Ibid.
6   Ibid., 254–255.
7   Based on language from Giegerich's discussion of this in Giegerich, *The Soul's Logical Life*, 9–38.
8   Hillman, *Blue Fire*, 114.
9   Hillman, *The Dream and the Underworld*, 49.
10   Ibid., 1.
11   Ibid.
12   Jung, *Aion (CW9ii)*, §240.
13   Panisnick, "The Philosophical Significance," 201.
14   In all fairness to Giegerich, he responded to this criticism by noting:

> It is true that I did not talk much about coagulation, although it is certainly part of alchemy. But I think it is part of alchemy in a different sense from sublimation, distillation, etc. I make a difference between the particular instantaneous operations and the overall direction of the work. Coagulation is not essential as far as the overall purpose of the work is concerned. Beware of the physical in the matter, the stone that is NOT a stone, vinum ardens, the freeing of Mercurius from the imprisonment and Mercurius itself as QUICKsilver. These are a few indications of the goal of

alchemy. The end-product is not supposed to be coagulated. By contrast, in the day-to-day work coagulation may be necessary, for example if the prime matter, as in hysteria, begins so to speak with a prime matter in the status of 'diarrhea.' So my point is this distinction between two levels.

(Personal communication, October 3, 2012)

15 Giegerich, "The Unassimilable Remnant," 199.
16 Giegerich, *What Is Soul?*, 315–316.
17 Ibid., 316.
18 Ibid., 322–323.
19 Ibid., 332.
20 Ibid.
21 Ibid.
22 Ibid.
23 Ibid., 316.
24 In all fairness, I would like to include here a response that Giegerich made to my criticism:

[Y]ou contrasted [James Hillman] and me with respect to the topic of hope. I think, however, that there is no difference between his and my view about this. The sentence you used as basis for your comment was one in which "hope" was used in the trivial everyday sense. But Hillman probably also hoped that when he said something it was sound and not erroneous Concerning the deeper psychol. sense of hope, I voiced my criticism of it repeatedly and consistently, e.g., my Coll. Engl. Papers vol. III, p. 12 (or 9–12).

(Personal communication, October 3, 2012)

25 Ibid., 334.

Chapter 8

The problem of the remainder

The unassimilable remnant – what is at stake?[1]

In the last chapter, I discussed my own view of the psychologist and the experience of the human-all-too-human in the consulting room. My own experience of this was described in my work on *The Black Sun: The Alchemy and Art of Darkness*. In that book, I addressed what I considered to be an unassimilable darkness through experiences that resisted conscious assimilation, in particular with an image of the black sun that would not yield to or be incorporated into consciousness. It would not dissolve, go away, or be lifted up, and it challenged my own theoretical and psychological narcissism to the core. Since the image of the black sun did not allow itself to be fully integrated into consciousness, it remained an unassimilable remnant, which left me with the question of whether or not this darkness could ever be sublated.

My idea of the unassimilable remnant was catalyzed while treating a woman who reported that she felt something ominous in her chest. She described it as a dark ball that had long strands reaching throughout her body. Her inclination was to reach down and pull it up. Between sessions, in and through her active imagination, she drew the image that she felt was lodged in her chest. It was a brilliant sun with a dense black center and long fibrous tentacles. After drawing it, she felt the image was not menacing enough and felt a need to draw it again. Shortly afterwards, she reported a dream in which she felt a nuclear war was inevitable.

No psychological interpretation seemed to do justice to the monstrosity of the image. The long black fibers remained and there were many circular black shapes that my patient described with horror as an expression of dead skeletal embryos. In spite of this retrieval and the process it stimulated, the image, like a devouring demon, did not subside and no conceptual

DOI: 10.4324/9781003215905-9

translation seemed adequate. While grappling with these images, she suffered an aneurism of the anterior region of her brain and came close to dying. She lost sight in one eye but survived.

The power of these clinical images left me with an experience of their unassimilable monstrosity and an incapacity to dialectically move through or beyond them. I began to research the image of the black sun and, surprisingly, discovered many other instances of such images intimately linked to the most literal and destructive experiences of narcissistic mortification, humiliation, delusion, despair, depression, physiological and psychological decay, cancer, psychosis, suicide, murder, and death. I found these images were resistant to any kind of meaningful explanation or any kind of process that would attempt to sublate them. Rather, the images paradoxically seemed to be the archetype of negation itself, and I found it impossible to bypass their dark aspects. In the face of such a monstrous image of destruction, darkness, and negation, the question of how to come to terms with the unconscious is problematized.

For Jung, this meant opening oneself to the depths of the unknown and yet not abandoning the precious gift of the intellectual differentiation of consciousness. Jung states in *Psychology and Alchemy*:

> It is rather a question of the *man* taking the place of the *intellect* – not the man whom the dreamer imagines himself to be, but someone far more rounded and complete. This would mean assimilating all sorts of things into the sphere of his personality which the dreamer still rejects as disagreeable or even impossible.[2]

For Jung, this was no easy task and required facing the perils, threats, and promises that often show themselves in the context of deep analytic work. Part of this process Jung called "facing the shadow." Facing the shadow is one of the more important goals of Jungian analysis, a key aspect of the overall work. "Coming to terms with the unconscious [shadow] means calling into question the illusions one clings to most dearly about oneself, which have been used to shore up self-esteem and to maintain a sense of personal identity."[3] Confronting the shadow and confronting one's illusions are understandably painful and, at times, dangerous moments in analysis. One danger is that the daimonic can become demonic. Stanley Diamond differentiated the daimonic from the demonic by noting that the demonic remains one-sided, frozen, locked into irrevocable ontological convictions – personal, professional, political, religious, unconsciously self-certain.[4] We worship ourselves or others, Plato or Aristotle, Freud or Jung, Hillman or Lacan, Democrats or Republicans, God or the Devil, Good or Evil – our biases are inner or outer, yin or yang. Rodrick Main has noted that "[w]here ambiguity and intensity are found together, as in the numinous . . . there is indeed a high risk" of splitting and projection.[5]

The daimonic, unlike the demonic, contains the seeds of its own redemption, while fixed ontological convictions lead to fundamentalisms of every sort that silently invade and possess us. They press us toward premature clarity and philosophical closure. Our inspirations and ideas become "gods" in whose thrall we labor to work out our ends and in whose service we become warriors for their "truth." We become purveyors of absolute points of view. These "truths" may be rooted in biology or physics, psychology, poetry, philosophy – or even the deconstruction of all points of view. Perhaps we cannot escape the gods. We think them necessary not only in our inner but also in our outer world, in our personal and professional lives, in our organizations, university classes, consulting rooms, and private studies. In short, our demons inflate us, become our shadows, and our shadows often have roots in our deepest wounds.

In the most general sense, one might define the shadow as referring to the darkness of the unconscious, to what is rejected by consciousness, but also implicit in what we hold dear, as well as that which has not yet or perhaps will never become conscious. Turning toward this darkness means facing the unacceptable, undesirable, and underdeveloped parts of ourselves, the crippled, blind, cruel, ugly, inferior, inflated, and sometimes vile, as well as discovering the potentials for further development of which we are unaware. For Jung, our attempt to fit in with our historical, cultural, and religious values results in the personality's developing what he called a persona, a mask through which adaptation is facilitated.

In order to adapt, parts of our soul are rejected, aspects of ourselves are deemed unacceptable, denied or too highly valued, frozen, repressed, and split off from the developing personality. As a result, they can become tortured, wounded, maimed, and can recede into the dark where ultimately they may be killed and buried. In spite of banishment to a nether world, the shadow continues to play a dynamic role in our psychological life. We are plagued by neuroses.

Jung explored the way in which the shadow emerges into awareness, often through irrational eruptions that impede consciousness. The shadow's trickster-like behavior acts as if it had a mind of its own, sending conscious life into a retrograde movement, where something other than the conscious person seems to hold sway. The shadow appears as well in dreams, projections, transferences, and counter-transferences. On the one hand, it resists consciousness, seeking confrontation, threatening, often leaving us terrified and retreating from contact; while on the other hand, it pursues consciousness, challenging us to engage it.

Angst about the shadow is not surprising. Some current dream images of patients reveal the shadow emerging in the form of primitive, disembodied voices and spirits, wounded animals, impervious cold-blooded prehistoric and mythical beasts, stalkers, murderers, and sexual perverts. In addition, patients' dreams have presented images of disgusting beer-drinking alcoholics, down-and-out gamblers, heavily made-up unattractive women, men with outrageously bad taste, dull-witted jerks, and paralyzed figures locked into frozen rages. Deep emotion has often accompanied images such as those of severe and at times incurable illnesses, as well as scarred, disfigured, and sometimes dead infants and children haunting graves and burial grounds.

Parts of the Self are experienced as poisoned, tortured, killed, decomposed, rotting, and moving toward death. Hillman has warned that the *nigredo* speaks with the voice of the raven, foretelling "dire happenings," echoing and amplifying Dante's classical admonition: "Abandon hope all ye who enter here." In short, following darkness into its most destructive aspects is to enter the dark night of the soul, the heart of darkness, into the world of Hades and Ereshkigal, to Kali's cremation ground and Dante's world of ice, where idealistic and youthful visions of light, eternity, truth, and bliss give way to Saturnine time, the perils of night, and the death of God. Here rational order breaks down and traumatogenic defenses come into play to prevent the unthinkable. At times, one must ask oneself, as a human being and as an analyst, how is it possible to engage such monstrous realities?

Unfortunately, these experiences cannot be simply written off as pathological states, but rather are often the very passageways to individuation, perhaps one aspect of fate or of an individual destiny. One might ask: Why do terrible things happen to good people? I believe it is an illusion to think that such experiences can simply be avoided, rejecting them while imagining that life can or should always be fair or rational. The alchemists called such fantasies "virgin's milk," naïve fantasies of purity and perfection that everything will eventually come out ok. Typical virgin's milk fantasies are often maintained emotionally in intellectually sophisticated and otherwise developed people who unconsciously hold onto ideas that might include sentiments like: God will protect and care for me like a good parent. Bad things won't happen to me because I have lived according to this or that principle. I have been good or faithful, eat healthy foods, meditate and exercise, regularly interpret my dreams, study hard.

When life does not conform to such ideas, the innocent or immature ego is wounded and often overcome with feelings of hurt, self-pity, anger, oppression, and feeling victimized. The injured ego can carry this wounding in many ways. The darkening process can lead to a kind of blindness and dangerous stasis of the soul that then becomes locked in a wound, in hurt or rage, frozen in stone or ice, or fixed in fire. From an alchemical point of view, these innocent attitudes resist undergoing a *mortificatio* process – and as the inevitable experiences of life cause wounding, the soul enters the darkening process. Jacques Lacan likens facing such horrific images to facing cancer, not necessarily manifested physically, but psychologically, proliferating and often leading to humiliation, despair, or depression. What is often not seen is what is happening under the surface – the ripening of innocence that opens the dark eye of the soul.

Facing the darkness: imbibing philosophical vinegar

The suffering in the depths of this descent has been known from ancient times and in various cultures. Traditional approaches to taking in and engaging these realities have been recorded in wisdom traditions, in ritual art, poetry, and spiritual practices. These traditions have also inspired modern poets and artists.

May Sarton, in her poem "The Invocation of Kali,"[6] describes this Tantric goddess as a destructive savage who makes it difficult to become ourselves. She is maddening and reflects our primordial fears, which are so difficult to confront. Swami Vivekananda[7] describes the impact of facing this goddess as not unlike facing the horrors of blackness and death. It is hard to imagine facing a shadow figure as potent as the goddess and inviting her in. It is difficult to translate this into analytic principles, but clearly the hard work of facing the shadow and of analysis is in part learning to turn toward the painful, unpleasant and at times horrifying figures of the psyche, and thus toward the unacceptable aspects of the Self and of life. Moreover, the deepest recesses of the archetypal shadow may be unredeemable, and we may need to relativize salvationist hopes or we will be driven to do so. These images remind us that life at times can be tragic and that the unconscious is not invariably benevolent.

Recalling my patient's dream of the black sun, in its aftermath one realizes that there appear to be limits to what our efforts – religious, spiritual, analytic – can accomplish, and this is sobering to our overzealous expectations. In such instances, the analyst may be called upon to sit with the analysand in and through loss, grief, despair, and the tragic experiences of life, and be company on the ship of death and in silence be witness to the limits of analysis and to the hopes and dreams of the human soul. And yet, there will be moments when the "death" we face may turn out to be a symbolic one, heralding an alchemical process of *mortficatio* and *putrefactio*, which can lead to renewal and the opening to a deepened symbolic life.

Stein has noted that "[p]ersons in analysis are asked explicitly or implicitly to stay receptive to the unconscious – to the less rational, more ambiguous, and often mysterious side of the personality."[8] It is important that the analyst as well be prepared to venture into the darkest recesses of the shadow as a participant and guide with the capacity to sit still, stay present, accompany and facilitate facing the darkest aspects of psychic life, in so doing, the shadow figures may show themselves to compensate or complement a one-sided conscious position, and facing them can lead to a more integrated personality. Still, the question remains: how to face such figures? And to what extent can we do so?

How can we take in what Hillman speaks of as broken, ruined, weak, sick, inferior, and socially unacceptable parts of ourselves? For him, curing these shadow images requires love. He asks: "How far can our love extend to the broken and ruined parts of ourselves, the disgusting and perverse? How much charity and compassion have we for our own weakness and sickness? How far can we. . . [allow] a place for everyone?"[9] Because the shadow can be socially unacceptable and even evil, it is important that it is carried by us, which means that we do not project our unacceptable parts on to others and or act them out. This is an ethical responsibility.

The importance of refraining from creating scapegoats loaded down with our own evils is particularly urgent in today's world situation. For Hillman, a moral stance toward the shadow is essential and cannot be abandoned, but this is not enough: "At one moment something else must break through."[10] Facing the shadow and its cure requires a conjunction of seeming opposites, a confrontation, and a paradoxical union of two incommensurables: "the moral recognition that these parts of me are burdensome and intolerable and must change, and the loving laughing acceptance which takes them just as they are. . . . [o]ne both . . . judges harshly and joins gladly."[11] Each position "holds only one side of the truth."[12] Hillman gives an example from the Jewish mystical tradition of the Chassidim, where "deep moral piety [is] coupled with astounding delight in life."[13] To achieve such an attitude requires considerable psychological development, but it still seems almost impossible to imagine taking delight in the deeply heinous and virulent aspects of the shadow. How can we participate in the implications of perversity, with Nazi images of the Holocaust, and with the terrorist shadow? Did Job join gladly with the dark side of God, which according to Jung required a moral transformation?

There hopefully is a moment where moral outrage turns to moral conviction and the moment where one challenges the gods – inner or outer – and speaks out. One deep shadow of psychoanalysis is the danger of an introverted bias, thus bypassing the atrocities of everyday life. But psychoanalysis has also taught us about the shadow of premature acting out in the naïve name of the good, the "truth," that righteously brings even more darkness into the world.

We spoke above of the kind of love necessary to embrace the shadow. It is difficult indeed to make real the cliché to love ourselves when our selves contain not only the noblest but also the vilest aspects of our human condition. It is too easy to fall into the clichés of love and self-acceptance – residues of virgin milk may still be operative in the fantasies of wholeness unification and oneness.

Jung early on spoke of this oneness as "a melting together of sense and nonsense" – a *complexio oppositorum* or *mysterium coniunctionis* – but such ideas can too easily become assimilated and intellectualized, thus becoming clichés for a dark chaosmos that pushes the soul toward the unthinkable and to the limits of mind and language bringing with it the danger of being used by the powers we pretend to understand.

It is clear to me that Jung's idea of the mysterium and Hillman's idea of love are no simple clichés. What both Jung and Hillman call for in the name of love is an ability to endure and embrace the darkest and most offensive and unacceptable parts of ourselves and to resist projecting them on others. This requires a breadth and depth of soul and an ability to tolerate the tension of moral paradox. In "Silver and White Earth," (Chapter 6 in *Alchemical Psychology*) Hillman considers such a paradox as a kind of "illuminated lunacy"[14] and, in addition, he sees the work of psyche as a return of the soul to the world, a reality that goes beyond insular subjectivity and moral passivity.

The inexpressible mysteries of life remained with Jung throughout his life and in his works from *The Red Book* to his final works on alchemy. Jung's vision of the unity of opposites was never a simple or benign cliché, but, as noted above, there has been a tendency to pass over the shock and radicality that Neil Micklem has called grotesque and monstrous. The teleological future that Jung intends in his idea of the transcendent function that "unifies" opposites is indeed monstrous! Jacques Derrida likewise has noted that the future is necessarily monstrous – surprising – that for which we are unprepared. And Casey, at the end of his book *Spirit and Soul: Essays in Philosophical Psychology* has noted that "we must allow ourselves to be surprised at every turn. We must, in Heraclitus' trenchant fragment, 'expect the unexpected.'"[15] Like innocent Persephone, we are sometimes drawn downward kicking and screaming into the depths, a descent into darkness and to an underworld marriage with Hades. Whether in the story of Orpheus and Eurydice, Demeter and Persephone, Ishtar and Demuzi, all symbolize the potential for loss and the redemptive power of darkness, and perhaps even more that at an archetypal level these potentials are somehow linked together.

I believe this is the "mystery" of the black sun, an image that carries both darkness and illumination. If, as noted earlier, we do not avoid the monstrous paradox of the black sun and simply attempt to reach beyond it to the light, we may notice that the archetype of negation itself is indeed a sublated image – a darkness that negates itself not through an external light that dispels darkness, but rather through what the alchemists called the *lumen naturae*, an intimate intertwining that is called "the light of darkness itself." It is clear that, if indeed there is anything like a sublation, the human-all-too-human element remains an ongoing presence never simply transcended by any intellectual abstraction. The mess of our everyday existence is a never-ending remainder that is part of our experience of otherness and of life itself and that shows itself in our neuroses and in history. If we can tolerate or even learn to appreciate this differentiated oneness, perhaps we can begin to free ourselves from virgin's milk and turn vinegar into wine, which may allow one to live on in the face of insult and loss, or as Shakespeare has put it, with "the slings and arrows of outrageous fortune." Perhaps it is a recognition of such duplex images that can catalyze a linking of soul and spirit and that can be instrumental in the development of a more intimate relationship between psychology and philosophy. It is this integration that leads us toward an understanding of the Philosophers' Stone as an initiatory experience involving both spirit and soul and the fullness of life, which the philosophers have sought since the earliest expressions of the alchemical imagination.

Notes

1 This chapter is a modified version of Marlan, "Facing the Shadow," a chapter in *Jungian Psychoanalysis*, 5–13.
2 Jung, *Psychology and Alchemy (CW12)*, §84.
3 Stein, "The Aims and Goal of Jungian Analysis," 40.
4 See Diamond, *Anger, Madness, and the Daimonic*, Chapter 3: The Psychology of Evil: Devils, Demons, and the Daimonic.
5 Main, "Numinosity and Terror," 163.
6 Sarton, "The Invocation of Kali."
7 Vivekananda, *In Search of God*, 25.
8 Stein, "The Aims and Goal of Jungian Analysis," 39.
9 Hillman, "The Cure of the Shadow," 242.
10 Ibid., 243.
11 Ibid.
12 Ibid.
13 Ibid.
14 Hillman, *Alchemical Psychology*, 125.
15 Casey, *Spirit and Soul*, 348.

Chapter 9

The alchemical stove

Continuing reflections on Hillman's and Giegerich's views of alchemy and the Philosophers' Stone[1]

In this chapter, I first return to alchemy, the Philosophers' Stone, Jung, Hillman, and Giegerich, and then move on to Hegel and other philosophers, in order to rethink the question of soul and spirit in the light of analysis and philosophy. One way to imagine the psychological work on the Stone is to follow in the steps of the old alchemists and claim that each thinker advances over those who came before, each representing a version of the best or truest vision of the goal. While such a perspective ultimately may prove to be true, I must confess that I am not yet ready to make such a move. Rather, I am still at work trying to understand Jung's alchemical vision *alongside* those of Hillman, Giegerich, and others. While there are many scholars who have presented a number of valuable contributions to the alchemical work, I will continue to focus here on Hillman and Giegerich, both of whom offer astonishing insights into the psychic reality of the Stone. Each of their perspectives can be read independently or as contributing to a larger and subtler vision still being articulated.

For me, reading Jung side-by-side with Hillman and Giegerich evokes an image of the alchemical stove: Jung in one alembic cooking on a back burner over a steady low heat, Hillman and Giegerich in differently shaped vessels boiling up front, while I attempt to prepare my own concoction utilizing the vapors produced by them and others, and seeking to further distill the essences and elixirs necessary for the difficult production of the Stone.[2]

For the moment I will leave Jung's vessel closed and on the back burner, and return again for another look into Hillman's alembic which reveals a phenomenology of the soul's colors: an imaginal rainbow of black, blue, white/silver, yellow, and red. For Hillman, the Stone is first an "idea" of

DOI: 10.4324/9781003215905-10

the goal, since the goal must be deliteralized from the beginning.[3] While the Stone has facticity and objectivity, duration and substantiality, it is too complex to be described simply in *senex* metaphors. The Stone is also sensual, soft, waxy, and wounded. It is tender and flexible, oily, rich, and fat. It is vital and combustible and, though emotional, it has a kind of stability and timelessness. It moves in a circular way, turning like a wheel, returning *telos* to itself – "to the subjective urge that has impelled the entire work from the start . . . the snake eats its own tail"[4] – and the *rotatio* announcing "that no position can remain fixed, no statement can be finally true."[5] It is ultimately the objectification of our subjectivity, yet it oozes with libido. It is Freudian, pagan, neo-Platonic, Greek, and Italian – a pleasurable pull towards Beauty, toward Voluptas, rather than the "mediocrity of ataraxic rationality."[6] Hillman's patron saints, Corbin, Ficino, and Valla, among others, stimulate a reddened psychology dripping with an Aphroditic language, exalting, revivifying, and crowning matter. The goal is not growth, health, development, or transformation "but seeking and searching of the awakened mind . . . like a burning jewel in the stone."[7]

As we noted earlier, a look inside the Giegerich vessel suggests the need to refine the Stone further. Its inner essence emphasizes the *logical* rather than the *imaginal*. The work of the adept, for Giegerich, would be to liberate the Stone from the confines of "sensate intuition" and "picture thinking." With the dissolution of the imaginal and of sensate intuition, one might be left imagining the Stone as colorless rather than colorful. If Hillman's tincture leans toward "*coagula,*" Giegerich's move is toward "*solve*" – toward the freeing of Mercurius through sublation, through the dialectics of the Negative, the "NOT" or "ou" (from the alchemical saying "*líthos ou líthos,*" that is, "the not-stone stone").[8] For Giegerich, the highest mystery of the whole work is the physical dissolution into mercury, a movement out of the imaginal into the logical. Here I imagine Kundalini shedding her skin and Thales remarking that all is water (liquidity). Giegerich also notes that *aqua permanens* is "a solid ground that in itself is not solid, not 'ground' at all, but rather liquidity, pure movement, that. . . *is* nevertheless solid ground."[9]

So, if Hillman emphasizes wax (the body of the image), Giegerich thinks water (the *solutio* of its body). If Hillman finds soul in the valley, Giegerich points to the peaks. If Hillman critiques sublation,[10] Giegerich considers it to be the *elixir vital*. If Hillman draws inspiration from the Italians, Giegerich finds his in Hegel.

However, if one has read Hillman and Giegerich carefully, one soon begins to see that all of the above caricatures are at best misreadings. As we have seen in the last chapters, both thinkers are far more complex than such sketches suggest and, while there are crucial differences between them, there are also considerable overlapping themes that call for further study. Placing the above ideas into a double pelican and reheating the entire mixture will allow us to see their similar essences circulating and rising up. Both thinkers emphasize the importance of "ideas," and both see that it is essential to go beyond the physical and the literal. Both emphasize the intrinsic link between idea and image, peak and vale, *solve* and *coagula*, and both officiate at the puer/psyche marriage, although the way each tinctures his syzygy differs. And, most importantly for me, both emphasize some version of the "death of the ego." While both might be seen as privileging one side of the syzygy over the other, neither can be accused of disregarding the importance of that which is not given priority.

In order to understand their respective positions, it may be useful also to compare some of their mutual misunderstandings. For example, when Hillman critiques Hegel's notion of *Aufhebung*, what he seems to have in mind is the spirit detached from psyche, the puer drawn apart from psyche, or anima separated from animus – a procedure that he uses as a heuristic device in his essay "Peaks and Vales." However, to read Hegel's or Giegerich's notion of sublation in this way does not do justice to the complexity of their ideas. Nor does it recognize that for both of them sublation should never be understood as an either/or. Giegerich clarifies his position on this by noting: "What I offer instead [of an either/or interpretation] is a psychology of interiority. There are not two, but only one, and this 'one' contains its own 'other' within itself."[11] In other words, for Giegerich, thought is not an external other to the image, but the very soul of the image itself. Put in this way, Hillman's critique of sublation, if it is understood as a "climb into the thin air of mountain peaks,"[12] does not hold. Giegerich's notion of sublation already assumes a puer-psyche, anima-animus syzygy. If his thought can be said to lean towards the animus, it is because Giegerich feels that "thought" has been underdeveloped under the weight of the image in imaginal psychology. Giegerich makes it clear that his "pleading for 'thought' [an appeal Hillman makes as well] is not a call to turn our backs on 'image' and on what archetypal theorizing ha[s] accomplished, 'but rather to continue it radically in an attempt to complete it. . . .'"[13]

However, in spite of his desire to develop Hillman's thought, Giegerich actually misconstrues the way Hillman defines image. He believes that Hillman's understanding of image is based on "sensory intuition" and that it is a form of "picture-thinking" in contra-distinction to "thought" or thinking proper.[14] But here, just as Hillman's critique falls short of Giegerich's idea of "thought," so Giegerich's critique of Hillman seems to miss Hillman's more radical understanding of "image." After all, in "Image-Sense," Hillman writes: ". . . images are not the same as optical pictures even if they are like pictures. . . . We do not literally see images."[15] He adds, giving credit to Casey, that "An image is not what you see but the way you see."[16] That is, we do not see images but see through them. In fact, Giegerich knows that his critique is different from what archetypal psychology actually proposes and that its notion of image has a deeper and more fundamental meaning than he has attributed to it. Seeing images as pictures might be considered to be a remnant of a sensationist psychology that understands images and even the imagination as epiphenomenal to actual things. Although he claims that he does "not want to *reduce*"[17] archetypal psychology's understanding of image to this limited representationalist notion, his critique is primarily aimed at image and the imagination in the narrow sense just described.

David Miller also alludes to this issue of "the nonperceptual and nonsensate 'image.'"[18] While Miller's view of image is closer to Hillman's and different from Giegerich's, this difference for Miller is very small and does not diminish his deep appreciation for Giegerich's contribution. Likewise, Greg Mogenson is aware that Hillman's understanding of image is non-representational and that it functions, in some ways, not unlike the work of negative interiorization as described by Giegerich. This is clear from Mogenson's choice of quotes from Hillman: "The soul's life is not upheld as correct by virtue of exteriority"[19] and "What is reflection then when there is no subject reflected, neither emotion nor external object?"[20] For Hillman, the image is most clearly "a metaphor without a referent."[21] While in many ways I share Miller's sense that in a larger perspective such issues are trivial, and perhaps heuristic on Giegerich's part, they nonetheless point to matters that require further distillation and a "labor of the concept,"[22] as Giegerich might describe it. This is particularly true in the face of the provocative question raised by Mogenson at the end of his chapter "Different Moments in Dialectical Movement." He acknowledges that Hillman, like Giegerich, conveys "the negativity of the image"[23] – but he then calls attention to an even more radical interiorization. Pointing beyond Hillman toward Giegerich's notion of logical form, he asks: "But what of the gold that is to follow?"[24] Here he alludes to Giegerich's view that "the 'gold' of true psychology is the further negation of the image's silvery negativity into the absolute negativity of a consciousness that can *think* the various moments of each image all at once."[25]

But just what does absolute negativity mean when it comes to Giegerich's "gold," which, like the "stone that is not a stone," is a subtler "gold that is not gold" – a gold that is spirit? How is this subtle gold to be differentiated from Hillman's idea? Hillman, too, speaks of gold, not only of silver's imagination of it. What is the difference when we "think" gold in the context of absolute negativity versus when we see it from Hillman's standpoint – particularly when we no longer define the imaginal as simply representing the real? Once we have Giegerich's subtle view of "gold" as totally liquefied Mercurius, can we still distinguish it from lead, silver, or mercury? Are all sublated concepts dissolved in the grand solution of the dialectic? Is "the gold that is not gold" the spirit of gold, the ghost of gold, a tincture of gold, the idea of gold, or no gold at all? I suspect that these questions mistake what Giegerich means and that we can distinguish gold's particularity once we have a deeper understanding of the dialectic he proposes. However, just how his gold can be "thought" in comparison to Hillman's "seeing," its sensuous particularity requires further elaboration. When Hillman sees through gold, pushes off from it, he does not go "all the way" according to Giegerich – and for which he faults him. While Hillman's gold is also clearly not the "vulgar gold"[26] but rather the "fantastical gold" of alchemy, his way of speaking about it retains the "golden touch,"[27] the sensate "heart of gold," the "winners gold," images of gold as "permanently glowing and untarnished," visions of "a consciousness ever shining like dawn, like the sun, without fits of darkening," ever "able to be beaten and beaten yet never crack under the hammer, to be bent, thin as a leaf and so cover mundane things with the shine of glory."[28] Images such as these are ideas of gold released from simple physicality, but they retain a pigment recognizable to the metaphoric ear. While Hillman's move takes him beyond the physical, he stays with the material, the concrete, what I have called here the pigment, a certain impurity that for him saves gold from the "poisonous state of splendid solar isolation."[29]

Therefore, the question about the gold that is to follow (Mogenson's question) is also a question that ultimately applies to the Philosophers'

Stone and to the goal of the work. In considering the vision of the Stone in Hillman and Giegerich, it is important to place Hillman's most radical view of image and of the Stone alongside Giegerich's ideas of "absolute-negative interiority, spirit, thought."[30] For Giegerich, the goal of both alchemy and a "true psychology" is to go *beyond* a psychology rooted in images and the imagination to a psychology rooted in the logical life of the soul. Such a move, for Giegerich, is a true working through of the hierarchical possibilities present in the dialectic and is superior to a psychology that remains rooted in the flesh of images. Since Giegerich does not propose that we eliminate images, the question remains how to understand the similarities and differences between Hillman and Giegerich in a way that moves beyond a side-by-side view of simple difference.[31]

This brings us full circle to my image of the alchemical stove and to my own side-by-side placement of differing views of the Stone. Is it adequate simply to allow different views, perspectives, archetypal stances – or does the "labor of the concept" demand that all views be subject to a dialectic in which "Reason" will produce one position more developed than others? Following Hegel, Giegerich notes that "items that are 'simply different' (*verschienden*) are indifferent to the difference between them."[32] Here I take Giegerich to be calling for an engagement of ideas versus simply settling for alternative perspectives; for instance, holding that the fundamental basis of psyche is imagistic versus logical rather than working through the two positions to a conclusion. He has done much to argue for his well-worked-through positions, and his critiques of imaginal psychology merit careful reading and consideration. Miller and Mogenson have done a masterful job of giving us strong readings of Giegerich's work and of helping us toward a careful consideration of his ideas. What follows is my beginning attempt to work through an interface between Hillman and Giegerich and to raise a number of concerns about any move that relegates images to a status secondary to thought. In opening up the problematic of moving from image to thought, it is unclear whether, or in what way, thought is more fundamental than image, particularly when the image is understood in its most radical way. In addition, a number of philosophers have resisted this move and raised critical questions that must be explored before we can consider abandoning the primary place of image in the work of Jung and Hillman.

Resistance of the remainder

My own hesitation and resistance about a move to spirit/thought is rooted in my belief that Jung and Hillman each brought about an advance in consciousness by re-envisioning image and imagination, both of which had been in the shadow of Western thought and metaphysics since Plato. Jung's resuscitation of images was a return to the soul and began a reversal of the dominant historical process that had de-potentiated images and reduced soul to rational intellectual spirit. Hillman's archetypal psychology continued and radicalized Jung's reversal. Hillman has taken note of the hatred for image. The battle between spirit and soul, thought and image, is an old one and even now continues to be fought. The fear of the power of image and of the imagination is very deep in our culture. Giegerich himself has acknowledged that the work of Jung and Hillman was a major step from which "there is no way back."[33]

Given that Giegerich's return to the "rational" and to "thought" *is* so powerful, I am concerned that his perspective may be too easily assimilated into the cultural undermining of image, especially since image is still in a fragile revival of its importance, if not its primacy. We must give Giegerich full credit for the complexity of his ideas and for his recognition of the rational. However, although his work does suggest that the rational and the soul are integrated notions, the idea of the rational is so emotionally and psychologically laden with profound cultural implications that Giegerich's perspective, in spite of its sophistication, may serve to continue the repression of the imagination and to turn readers away from the radical innovations of Jung and Hillman. While this, in itself, is not an argument against Giegerich's position as such, it is an expression of my concern about how his work may be heard and taken up by others.

A move to spirit is an earmark of Hegelian and post-Hegelian Idealism and neo-rationalist philosophies. An example of this, perhaps another misreading, can be seen in the work of Paul Ricoeur, who – in spite of his creative valuing of the symbolic – nevertheless ends up ultimately in a neo-rationalist position in which thought/philosophy transcends mythopoesis. This can be seen in his formulation "the symbol gives rise to thought,"[34] which privileges thinking and tilts the balance away from the primacy of the metaphoric toward the superiority of the rational and the philosophical. My concern here is with the dangers of logocentrism, with what happens when an interpreter, philosophical or psychoanalytic, gives primacy to thought over image, to the rational side of a metaphoric copula, to a formulation in which image and metaphor could be reduced to being simply instrumental, as literary critic Dominick LaCapra has noted.[35]

LaCapra's analysis echoes both archetypalist and deconstructivist critiques of the traditional position, which has its roots in the whole history of thought that gives priority to logos over mythos. It is a position resisted as well by a number of philosophers who take a critical stance toward the Hegelian dialectic and post-Hegelian neo-rationalist thinking and toward Hegel's attempt to sublate the image into the rational. Martin Heidegger, for instance, has commented that the "not" or "negative," referred to as a moment in Hegel's dialectic, cannot be simply overcome or assimilated by reason. The "not" is more than a dialectical alienation on the way to a sublation. In fact, it resists assimilation into the movements of thought. The negation of a negation does not culminate in an unconditional "yes" (i.e., a full assimilation of the "not"). For Heidegger, Hegel's interpretation of negativity is an inauthentic modification of an insurmountable "not" – a "not" that can serve as an access point that transitions from a logical understanding of the soul to a poetic one. For Heidegger, the more important category is not rationality but Being.

Similarly, Edgar Morin "faults Hegel for considering contradiction a transitory 'moment' of the *Aufhebung*, a moment which is ultimately annulled."[36] Like Heidegger, Morin is arguing, in effect, that the "not" cannot be sublated by any movement of thought and that it represents an unassimilable difference that resists any form of engulfment.

In a spirit similar to Heidegger's and Morin's, Jacques Derrida also recognizes the problem of the unassimilable "not." For him, trying to undo Hegel is like trying to decapitate the hydra. He argues that Hegel's dialectic incorporates all contradiction, and that every attempt to refuse such "engulfment" is seen as an error to be overcome by the continuing dialectic. He asks: how then to interrupt the operation of *Aufhebung*, how to handle a negative that is more than just a moment in an all-embracing process? How do we escape the perpetual reversal entailed in any oppositional system of thought? What would bring the death knell (*glas*), or laughter (Nietzsche) to bear on Hegel's attempt to achieve absolute spirit without remainder?

For Derrida, Hegel's insistence on absolute spirit implies a drift towards rationalism and idealism and requires the creation of a metaphysical edifice, which for Derrida is rooted in a trembling ground of double entendre. He describes this trembling ground as a "fabulous scene" which any metaphysics of certainty effaces and yet this scene remains, stirring beneath it.[37] For Derrida this scene provokes "an endless confrontation with Hegelian concepts, and the move from a restricted, 'speculative' philosophical economy – in which there is nothing that cannot be made to make sense, in which there is nothing *other* than meaning – to a 'general' economy – which affirms that which exceeds meaning, the excess of meaning from which there can be no speculative profit – involves a reinterpretation of the central Hegelian concept: the *Aufhebung*."[38] In order to engage Giegerich's particular vision of the Philosophers' Stone, and while realizing that Giegerich's thought is to be distinguished from Hegel's, I find myself struggling with the above critiques naming the unassimilable "not" as a remainder rather than as a momentary hiatus in the dialectic. In my own work, an expression of the negative that is unassimilable showed itself as the image of *sol niger*, a darkness that refuses conscious assimilation.

This unassimilable darkness was a theme of my book *The Black Sun: The Alchemy and Art of Darkness*. The alchemy and art of this darkness require a further exploration of the light of darkness as an expression of both *sol niger* and the Philosophers' Stone. As I've stated, my work began with the recognition of that which resists conscious assimilation, with a black sun that would not yield or be incorporated by an ego stance. It would not dissolve, go away, or be lifted up, and it challenged my own psychological narcissism to the core. While *sol niger* did not allow itself to be possessed by ego and the ego at times felt more in danger of being possessed by it, a perceptual awareness occurred. The wounded and by now somewhat emaciated ego noticed that what it called darkness had a shine that Jung called the shine of darkness itself, the *lumen naturae*. My book was the beginning of an exploration of this darkness and of its odd luminosity. This strange lumen was my impetus to explore the Philosophers' Stone as I imagined it, present in a darkness that is no darkness. Could the lumen of the Philosophers' Stone be an image in Hillman's sense – something that is not simply an object of consciousness but something we can see through? Could this darkness be called sublated?

My ongoing work on the Stone owes a continuing debt to Jung, Hillman, Giegerich, and others – and, as I have noted, is a work in progress. It began in *The Black Sun* with the blackness of *sol niger*, with the *mortificatio* of brokenness, incision, and wound, castration, cut, negation, with an ultimate "No" to the ego, with what felt unassimilable. But now my attention is turning from the black sun per se to the Philosophers' Stone. To bring the Stone into focus is not to leave the black sun behind, nor to simply move to an *albedo* psychology. Rather, it is to pursue my suspicion that the Philosophers' Stone has been there all along in the shine of darkness itself and that darkness will be there at the end as well, perhaps as an indispensable *caput mortuum*, the dross or residue that remains in the retort after distillation. In some philosophical and alchemical views, this residue is ultimately eliminated, but my wager and anticipation is that the Stone – whether in the language of revivification and Aphroditic pleasure or in the sublation to pure mercurial liquidity – is always accompanied by a remainder. This remainder, while not best understood as a Kantian thing-in-itself, is nonetheless that which resists a consciousness that does not account for its differentiation. At times, to accommodate this difference, one can see the Stone described as "the unity of the unity and difference."

Such a description attempts to address the monstrous complexity of the Stone, but even the idea of "the unity of the unity and difference" privileges unity, although at a higher "logical level." The "unity of the unity and difference" is still a tincture of the syzygy that emphasizes unity as the major trope. The syzygy can also be tinctured to emphasize difference. This would call out for the complementary idea of "the difference of the unity and difference," a difference that resists being lit up by consciousness and which protects the remainder that emits a mysterious light of its own as opposed to a light that consciousness would shine on it. This complementary idea is itself similar to one of the stages of the logical dialectic discussed by the Buddhist sage Nargarjuna. His formulation resists any transcendent unification and reinstates a darkness, a void (*sunyata*) that can also be said to shine.

My exploration here of the shine of darkness begins with two images of *sol niger*. In the first, a skeleton stands on a blazing black sun; the image reads "*Putrefactio*."[39] In the second, a black sun burns down on a primarily desolate landscape in the alchemical text *Splendor Solis* (1582). These are images of a place an adept must enter if anything is to be learned about the light of nature and the Philosophers' Stone. Jung writes about this light, the *lumen naturae*, in his *Alchemical Studies*, where he calls it "the light of darkness itself."[40] It is a light "which illuminates its own darkness. . . [and] turns blackness into brightness." It is a kind of light that the "darkness comprehends." This light is not the light of our day-world sun, but rather the *lumen naturae* that shines in *sol niger*. It can be seen in the rising of the black Ethiopian (also referred to as *caput mortuum*, *nigredo*, "matter to be calcined," "dragon," "black faeces," and "shadow stuff"[41]), whose rebirth takes on a new name "which the philosophers call the natural sulfur and their son, this being the stone of the philosophers."[42] Likewise this transformation is seen in the reconstituted Kali, and is cultivated in Taoist alchemy. It shines in *The Secret of the Golden Flower*, and in the *filius philosophorum*, imagined by Paracelsus as a luminous vehicle and referred to by Jung as "the central mystery of philosophical alchemy."[43] It is to this mystery, to this "luminous vehicle," that we turn as we imagine a move from *sol niger* to the Philosophers' Stone. Just as this light is not separate from darkness, so the Philosophers' Stone is not separate from *sol niger* but is intrinsic to it.

How can darkness shine? In my work on the black sun, it is the shining that seems most enigmatic. Is it a question then of presence and absence, or of a present absence, or of absence itself? The negation and presence of light is at the heart of the archetypal image/idea of the black sun. The Sun King is mortally wounded by darkness and in the negation of negation, *sol niger* shines; a strange reversal takes place or perhaps is "logically" present from the beginning.

One could say that *sol niger*, the black sun, is already a sublated sun, a philosophical/psychological sun, a sun that is not a sun (as the alchemists say of their Stone). It is black and yet, at the same "logical" time, it shines. What is the nature of such a shining, such a consciousness? Is it an image, an idea, or both? Is consciousness too dull a word to express this complexity? Philosophers and psychologists have often found difficulty with words like consciousness, image, and idea, and have struggled to give expression to their meanings in a way not encumbered by the metaphysical and metaphoric prejudices of their times – a seemingly impossible task that on occasion has silenced the best of philosophers. How then to let be manifest what is gathered into the shining?

In our postmodern world, our efforts have often left us with a virtual apophatic orgy of dissemination, of a negation of master tropes (and, in their place, sliding signifiers), and of neologisms that require another language to follow the discourse. Yet our simple common language will not do either. Our best efforts are marked by traces of darkness, perhaps penetrating to the core of language itself, into a darkness that matters – and still there is the shine. How then to speak of it, of what Roger Brooke has called the "fertile and hospitable emptiness within which the things of the world could shine forth?"[44] To speak of the shining is not only to speak in the context of the metaphor of light, but also to speak of the shining in a way that aims at expressing an insight that goes beyond the traditional divide between light and dark, and in a way that approaches a more primordial awareness closer to Jung's more mature vision of the psyche, a vision influenced by the alchemical tradition.

Sparks of reiteration

In *The Black Sun* I began a consideration of this shining and wrote of it as an image of light at the core of ancient alchemical ideas. The aim of alchemy, according to Paracelsus, was to discover this light hidden in nature. It is a light very different from notions of light as simply separate from darkness and by extension different from any conception of a consciousness separate from its dark background. My strategy in *The Black Sun* was to hesitate before this darkness, to pause and then to enter its realm of corpses and coffins, of monsters and monstrous complexity, and to engage its most literal and destructive demons. Such kinds of experiences can traumatize and kill. They can also drive the soul toward the unthinkable, a condition which archetypal defenses seek to avoid. To experience the above means to be in the grip of the *mortificatio*, a condition the alchemists knew was essential to reaching the depths of the transformation process. Through illness and/or a shamanic-like initiation, the *mortificatio* drives the psyche to an ontological pivot point, to a desubstantiation of the ego, and to what Theodor Adorno might call an emaciated subject,[45] leading to a gateway that is both a dying and a new life.

   The black sun is a complexity. Its "blacker than black" dimension shines with a dark luminescence. It can open the way to some of the most numinous aspects of psychic life and can give us a glimpse of the miracle of perception at the heart of what Jung called the *mysterium coniunctionis* and of the Philosophers' Stone. I spoke above of such a vision in the Tantric rites of Kali who was worshiped at the cremation grounds where she copulates with her consort Shiva on the body of a corpse burning on a funeral pyre. Kali worshipers enact ceremonials associated symbolically and ritually with the annihilation of the ego. These rituals often depict the death of the ego, out of which, it is said, the "human being arises shining."[46] How is it possible to embrace such a negative image? For Hegel, "only by looking the negative in the face, and tarrying with it," is it possible that the negative can be "the magical power that converts death [and darkness] into being."[47]

For the Tantrics, if one's worship is successful, if one is able to stay the course open-eyed, to dance Kali's dance, to welcome her, then her blackness is said to shine. This shining can be linked to the alchemical ideas of whitening and silvering, with the proviso that we see this shining *albedo* as part of the complexity of darkness itself and not simply as a literal phase following blackness. From one perspective, the theme of renewal follows from symbolic death, but from another, archetypally and logically, death and renewal are at the core of *sol niger*, and this is expressed in the simultaneity of blackness and luminescence.

Mystical death

How can we further our understanding of this mystical death? How to speak of it? The idea of ego death is a difficult one in the light of the acknowledged importance of the role of the ego in relation to the unconscious in our classical way of thinking. When we think of ego loss, our thoughts immediately go to the problematics of a weak, impaired, or nonfunctioning ego, to a concern with annihilation anxiety and the defenses of the Self against it, as well as to psychosis. Ego psychology has a dominant hold on our everyday psychological culture. Yet, the notion of ego death is and has been in the margins of our tradition: in Jung's idea that "*the experience of the self is always a defeat for the ego*,"[48] in Hillman's "psychotherapeutic cure of me,"[49] in Rosen's "egocide,"[50] in Miller's views about the "no self,"[51] in Giegerich's "death of the ego,"[52] and so on. Each has contributed to our understanding of a psychology that relativizes and/or dismembers the ego, and each has a stake in the transformation of our psychological theory.

Giegerich, for example, states that "the Self is real only to the extent that the ego has been negated, overcome . . . one might even say, it exists only as a reality 'over the ego's dead body'[53] . . . as one who has long died as ego personality."[54] "The art of psychological discourse," he continues, "is to speak as someone who is already deceased."[55] Here Giegerich extends the notion of ego death into the core of psychological discourse itself. For him, this is a necessary step toward the achievement of a "true psychology" and essential in understanding the goal of both alchemy and of a psychological life. For Giegerich, as noted, ego death also signifies the death of all positivity and serves as the gateway to a liquification of the subject and thus allows entrance into the logical life of the soul. There is a resonance between Giegerich's reading of Hegel and poststructuralist thought, both of which proceed toward if not a liquification of the ego, at least a displacement of the subject from the center of philosophical, linguistic, and theoretical activity.

Several postmodern philosophers have made this connection between ego death and philosophical activity. For example, philosopher Geoffrey Bennington has remarked that: "Taking something philosophically, then, *always* involves this more or less hidden relationship with death. Or, by a slightly violent *contraction*, whatever I take philosophically is death."[56] Surprisingly, Bennington ends his statement with an enigmatic image, but one which captures his point: "The philosophers' stone is an inscribed head stone." For Marla Morris, another postmodern thinker, what is true of the Philosophers' Stone is also true for the "psychoanalyst's stone."[57] She notes that for Bennington, at the end of the day, it is death that deconstruction is all about.

The philosopher Simon Critchley argues in a similar spirit, noting that "ancient Ciceronian wisdom says that to philosophize [and, in light of Morris' comment, to practice psychoanalysis] is to learn how to die."[58] Critchley's exploration echoes the theme of *Sol niger* in that it seeks to "*de-create* narratives of redemption" and to "strip away the resources and comforts of story, fable and narrative."[59] Here Critchley sounds like Giegerich and, following the work of Samuel Becket, he seeks to understand "the meaning of . . . meaninglessness," what he calls "a redemption from redemption."[60] He notes how Becket's work "frustrates our desire to ascend from the flatlands of language and ordinary experience into the stratosphere of meaning"[61] and comments:

> As is all too easily seen in both contemporary New Age sophism, crude scientism, and the return to increasingly reactionary forms of religious fundamentalism, there is an almost irresistible desire to stuff the world full of meaning and sign up to one or more salvific narratives of redemption.[62]

Critchley, like Becket and in the spirit of Giegerich's "Birth of Man,"[63] leads us away from the temptation to redemption and toward a Zen-like perception of the ordinary, the "sheer mereness of things."[64] He turns to a number of poets – Wallace Stevens, Rainer Maria Rilke, Ralph Waldo Emerson – to give voice to this perception of the ordinary, a perception not unlike Hillman's whose reading of alchemy seeks to move our understanding and our language outside of redemptive, metaphysical systems and salvationist programs. Like Stevens' expression of particulars, "pond," "leaf," "tree," – and, I would add, stones.

So, what kind of "thing" is a Stone? For Critchley, like Hillman, perception yields a simplicity of awareness in which the subject/object, person/world dichotomy is altered. In such an awareness, we are like a "thing among things," displaying a shining world of sheer "isness," or, as the Buddhists would say, of "suchness." In such a world, a "stone is not a stone," because stones are part of the alchemical white earth and of matter illuminated from within itself. Ordinarily we think of matter as illuminated by virtue of an external consciousness separate from its object, but matter, in truth, is better understood as part of the complexity of the materialized soul. Such a soul can alchemically be said to be a Stone "cleared of moistures"[65] and objective in the "psycho-alchemical" sense as Giegerich has described.[66]

Hillman has noted that depth psychology, including Jung's, has had difficulty in finding a way to express the complex/simplicity of psyche's need to substantiate[67] or likewise of substance's need to speak. For Hillman, the problematic is in part rooted in the way conceptual language splits apart a fundamental unity, "abstracting matter from image."[68] When this occurs, there is a powerful psychic demand to heal the split, to substantiate psyche and to bring it back in touch with something solid. The problem of "languaging" the soul was present for Jung throughout his life and work. The need to substantiate, to go beyond words and paper, played a role in his desire to personify and in his urge to turn to stone.

Turning to stone

Ultimately for Jung "words and paper . . . did not seem real enough. . .; something more was needed."[69] He had "to achieve a kind of representation in stone of [his] innermost thoughts and of the knowledge [he] had acquired." Or, to put it another way, he "had to make a confession of faith in stone." Jung's need to substantiate was responsible for the building of his tower at Bollingen where he felt he was "reborn in stone" and through which he was able to express a concretization of his ideas.[70]

Jung carved his way to self-expression through architecture, sculpture, and his focus on alchemical language and poetry, but even more one might say that he opened himself to the call of stone – to its message and to the way the world came to him. Jung reports the story of the cornerstone he had ordered for his garden when he was building his tower at Bollingen. When the stone arrived it was the wrong shape and measurements, and the stonemason, furious, wanted to return it. However, when Jung saw the stone, he claimed it as *his* stone. He felt he "must have it!"[71] even though, at the moment, he was not sure what he wanted to do with it.

In short, Jung welcomed whatever arrived unwanted and unexpected, unlike Faust who murdered Baucis and Philemon. In other words, Jung opened himself up to experiences the ego would often reject, seemingly in good sense. As Jung contemplated the stone, a verse from the alchemist Arnoldus de Villanova came to him and he chiseled it into the stone:

> Here stands the mean, uncomely stone,
> 'Tis very cheap in price!
> The more it is despised by fools,
> The more loved by the wise.[72]

Jung was aware that this verse referred to the Philosophers' Stone and, as he contemplated it further, he saw in its "natural structure" a sort of eye[73] that looked back at him, a living other, who appeared to Jung as "the Telesphoros of Asklepios," the healing figure of a child who was seen as roaming through the dark regions of the cosmos and glowing like a star out of the depths, a shining "pointer of the way."[74] In this image and in the stone, Jung captured something in the heart of darkness itself, something that he found in the depths of inorganic matter, something that looked back at him and made a stone a living stone, a Philosophers' Stone that shines. For Jung, stones speak a shining truth and such a truth touches the core of what we have come to call, inadequately, psyche and matter.

Jung's attempt to repair this split in his life and work led not only to stone, but also to innovative formulations in the language of his psychology by which he attempted to embrace both sides of a linguistic divide – subject and object, spirit and matter – using terms such as "psychoid," "synchronicity," and "*unus mundus*."[75] Such terms expressed Jung's urge to go beyond the subjectivity of words and paper in order to express psyche's need to substantiate and the need of substances to speak.

For Hillman, however, such words not only fall short of Jung's goal, but also actually "reinforce the splitting effect inherent" in the neurosis of one-sided abstract language.[76] If this was a problem for Jung, it is also one which is deeply rooted in our collective, historical, cultural, and linguistic consciousness. It is an issue that penetrates into the problematics of perception and language, and into the archetypal psyche itself. How then to express psyche's need to substantiate and substances need to speak?

In his book entitled simply *Stone*, philosopher John Sallis speaks of his desire to substantiate, to find a way to articulate, philosophical ideas adequate to the powerful stone monuments he is drawn to investigate, and in and through which he finds a "shining truth."[77] In his book, he explores the power of stone in "the various guises and settings in which stone appears"[78] – in monuments, the complexity of Gothic cathedrals, Greek temples, and the tombstones of a Jewish cemetery in Prague; in fossils, stone houses, and the power and beauty of wild nature in the mountains of Haute Savoie, France. In his search, he attempts to give voice to the power he discovers in these profound expressions of stone. Sallis writes:

> I would have liked this discourse to be inscribed by a very skillful stonemason, by one who knew just the right slant at which to hold the chisel so as to cut obliquely into the stone and produce well-formed, clearly legible letters, chipping away the stone so as to leave the inscription both in place of stone and yet still in stone, practicing thus a kind of lithography. I would have liked the well-measured strokes of his hammer to be audible, as he practiced his venerable craft of making stone, in its silence, nonetheless speak.[79]

One might imagine Jung, Hillman, Giegerich, and Sallis as such stonemasons, adepts who inscribe the *materia* of rock and word such that stone has words and words matter. In these thinkers, we find stones that speak, living objective stones that shine, modern day expressions of the alchemists' quest for life in the heart of matter.

Must we turn to stone? The stone that is not a stone

The well-known alchemical saying "Beware of the physical in the material" provides us with a warning not to confuse what the alchemist is after with literal materiality – but it is also important to recognize that a simple psychological or spiritual abstraction misses the mark as well. "The precious goals of alchemy are neither physical achievements . . . nor metaphysical truths. . . . We are not in the realm of metaphysics or physics,"[80] says Hillman. Sallis makes a similar point, noting that when trying to give expression to what we mean by "stone" it is important to do it in a way that does not split off our subjectivity from the voice of stone itself, nor turn this voice into a projection onto stones.[81] To fall into either one position or another fixes thought into a false subject/object dichotomy. Either the stone that we seek is literally over there in a mind-independent world, or it is simply part of our subjective inner life projected outward. Jung's psychology of alchemy is usually understood in the latter way and, thus, the Philosophers' Stone is seen as a projection of the Self.

I submit that this is one plausible reading of Jung, but it remains unclear exactly what the nature of such a projection entails and just what it is that is projected. Ultimately, the Arcane Substance that Jung often spoke about remained as mysterious as his understanding of the unconscious and to assume that this projected substance is simply inside our subjectivity misses Jung's deeper understanding of "psychic reality," even if it was not adequately developed. In addition, the problem of projection itself requires a number of philosophical and metapsychological presuppositions that are taken for granted in classical analysis. Going beyond these assumptions requires a fundamental shift in metapsychology if not ontology.[82] Schwartz-Salant deconstructs the notion of "projection" and concludes that using this idea as a framework for understanding what the alchemists are talking about is inadequate. Alchemical "experiences do not always, or even primarily, fit into an inside-outside structure."[83] In its place, Schwartz-Salant constructs a field theory, an intermediate realm between subject and object, mind and matter. While he applies his field theory primarily to the analytic interaction, it is a move that also has consequences for how we understand both Jung's work with stone and the nature of the Philosophers' Stone.

Although Jung actually worked with literal stone, his more enduring corpus was what he produced through his imagination and with words and paper, that is, his ideas. And, likewise, it is with ideas and the imagination that Hillman finds a "rock-hard standpoint from above downward, just as firm and solid as literal physical reality."[84] From this perspective, the Philosophers' Stone that is not a stone seems indestructible. It is solid, has objectivity, thing-likeness, facticity, and duration. It is an example of philosophical permanence. Yet, while its hardness wounds, it is also wounded, easily affected. The Stone is complex and resists one-sided descriptions and simple dichotomies. As David Miller has shown, "the course of wisdom consists in deferring one-sided judgment concerning meaning."[85] The *imaginatio* is as much a part of what is imaged as the world is itself the substance of imagination. Robert Romanyshyn makes a similar point:

> Imagining is not something which a subject adds to a merely perceivable world. On the contrary, we imagine and the world is imagineable. To say one is to say the other. Each is the obverse of the other. In other words, imagining belongs as much to things as it belongs to us. Perception is always less certain than we naively believe it to be, and things are more shadowy than we often dare admit.[86]

In this passage, and throughout his analysis, Romanyshyn cautions us not to collapse the difference between perceiving and imagining. He underlines how the perceivable and the real exhibit a stubborn intractability which marks them as different from the imagination even if we have destabilized their absolute difference. Romanyshyn holds this distinction in place as he continues to subtly refine our understanding of the imaginary and the real. He demonstrates, following Merleau-Ponty and reminiscent of Schwartz-Salant, how perception and imagination are like mirrors "facing each other,"[87] forming "a couple more real than either of them"[88] would be independent of each other. For Romanyshyn, "the imagine-ability of things is their very depth: that is the image of a thing, seen through other things, describes the depth of the real."[89] Romanyshyn's analysis gives amplification to Critchley's insight that things merely are and that we are things too. He sees into the complex materiality of the soul and into a substance's need to speak. For Romanyshyn, the "voice of things" is best served by the language of metaphor and imagination which "inhabits neither the brilliance of the day [spirit] nor the darkness of night [soul], but speaks simultaneously in light and shadow."[90]

If the imagination can be seen to be the voice of things, then one might also understand how "imaginal realities" exhibit a stubborn intractability. The Philosophers' Stone, as we have noted, exhibits facticity and thingness. It refuses to be altered by the manipulating ego subject, and yet subjectivity is part of its intrinsic reality, a subjectivity that appears as the ego subject dies or is negated and relativized. It is a subjectivity that has been touched by ego death and therefore is no longer subjective. It is a subjectivity that is not subjectivity, a subjectivity in which the me-ness has been "cooked out" and redeemed from essentialist narratives of meaning.

As Hillman, making reference to Miller, points out, the stone "does not allow itself to be held in meaning"[91] and generality. "It does not yield to understanding." For Hillman, the alchemical process of *ceration* is "designed to obliterate a psychological *episteme* of . . . anything that would rigidify the idea of the goal into categories of knowledge."[92] And yet, as Sallis has noted, the stone exhibits a "shining truth,"[93] a truth discovered in a "suspension of the difference that otherwise separates the eidetic from the singular, a *peculiar* suspension in that its very force requires that the difference remain, in the moment of suspension, also intact."[94] If I understand Sallis correctly, such singular yet eidetic moments of "shining truth" recall the sheer "isness of things" discussed above, the metals, planets, minerals, diamonds, pearls, stars and stones, the shining particularities that are also oddly universal but which can "never simply be assimilated to the purely eidetic."[95] Such singular moments of perception/imagination are neither inside nor out and must show themselves, be exhibited like pearls so as not to lose their luster, again to use Hillman's metaphor.

The bringing forth of such particulars allows them to shine, and this shine is for Hillman the revelation of Beauty, a term Plato used as well for that "shining truth" which he considered "the most radiant, that which most shines forth amidst the visible, in the singular things that come to be and *pass away*."[96] Is the Philosophers' Stone such a radiant truth, a truth that must as well remain in touch with negativity, death and darkness? It is "not enough," Hillman reminds us, "to shine in the dark."[97] The Philosophers' Stone is linked intrinsically with *sol niger*, "no matter how exalted the stage of any process in life, that stage lives within the context of whatever despair and failure accompanied its creation."[98] Thus, it is not surprising that Schwartz-Salant observes, in relation to the last image of

the *Splendor Solis*, that there are "two states – a created self and its puri-
fied consciousness . . . joined not only with life and body but also with a
history of despair and failure."[99]

Likewise, as Hillman notes, in alchemical psychology "sorrow, solitude
and misery can break even the most indomitable spirit."[100] The Philosophers' Stone requires a relationship with the ongoing negativity of the
deconstructive principle of the black sun. Perhaps this recognition of *sol
niger* is related to why, for Giegerich, the imaginal requires continuing
negative interiorization. But if this is so, just as Giegerich deconstructs
the literal residues of the imaginal, so imaginal psychology continues to
give flesh to the unseen. *Solve et coagula*, say the alchemists. In Hillman
and Giegerich we have two moments of the Stone that not only can live
together but also belong together in the same living mosaic – or do they?
Jung has noted: "sometimes Mercurius is a substance like quicksilver
[image], sometimes it is a philosophy [thought]."[101] To put it yet another
way, if Paul Ricoeur is correct that the symbol gives rise to thought, then
perhaps it is also the case that thought gives rise to symbol. What has priority may well be, as Giegerich has noted, a matter of personal and philosophical conviction "of the psychology [and philosophy] that one *has*,"
"that one *is*," "that one lives."[102] Perhaps in the end, thought and image
may best be spoken of in a variety of ways: as an alchemical *circulatio*, or
in a monstrous *coniunctio*, or as a trembling ground of poetic undecidables
(Derrida), or a unity of unity and difference (Hegel/Giegerich), or as the
difference of unity and difference (Marlan). Perhaps all of the above might
be thought/imagined as metaphors that attempt to speak the unspeakable,
an idea perhaps captured in the title of Paul Kugler's latest book, *Raids on
the Unthinkable*. To struggle with these seemingly irreconcilable moments
is well articulated by Alain Badiou who gave expression to the importance
of attempting to speak the unspeakable when he stated:

> Let us struggle then, partitioned, split, unreconciled. Let us struggle
> for the flash of conflict, we philosophers, always torn between the
> mathematical norm of literal transparency, and the poetic norm of sin-
> gularity and presence. Let us struggle then, but having recognized the
> common task, which is to think what was unthinkable, to say what
> it was impossible to say. Or, to adopt Mallarmé's imperative, which
> I believe is common to philosophy and poetry: "There, wherever it
> may be, deny the unsayable – it lies."[103]

In our attempt to express psyche's need to substantiate, we have come to see that the Stone to which we have turned is a "stone that is not a stone." It is rather a Philosophers' Stone. It is a Stone linked to the *lumen naturae* of *sol niger*, a luminous vehicle, a central mystery of alchemy. It is an alchemical achievement involving the death of the ego out of which something emerges shining and yet the shining was already there at the core of darkness. It is a part of the complexity of darkness itself, reflecting the death and shine of a positivity that is perhaps no positivity at all, but rather an image/idea requiring a liquification and/or displacement of the subject. The Stone requires learning how to die, how to de-create narratives of redemption, and thus allowing one to see, with Zen-like astonishment, the perception of the ordinary, the sheer mereness of things. As the poet Theodore Roethke once indicated, when we encounter the power of death, even stones express themselves.[104]

Notes

1 This chapter is a modified version of my previously published paper entitled Marlan, "From the Black Sun," 1–30.
2 A more comprehensive outcome of these distillations, however, must await a longer work still in progress. Here I can offer only a glimpse at the work emerging from the alembics of my colleagues, each with his own ideas and his own compelling images of the Philosophers' Stone.
3 The description which follows is a condensation of Hillman's ideas drawn from his essay "Concerning the Stone" (Chapter 8 in *Alchemical Psychology*, 231–263).
4 Hillman, *Alchemical Psychology*, 260.
5 Ibid., 259.
6 Ibid., 262.
7 Ibid., 253.
8 Giegerich, *The Soul's Logical Life*, 111.
9 Ibid., 148.
10 For example, Hillman argues that the goal is "not the lifting, the *Aufhebung,* of material worldliness, but the full realization of desire for the world that pulsates in the materials of the elemental psyche, those substances that compose the stone and give its enduring life . . ." (Hillman, *Alchemical Psychology*, 261).
11 Giegerich, "Afterword," 109.
12 Ibid.,
13 Ibid., 108.
14 Giegerich, *The Soul's Logical Life*, 107.
15 Hillman, "Image-Sense," 130.
16 Ibid., 134.
17 Giegerich, *The Soul's Logical Life*, 107.
18 Miller, "The End of Ending," 85.
19 Hillman, "Silver and the White Earth (Part Two)," 49; quoted by Greg Mogenson in "Different Moments," 106.
20 Hillman, "Silver and the White Earth (Part Two)," 49; quoted by Greg Mogenson in "Different Moments," 105.

21 Ibid.
22 This is a phrase used by Hegel and borrowed by Giegerich, and here refers simply to the process of working through.
23 Mogenson, "Different Moments in Dialectical Movement," 106.
24 Ibid.
25 Ibid.
26 Hillman, *Alchemical Psychology*, 239.
27 Ibid., 240.
28 Ibid., 241.
29 Ibid., 240.
30 Mogenson, "Different Moments," 106.
31 Giegerich, "The End of Meaning and the Birth of Man," 115.
32 Ibid.
33 Giegerich, *The Soul's Logical Life*, 104.
34 Ricoeur, *Freud and Philosophy*, 38.
35 LaCapra, "Who Rules Metaphor?," 15–28.
36 Kelly, "Atman, Anatta, and Transpersonal Psychology."
37 Derrida, *Margins of Philosophy*, 213.
38 Alan Bass (translator) in Derrida, *Margins of Philosophy*, 19–20, footnote 23.
39 Jung, *Psychology and Alchemy (CW12)*, 85.
40 Jung, *Alchemical Studies (CW13)*, §197.
41 Edinger, *Anatomy*, 21.
42 Melchior, quoted in Jung, *Psychology and Alchemy (CW12)*, §484.
43 Ibid., §162.
44 Brooke, *Jung and Phenomenology*, 99.
45 Kuspit, "Negatively Sublime Identity."
46 Sinha, *Tantra*, 52.
47 Hegel, *Phenomenology*, 19, §32.
48 Jung, *Mysterium Coniunctionis (CW14)*, §778.
49 Hillman, *Alchemical Psychology*, 259.
50 Rosen, *Transforming Depression*, xxi.
51 Miller, "Nothing Almost Sees Miracles!," 15.
52 Giegerich, *The Soul's Logical Life*, 18–24.
53 Ibid., 18.
54 Ibid., 24.
55 Ibid.
56 Bennington, quoted in Marla Morris, "Archiving Derrida," 44.
57 Ibid.
58 Critchley, *Very Little*, xvii.
59 Ibid., xxiii.
60 Ibid.
61 Ibid.
62 Ibid., xxiv.
63 Giegerich, "The End of Meaning and the Birth of Man."
64 Critchley, *Very Little*, xxiv.
65 Hillman, *Alchemical Psychology*, 252.
66 Giegerich, "The Ego-Psychological Fallacy," 55.
67 Hillman, "Therapeutic Value of Alchemical Language," 40.
68 Ibid., 41.
69 Jung, *Memories*, 223.
70 Ibid., 225.
71 Ibid., 226.
72 Ibid., 227. This carved stone became a monument for what his tower meant to him.
73 Ibid.

74 Ibid.
75 Hillman, "Therapeutic Value of Alchemical Language," 41.
76 Ibid.
77 Sallis, *Stone*, 2.
78 Ibid., book jacket.
79 Ibid., 1.
80 Hillman, *Alchemical Psychology*, 241.
81 Sallis, *Stone*, Chapter 1.
82 Nathan Schwartz-Salant, personal communication, 2000.
83 Ibid.
84 Hillman, *Alchemical Psychology*, 239.
85 Miller, "The 'Stone' Which Is Not a Stone," 116.
86 Romanyshyn, "Psychological Language," 79–80.
87 Ibid., 73.
88 Merleau-Ponty, *The Visible and the Invisible*, 139; quoted by Romanyshyn, "Psychological Language," 73.
89 Romanyshyn, "Psychological Language," 73.
90 Ibid., 79.
91 Hillman, *Alchemical Psychology*, 250.
92 Ibid., 255.
93 Sallis, *Stone*, 2.
94 Ibid., 4.
95 Ibid.
96 Ibid., 2–3.
97 Hillman, *Alchemical Psychology*, 239.
98 Schwartz-Salant, *The Mystery of Human Relationship*, 216.
99 Ibid.
100 Hillman, *Alchemical Psychology*, 239.
101 Jung, *Aion (CW9ii)*, §240.
102 Giegerich, "Afterword," 108.
103 Badiou, *Theoretical Writings*, 241.
104 Roethke, "Fourth Meditation."

Chapter 10

The philosophical basis of the remnant in Kant's thing-in-itself and in Hegel's move to surpass it

In 2008, Wolfgang Giegerich published a response to the ideas in the last chapter, which had been previously published as an article entitled "From the Black Sun to the Philosophers' Stone." Giegerich's response to my analysis was called "The Unassimilable Remnant – What is at Stake? A Dispute with Stanton Marlan." In a later essay entitled "Jung's Betrayal of His Truth: The Adoption of a Kantian-Based Empiricism and the Rejection of Hegel's Speculative Thought," he reiterated some of these points and made additional comments about my interpretation of his position. His criticisms of my article motivated me to reconsider my understanding of Kant and my criticisms of Hegel and their importance in the ongoing ferment about soul and spirit within the Jungian tradition. These re-readings are reflected in the remainder of this study beginning with this chapter.

Giegerich's thoughtful response to my interpretation of his work was a welcome furthering of the issues at stake in our exchange. In his articles, he addresses a number of issues, including: (a) differing views on the Philosophers' Stone, (b) the relationship between image and dialectical thought, (c) my complement to his Hegelian view of the "union of the unity and difference," with an additional formulation of "the difference of unity and difference," (d) my insistence on what I referred to as an unassimilable remnant, and (e) my historical assessment of Jung's and Hillman's emphasis on the primacy of the image as a reversal of a dominant trend in the historical process that has repressed images. In addition, Giegerich clarifies a number of points. My criticism of Giegerich was that his interpretation of Hillman's view of image was limited because he only understood "image" in the traditional sense, as being based on a sensationist psychology, as representational and epiphenomenal with

DOI: 10.4324/9781003215905-11

respect to literal objects, and seen in the Hegelian sense as "picture thinking." He argues, however, that his criticism was not based on seeing "images as contents of consciousness or as 'copies' in the mind at all. Rather than the image in the narrower sense, [he was] critiquing the imaginal style of thought as picture thinking."[1] He takes for granted that the image was understood by Hillman as "a metaphor without a referent." Still, his point is that with "the charge of picture thinking, it does not make any difference whether an image is 'what you see' or whether it is – 'understood in its most radical way' – 'the way you see,'" that is, whether you see the image as content of consciousness or as a perspective with which you see. "In either case, the sphere of sensory intuition (*sinnliche Anschauung*)" has not been exceeded. "To be sure," he continues, "the image has now [with Hillman], through this quasi-transcendental-philosophical move been deliteralized; it may no longer be visual in the empirical sense, but it stays *logically* visual" which does not for Giegerich "advance to *sublated* seeing as thought or conceptual comprehension: 'insight,' 'intellegere.'"[2]

> The point here is that it does not make any difference whether there is a literal external referent or whether the "referent" has been totally internalized into the structure of image or imaginal seeing itself so that the image is now its own referent: the structure or form of representation has not been overcome merely by overcoming the externally existent referent. The form of representation would be overcome only with a transcendence of the form of image as such, that is, with *thought*. Thought does not see or imagine; it thinks. Here one sees how important it is to become aware of the dimension of logical form or "syntax." A merely semantic approach is naturally already satisfied with the difference between "image without external referent" and "epiphenomenal representation of an external referent."[3]

Giegerich then proceeds to address my concern about how his idea of total sublation or "liquification" of Mercurius, absolute-negative interiority, spirit or thought, if pushed to the limit, cuts all the way through, thus losing its phenomenality, what I have called the "pigment,"[4] while giving gold its metaphoric potency and particularity. In my questioning of this reaction, I felt it important to place Hillman's most radical view of image and of the Philosophers' Stone alongside Giegerich's idea of sublation to determine the validity of Hillman's and my shared concern that there may be an important loss if one goes too far beyond imaginal awareness. For Hillman, that would lead to what he called a "poisonous state of splendid solar isolation."[5] Giegerich argues that for Hillman it is, in fact, the impurity that gives his gold its qualitative reality, its phenomenality, and saves it from that abstract isolation. Here Giegerich turns his concern back toward Hillman's point of view, noting that his own

> critique of imaginal psychology had precisely always been that it cocoons itself in the unreality of a kind of "Platonism," as I once termed it. I had challenged psychology with the thesis that a real cut into the naturalism of the imaginal and metaphoric is indispensable to reach actuality. And I believe that it is precisely by trying to save his "gold" by means of those so-called impurities (that is, through the logically unbroken tie to naturalistic apperception) that this cocooning in unreality takes place.[6]

For Giegerich, it is the fear of the poisonous isolation that he thinks is the problem.

> This is what makes consciousness shrink from going *all the way* forward and instead makes it turn back again to what it was itself, after all, intent upon leaving through its very move away from the physical in the material. It makes this move, but halfway there (namely after having moved from the literal to the metaphorical), it stops. Of course, the danger of splendid solar isolation exists. But the point is that it must be met, not avoided. . . . If you avoid the danger, you have psychologically succumbed to it unawares. You truly avoid it only by facing it.[7]

While Giegerich attempts to turn the table on Hillman's halfway metaphorical move and again proclaims the necessity of "a real cut into the naturalism of the imaginal" viewpoint, he does not demonstrate how his view of gold or of the Philosophers' Stone and all of their metaphoric resonances are not lost, bypassed into the isolation of which Hillman accused him. Giegerich's emphasis on the *actual* place of action and his assertion of logical form *rather than* semantic content begins to split syntax from semantics, form from content. Giegerich rightly attempts to see these two levels as always belonging together; however, he speaks in such a way as to emphasize one side of the binary and uses that to drive forward his perspective. For him, syntax is emphasized as somehow more important than semantics. Such emphasis then takes on a rhetoric of division and a polemical style of aggressive challenge. A similar martial style was also present in Hillman's writing and he reiterated many times that his creative work was motivated by his anger.

I should add as an aside here that with regard to my personal dialogue with Giegerich, he has always been most cordial, if still polemical. Perhaps it is also the case with both Hillman and Giegerich that the polemical style is an effective way to awaken one from the status quo, but I also believe that it lends itself to exaggeration and worse at times, a one-sidedness and the entrenchment of binary thinking. To point to this tendency does not, however, "resolve" the issue of what is at stake in the differing positions. That continues to remain for me an open and ongoing question. Implicit in these questions are some important philosophical issues.

One important tension has been the difference in perspectives between the imaginal psychology of James Hillman and the dialectical approach of Wolfgang Giegerich. The philosophical tension between Hillman and Giegerich has its roots in the history of philosophy. Philosophy like alchemy and psychoanalysis is not a benign art. The questions I posed to Giegerich pushed him to clarify his position, and his responses to me were an occasion of considerable struggle with my own point of view, which is still developing. Image versus thought, soul versus spirit, semantics versus syntax, phenomenon versus noumenon, unassimilable remnant versus sublation, sticking with images versus the freeing of and liquefying of the mercurial spirit are not simply perspectives in my dialogue with Giegerich, but also tensions in my inner dialogue with myself.

As I have noted, in Jung, Hillman, Giegerich, and in my own thoughts these differences are not simple binaries, but interrelated complexities so to speak which get drawn apart. In addition, even to the extent that a body of thought integrates rather than splits these differences apart, the overall character of the thought that links them seems to emphasize and be marked more by one side of the dyad than the other. Just how these contrasts play a role in the philosophical orientation of any given thinker gives a particular character to their philosophy.

The above issues have played an important role is the philosophies of Kant and Hegel. Rockmore has noted the importance of Kant:

> Kant is not only a great philosopher, one of the very small handful of truly great thinkers in the Western tradition; he is also a singularly influential figure, whose position continues to impact on the later debate, often in decisive ways. Like post-Kantian German Idealism and German neo-Kantianism, central philosophical tendencies in the nineteenth century, in different ways the main philosophical movements in twentieth century philosophy are all responding to Kant.[8]

Kant's philosophy has been important to both Jung and Giegerich, and like Hegel both have pushed off from him, though, as Rockmore has noted, "[w]e are still in the process of finding out Kant's position [and] [t]here is continuing controversy about how to best interpret it."[9]

If, as has been suggested, Jung's psychology can be interpreted in a Kantian way, it likewise can be seen as moving beyond Kant. If Jung is read as a Kantian, it is not surprising that his critics would evaluate him from a post-Kantian position. I believe that both Hillman and Giegerich have read Jung as Kantian and this reading is one basis of their criticisms. Kant's work, like Jung's, is complicated and in the next section we will explore this issue.

Phenomenon and noumenon: the unresolved tension of limit and transcendence in the thought of Kant and Jung

In her introduction to Immanuel Kant's *Critique of Pure Reason*, Patricia Kitcher notes that Kant "is usually regarded as the most important figure in the history of Modern Western Philosophy,"[10] and that his first *Critique* (1781–1787) "is his *magnum opus*."[11] She also comments on how difficult a book it is to read and notes that H.J. Paton has compared its " 'windings and twistings' . . . to crossing the great Arabian Desert."[12] For many, the metaphor of a desert is an apt one and they find the work dry as dust. Kant himself made similar judgments and called his book "dry, obscure," and "long winded." He lamented that readers would skim through it and that seriously thinking it through was a "disagreeable task."[13]

Goethe is reported to have "read no more than twenty pages or so of Kant's *Critique*, leafed through the rest and then put it aside exclaiming 'Good heavens no!'"[14] Mendelssohn, on whom Kant counted to help demonstrate his ideas, called the *Critique of Pure Reason* "*dieses Nervensaft-verzehrendes Werk* – this nerve-juice consuming book,"[15] and Carl Jung admitted that he found the book "difficult and it had caused him much *Kopfzerbrechen* ['brain racking']."[16]

But if Jung found Kant dry and difficult, he also found him important if not fundamental in the development of his psychology. In Kant's "dry" critique of "watery" metaphysics, Jung found a spectrum of differentiations that became essential to his psychology, the most prominent of which was that between phenomena and noumena. One might imagine Jung's attitude as echoing the maxim of Paracelsus, which stated "colors result from dryness acting on moisture,"[17] and Hillman notes: "there is more color in the alchemical desert than in the flood, in less emotion than in more. Drying releases the soul from personal subjectivism."[18] For Hillman, as for Jung and Kant, simple subjectivism was not an adequate basis for knowledge. "Dry souls are best, said Heraclitus, which Philo turned to mean, 'Where the earth is dry, the soul is wisest,'"[19] and, for Jung, Kant's critique of speculative metaphysics was a stroke of genius.

Undisciplined metaphysical speculation was prone to "*schwärmen*" – a kind of madness, fanatic and raving. Such speculation leads nowhere and worse, to "shipwreck," "entanglements," delusion, and "empty hopes." In his preface to *Dreams of a Spirit-Seer*, Kant writes: "The land of shadows is the paradise of dreamers. Here they find an unlimited country where they may build their houses *ad libitum*. Hypochondriac vapours, nursery tales, and monastic miracles, provide them with ample building material."[20]

Kant's first *Critique* and his *Prolegomena to Any Future Metaphysics* might well be imagined as a lifeboat on the sea of philosophy, a laying down of some ground rules necessary to set things in order before venturing forth into any beyond. In this sense Kant like Jung might be imagined as a healer of madness, treating generations of raving philosophers, helping to check the impulse of pure reason from exceeding reason's reasonable boundaries. For Kant as for Jung, the fantasy of transcendence must first be firmly anchored to the experience of our senses if we are to have knowledge and not empty ideas that fly away into the unknown. In a gesture not unlike that of Kant and Jung, the figure below shows an ancient philosopher pointing to the necessary chain that grounds high-flying ideas.

Figure 10.1 Ancient philosopher and eagle chained to a ground animal. From Michael Maier, *Symbola aureae mensae*, 1617.

Source: Public domain.

While Kant's critique of metaphysics was for the most part written in a controlled if not burdensome way, his critique at moments waxes poetic, as if to take a respite after surveying the ground that he has covered. He begins his "Analytic of Principles" in a way that echoes Heraclitus' earlier point about strife and imagines Metaphysics as, "a vast and stormy ocean, where illusion properly resides and many fog banks and much fast-melting ice feign new-found lands."[21] "This sea," he says, "incessantly deludes the sea fairer with empty hopes as he roves through his discoveries, and thus entangles him in adventures that he can never relinquish, not ever bring to an end."[22]

Kant draws us back from this sea and points to dry land where every-thing has its proper place, to a "land of truth,"[23] and he appeals to his read-ers, as if hesitating on the shoreline:

> before we venture upon this sea, to search its latitudes for certainty as to whether there is in them anything to be hoped, it will be useful

Figure 10.2 From the Rider-Waite Tarot Deck: Two of Wands.
Source: Public domain.

to begin by casting another glance on the map of the land that we are about to leave, and to ask . . . whether we might not perhaps be content with what this land contains, or even must be content with it from necessity if there is no other territory at all on which we could settle.[24]

Against the madness and entanglements of wild speculation and the ephemeral fog of dogmatic metaphysics Kant in Cartesian fashion sought certainty, carried out by the sharp sword of epistemological limits. One of Kant's basic messages in the *Critique* – perhaps his most basic – is that "philosophy errs when it tries to draw metaphysical conclusions about the way the world is part from our knowledge on the basis of epistemological arguments about how we do or must acquire knowledge of the world."[25]

Deirdre Bair, in a much-applauded recent biography of Jung, notes his appreciation for Kant's "painstaking work of distinguishing what belongs to me, what is within my reach, and what lies beyond, and where we cannot reach."[26] For Kant, it was important to draw apart those cognitive structures that gave shape to our experiences and to that which appears but which itself is unknown and perhaps unknowable.

Jung based his distinction on Kant, who attempts to deal with what is beyond the plane of perception, and he refers to this beyond (which affects us) as an unknown x or thing-in-itself.

> Just as, in the Transcendental Analytic, Kant drew a distinction between the object as phenomenon (representation for us) and as noumenon (in itself), so Jung attempted a distinction between "archetypische Vorstellungen" ["archetypal representations"] and "der Archetypus an sich" ["the archetype in-itself"].[27]

The way both Kant and Jung deal with this unknowable x is filled with seeming inconsistencies, complexity, and, perhaps most importantly, ambiguity; but for Jung, Kant's epistemic limits were essential in his own theory of cognition. Jung cites Kant as the real basis of his philosophical education "insisting that whoever did not understand Kant's theory of cognition 'cannot understand my psychology.' He despaired that people confused his psychology with metaphysics"[28] and he continued to claim that his thought never exceeded the limits imposed on our possible knowledge by Kant. Kant's considerable influence on Jung's psychology has been traced by Germanist Paul Bishop who notes that "Jung referred to Kant nearly twenty times – more than any other philosopher" in his published correspondence and "repeatedly [tried] to assimilate the fundamental notions of analytical psychology to the key concepts of critical philosophy of Kant."[29]

Bishop further states that in Jung's letters he "frequently aligned himself with Kant to defend the epistemological stance of analytical psychology." In a letter of 8 April 1932 to the aesthetician and philosopher August Vetter, Jung wrote: "In a certain sense I could say of the collective Unconscious exactly what Kant said of the *Ding an Sich* – that it is merely a negative borderline concept."[30] In a letter dated 8 February 1941 to Josef Goldbrunner, a Catholic theologian, "Jung declared himself to be epistemologically speaking a Kantian."[31]

It is abundantly clear that Kant's epistemic limits were a bulwark for Jung and he used them again and again in defense of claims that he was a metaphysician, and that his thoughts were filled with transcendent judgments. Jung, however, did admit that "in spite of Kant and epistemology [such judgments] crop up again and again and can evidently not be suppressed."[32]

For Bishop "such 'transcendental judgments' could be least of all suppressed in Jung's own work,"[33] and he goes on to enumerate a number of ways in which Jung exceeds the epistemic limits set down by Kant. For example, in Jung's "'Psychological Aspects of the Mother Archetype' (1938/1954), Jung went so far as to suggest that the critical philosophy of Kant had prepared the way for his own analytical psychology which now, so he implied, had superseded the first *Critique*."[34] In this assessment I believe Bishop is correct. Despite Jung's protestations that he is not a metaphysician, his "psychology" is always on the edge of transgressing the limits declared by Kant, at least in respect to the limits set by the first *Critique*.

While Jung thought himself to be a Kantian, others have shown the ways in which he was (or is) "a most un-Kantian Kantian."[35] While I believe this is not a totally unfair assessment of Jung, I think it is also important to consider that in some ways Kant himself was a most un-Kantian Kantian; and perhaps so by philosophical necessity. By this I mean that Kant himself was not always consistent. Rockmore has noted that the thing-in-itself is subject to multiple interpretations which find textual support in Kant's writings, ranging from representationism to constructivism.[36]

While seemingly conflicting points of view run throughout Kant's *Critique of Pure Reason*, his notion of the *Ding an Sich* and the tension between Phenomenon and Noumenon is a high point. While Jung accepted the limits of Kant's epistemology, I do not believe he adequately understood the complex philosophical problematic implicit in it, or that he was aware of the numerous inconsistencies in Kant's position. Nor do I think Kant himself ever adequately resolved the differing strands of thought in his critical epistemology.

In pointing to Kant's inconsistencies, it is not with the intent to emphasize his errors but rather to read him in a Derridian manner and as Rockmore has, seeking in the margins of his text the anomalies which enliven the continuing philosophical tensions implicit in Kant's philosophy. Rockmore, referring to the constructivist moment in Kant's epistemological position "has the enormous merit of solving the problem of knowledge in another, very different, potentially more promising and exciting way."[37] I believe that Jung consciously or unconsciously was immersed in this tension between epistemic possibilities as is all post-Kantian thinking. From an analytic point of view, unresolved philosophical problems like psychic complexes repeat themselves in continuing generations of philosophy and psychology.

Post-Kantian philosophers have struggled with the problem of the thing-in-itself in many creative ways. I would like to consider a number of issues that I believe are opened up by looking at some of the problematic contained in Kant's distinction of phenomenon and noumenon, and in his idea of a thing-in-itself.

A major point in Kant's critique is that when we try to apply pure reason beyond its phenomenal limit to things-in-themselves, we come up against an absolute limit. We have no way to know if our mental apparatus can go beyond itself to "real" or noumenal objects as they exist in themselves in some trans-empirical world. We are restricted to what can be experienced in time and space, and there is no legitimate way to get beyond our epistemological limit. Taking Kant's *Critique* in this strict way seems to lead to a profound skepticism except in so far as we are satisfied to restrict our knowledge to "phenomena," or, in Jung's case, to a "psychological" one. For Jung, if we are unable to know the real world, what we can know is our psychological experience of something that is unknowable. In this sense, Kant and Jung are in agreement.

In his *Alchemical Studies*, Jung states that the thing-in-itself is merely a "negative borderline concept."

> Every statement about the transcendental is to be avoided because it is only a laughable presumption on the part of the human mind unconscious of its limitations. Therefore, when God or the Tao is named an impulse of the soul, or psychic state, something has been said about the knowable only, but nothing about the unknowable, about which nothing can be determined.[38]

Here for Kant – as well as for Jung – a seemingly unbridgeable gap is opened up between knowable phenomena and the unknowable thing-in-itself.[39]

This reading of Kant's thing-in-itself stimulates metaphysical desire and leaves the concept open to multiple fantasies or, in psychoanalytic terms, multiple projections. The thing-in-itself can be imagined as "absolute oth-erness" or "alien" or as the mystery of the "unconscious," which Jung simply defined as the unknown and ultimate unknowable. Such designa-tions recall the medieval speculations about the mysterious inability to name God and the traditions of negative theology as well as the alchemical procedure of searching for the arcane substance by defining the unknown by the greater unknown. Such mystical ideas, fruitful as they are from one point of view, give us no knowledge in Kant's sense.

In contrast, as we have seen, Kant sought to limit such speculations in his *Critique*; but if his idea of the thing-in-itself set limits to dog-matic metaphysics and perhaps to our narcissism, it also kept open the door to metaphysical desire by its mysterious draw beyond the world of phenomenon. Ultimately, neither Kant nor Jung was fully content to simply stay within such absolute epistemic limits and both continued to struggle in their own ways with human limits, transcendence, and the tension between them.

Kant insisted "that in his theory he intends to navigate between dog-matic affirmation and skeptical doubt,"[40] between materialism and ideal-ism, and Jung, like Kant,

> suggests that while we may never know more than what the psyche
> presents to us, we must assume a transcendental reality – a thing-in-
> itself – which lies in back of and causes the phenomena which we
> experience. "One must assume that the . . . ideas . . . rest on something
> actual."[41]

Kant also held that there was something "actual" or "real" behind phenom-ena; the ontological question remained a continuing tension throughout his work.

While Kant continued to maintain that we cannot know things-in-them-selves, since knowledge is limited to possible experience, he also held that a thing-in-itself can be thought, "provided that it satisfies the condition of a possible thought which is not to be self-contradictory."[42] In the *Prole-gomena to Any Future Metaphysics*, "Kant uses things-in-themselves syn-onymously with noumena, namely in the application of pure concepts of the understanding 'beyond objects of experience' to 'things-in-themselves (noumena),'"[43] and in the *Critique of Pure Reason* he likewise speaks of things-in-themselves "as potential ideas of reason, and speaks of 'the *unconditioned* which reason, by necessity and by right, demands in things in themselves.'"[44] Caygill notes that "[w]hat distinguishes the things-in-themselves from the other forms of noumena are their property of being the 'true correlate of sensibility.'"[45] Here Kant assumes in a way similar to Jung that there "*must* be a correlate which can be thought, even if not known."[46]

Caygill also notes that on critical principles Kant can only say that the "thing in itself *may* be a correlate of sensibility. That he does not do so arises from his resistance to the 'absurd conclusion that there can be appearance without anything that appears.'"[47] Barker notes "that a world constructed merely of ideas could not by itself possess the power to be,"[48] and A.C. Ewing in addition states that for Kant: "if there were nothing but phenomena, then the intellectual ideals in question and the ethical ideals which led Kant to belief in God could not be fulfilled, therefore the ideas of reason at least suggest a reality beyond."[49]

In all, there are many passages in Kant's work that indicate commitment to a reality beyond appearances. Still to his critics this position remains vague, problematic, unclear, and indeterminate. Ewing notes a number of such inconsistencies. He states that:

> we cannot (even) say that things-in-themselves exist unless we mean something by the term thing-in-itself. But if we mean anything by the term, we are asserting something however vague and slight, about their nature when we assert them to exist, and therefore it is inconsistent to (even) describe them as unknowable, as Kant does.[50]

Ewing points to the paradox of claiming to know that there is in fact a reality behind appearances or "that it was of such a nature that we could know nothing about it without already inconsistently presupposing knowledge of its nature."[51]

Such inconsistencies multiply when what seems to be a common and natural attitude comes up against critical philosophical distinctions. In simply speaking of the "reality" or "existence" of a thing-in-itself, we must apply Kant's categories of the understanding beyond the phenomenal realm in which they are said to apply. Kant also inconsistently goes beyond the idea of the mere existence of the thing-in-itself to imagining it as the cause of appearances. Again in such moments Kant is "guilty of extending the category of causality beyond the realm of appearances," a procedure which, on the one hand, "he had explicitly repudiated,"[52] but on the other, there is "textual support"[53] for this in his writing.

The problem of causality continues to be debated in philosophical circles. For some scholars to apply causality to the thing-in-itself remains an impossibility in Kant's terms, while for others, such as Warren, it is essential to do so, and in his book, according to Watkins, he argues that

> insofar as the category of reality can be applied to the sensible qualities of objects, it can be distinguished from the pure, unschematized category (i.e., represented through the understanding alone) if and only if the sensible qualities or realities it represents are causal powers.[54]

Kant's text is filled with such tensions, and while for some modern Kant scholars such contradictions are reduced by the fact that things-in-themselves are not intuited but only thought,[55] for others such distinctions are still problematic. Perhaps it is the case that through such inconsistencies and complexity Kant walks a thin line between sensibility and understanding, knowledge and faith, skeptical doubt and dogmatic affirmation, between phenomenon and noumenon, limit and transcendence.

As noted earlier, Kant situated his work on the shoreline between dry land and the raging sea, between sanity and madness. For the most part Kant's work is dry and obsessional, while at other less frequent moments it takes flight as if on Plato's "wings of ideas" and ventures forth beyond the experienced world into that "empty space of pure understanding."[56] Still, if Kant's work is anything, it is the work of a philosophical genius which for the most part keeps its balance by staying in the tension between the opposites and hesitating to fly off in the traditional directions of "dogmatic affirmation and skeptical doubt."[57] At one point in the *Critique* Kant hints at bridging the gaps between "*sensibility*" and "*understanding*" by suggesting the possibility that "[h]uman cognition has two stems . . . which perhaps spring from a common root, though one is unknown to us."[58] By hesitating before the unknown, Kant maintains his dualism, but holds out a hint, for those after him, who might take up the perilous journey into metaphysics.

Heidegger, though also claiming to avoid traditional metaphysics, finds this common root (of sensibility and understanding) in the transcendental imagination,[59] and Jung, like Heidegger (whom he disliked), also leans away from dualism, likewise seeing the "opposites" as rooted in one world, the *unus mundus*. But, like Kant, for Jung this unifying principle remained unknown if not in principle unknowable.

In a passage that I believe links Kant to Jung, Kant states in regard to the thing-itself "we are completely ignorant as to whether it is to be found in us – or for that matter, outside us."[60] Likewise Jung's notion of the unconscious was paradoxical and although it is common to imagine that the unconscious refers to something inside the subject, Jung often spoke as if we are inside the unconscious. It was this fundamental paradox that characterized Jung's idea of the unconscious and what he meant by the "objective psyche." For Jung:

> The psyche is the starting-point of all human experience, and all the knowledge we have gained eventually leads back to it. The psyche is the beginning and end of all cognition. It is not only the object of its science, but the subject also . . . on the one hand there is a constant doubt as to the possibility of its being a science at all, while on the other hand psychology acquires the right to state a theoretical problem the solution of which will be one of the most difficult tasks for a future philosophy.[61]

Like Kant, Jung lived in an unresolved tension of opposites, though his work was aimed at overcoming them. Also, like Kant, while Jung was always in danger of contradiction and of overstepping the epistemic boundaries he espoused, I believe he more fundamentally lived in an ongoing tension, and thus he resisted metaphysical solutions and followed a critical path of interminable analysis.

Kant and Jung lived in an unresolved tension between limit and transcendence; both felt the power and importance of a noumenal reality beyond appearances, and approached it in their respective ways, all the while trying to avoid the pitfalls of dogmatic metaphysics. Possessed by what might be called a metaphysical desire, both Kant and Jung were continually drawn to the edge and beyond their self-imposed limits and, as a result, their voluminous works were filled with inconsistencies. It might be possible to imagine that if they each had more carefully followed the discipline they espoused, their works would be more consistent, but, if so, it remains a question if in so doing they would have, as Kant believed, brought "human reason to complete satisfaction in . . . its desire to know."[62]

This desire to know was a continuing impetus in post-Kantian philosophy as well as in post-Jungian psychology. Rockmore points out that in Kant's wake

> most able thinkers believed his position was incomplete and needed to be carried beyond Kant in order to complete the Copernican revolution in philosophy. If this is his standard, then arguably the most important later innovation, the biggest step in developing and completing Kant's contribution, lies in the post-Kantian transformation of the Kantian approach to knowledge from an ahistorical to a historical conception.[63]

As Rockmore notes,

> [t]he introduction of a historical dimension into the problem of knowledge totally transforms it. At least normatively, Kant's transcendental study of the general conditions of knowledge points to an a priori conception of knowledge unrelated to time and place, hence ahistorical. This changes immediately in Kant's wake. The post-Kantian idealist line of development up to Hegel leads to a thoroughly historical conception of knowledge claims indexed to time and place, hence to the historical moment. One way to put the point is that in building on Fichte and Schelling, Hegel rejects Kantian representationalism in favor of Kantian constructivism, which he understands not as an a priori but as an a posteriori construction by finite human beings in historical space.[64]

Movement from Kant to Hegel resonates with the aspects of Jung that exceed Kant's limitations with regard to the limits of knowledge. In the next section I will examine Hegel's struggle with what he considers the mistake of stopping at the notion of the thing-in-itself which Hegel considers to be an error. Hegel's philosophy is thus useful in understanding the way that Jung also exceeds these limits and is also a post-Kantian.

Hegel's introduction to the *Phenomenology of Spirit*: from clouds of error to the heaven of truth

This historical philosophical move is well illustrated in the Introduction to Hegel's *Phenomenology of Spirit*. Hegel's *Phenomenology of Spirit* is a difficult text that has been read in many different ways and there are end-less commentaries about it. It was Hegel's first great work and his Intro-duction to this work is instructive with regard to Hegel's departure from the limitations of Kant's epistemology and gives us a view of the direction of post-Kantian thought.

One way of reading Hegel's Introduction might be imagined in a Hege-lian fashion; that is, that Hegel leaps into the midst of a philosophical issue beginning with the thesis at the heart of Kant's epistemology, then entering into a dialectical engagement with it through a process of intense negation, and finally by offering articulation that both preserves something of Kant's original project and goes beyond it to envision a new scientific project for philosophy.

Hegel begins his Introduction by elaborating what he calls a "natural assumption" in philosophy: that before we deal with cognition of what is, an ontological concern, we must first understand cognition, the episte-mological instrument or medium through which we can discover the goal of philosophy as an object of knowledge. With Kant in mind and while acknowledging the naturalness of the above procedure, Hegel also con-fesses an uneasiness with Kant's procedure and ultimately concludes that it is unscientific. Hegel does not leap ahead to this conclusion, but, follow-ing Kant, he acknowledges that cognition is a particular "faculty of . . . kind and scope" and that "without a more precise definition of its nature and *limits*, we might grasp clouds of error instead of the heaven of truth."[65] Hegel's project is aimed at this "heaven of truth."

Next, Hegel articulates the concerns of Kant in his *Critique of Pure Reason*, noting that, without understanding the limits of Reason, one falls prey to the Metaphysical fantasy that one has arrived at the knowledge of a mind-independent reality, a "thing-in-itself." For a time, it is diffi-cult to discern exactly where Hegel is in agreement with Kant and where he differs, but as the Introduction continues Hegel's seemingly ambiva-lent response turns to a scathing if thinly veiled critique of the outcome of Kant's philosophical position, noting that it is ultimately absurd to assume an absolute boundary between cognition and the so-called mind-independent object. For Hegel, what is absurd is that we "make use of a means at all" ultimately putting into question the idea of cognition as a medium.[66] For Hegel, focusing on cognition as a medium is born of mis-trust and, turning mistrust on itself, he asks "whether this fear of error is not just the error itself?"[67] What Hegel seems to have in mind is that, in the grip of fear, our reflection focuses on a self-conscious concern with cognition, overemphasizing and splitting off our consciousness from its object. Thus, we presuppose that cognition stands outside the truth that it seeks. Ultimately for Hegel, this so-called fear of error is actually a "fear of the truth."[68] In short, Hegel destabilizes and challenges our notions of cognition, of subject and object, and of the Absolute. For him, these meanings remain "hazy" and to use them is deceptive and empty in the face of the recognition that science has not yet unfolded a true understanding of their meaning.[69]

For Hegel, a scientific philosophy must liberate itself from thinking in terms which only serve to maintain a separation of cognition from the true Absolute and creates an incapacity for a science to go forward with the hard work of what Hegel was to later call the labor of the concept. Instead of refuting these ideas of a prolegomena to metaphysics, Hegel simply rejects them "out of hand as adventitious and arbitrary."[70] In so doing, he turns his project away from Kant's natural attitude, noting that Science must now liberate itself and reflect on "*how knowledge makes its appearance.*"[71]

Hegel considers his new focus a science "free and self-moving" in its own particular shape, as opposed to Kant's focus on phenomenal knowledge of its object.[72] While Hegel remains critical of Kant's position, he is also able to preserve it as a historical standpoint on a path of natural consciousness and as a station on the way of the soul which journeys through its own configurations. For Hegel, the journey is a process of purification and a preparation for the life of the spirit. Through such a process, the spirit can finally achieve a completed experience of itself, the awareness of what it already is in itself. On the one hand, we can interpret this move as an abandonment of Kant's project, but from another perspective Kant's philosophy is a dead end and can lead no further.

Hegel continues to juxtapose Kant's natural one-sided and incomplete pattern of consciousness (which for him can only end in skepticism) with his own critique targeting Kant's phenomenalism and the structure of Kant's epistemology. For Hegel, this move liberates the spirit for the first time to examine what truth really is. This truth emerges from challenging Kant's thesis, a thesis which must suffer the negation of true despair. For Hegel, Kantian consciousness is negated and shown to be a bare abstraction, a nothingness that leads only to an abyss. Moving beyond this abstract nothingness, consciousness, like a phoenix arising from the fire of negation, finds a new and determinate form, which continues "unhalting" in its historical progression toward the goal.[73] Knowledge no longer needs to go beyond itself when Notion corresponds to its object, and the object to the Notion. Short of such a situation, there is "no satisfaction . . . to be found at any of the stations on the way."[74] For Hegel, consciousness is restlessly driven beyond itself by something else. It is a process in which our positions are always uprooted and surpassed. Formal positions must suffer a violence which kills, but it is a death necessary for the advancement of consciousness. It is due to this violent threat that consciousness retreats from truth and clings to its former position in unthinking inertia, but the unrest drives consciousness forward as well.

Hegel then takes another critical swipe at Kant who, at the end of his *Critique*, speaks of the importance of a burning zeal for truth. For Hegel, this zeal seems only to hide from itself and others a clinging to its position which is only vanity. In essence, one might say, Hegel considers Kant a philosophical narcissist who in his "conceit . . . gloat[s]s over [his] own [barren] understanding" – Kant flees from the Universal and is stuck in maintaining the structure of an in-itself.[75] For Hegel, what is needed is an "*examination of the reality of cognition*," but as yet no one has developed a standard by which science can be compared to phenomenal knowledge.[76] It is Hegel's own analysis that sets the stage for understanding this relationship.

Hegel approaches this relationship by examining an interesting paradox or contradiction: that consciousness simultaneously distinguishes itself from something and at the same time relates itself to it. Hegel notes that this something can be said to exist *for* consciousness, and that the determinate aspect of this relating or of the *being* of something for consciousness is knowing. But a contradiction seems to exist in that we distinguish this being-for-another from being-in-itself. Whatever is related to knowledge or knowing is also distinguished from it, and posited as existing outside of this relationship. It is this "posited. . . *being-in-itself* [that] is called *truth*."[77]

Hegel now makes an interesting observation that "if we inquire into the truth of knowledge, it seems that we are asking what knowledge is *in itself*. Yet in this inquiry knowledge is *our* object, something that exists *for us*."[78] A certain shift in focus seems to take place that hinges on Hegel's recognition that the so-called thing-in-itself *is posited by consciousness*. This move begins the restructuring of the true relationship of consciousness to its object. The nature of the object seems to undergo change such that consciousness, as it relates to its object, is now an object that "falls within it;" that is, any "comparison of consciousness" with its object is also a comparison "with itself."[79] In short, "the dissociation, or this semblance of dissociation" between consciousness and its object "is overcome by [recognizing] the nature of the object we are investigating."[80] This theme is refined and repeated throughout the Introduction and Hegel can be seen attempting to both acknowledge and leave behind the thing-in-itself as Kant understood it. For Hegel, within consciousness "one thing exists *for* another," yet, "at the same time, this other is to consciousness not merely *for* it;" this other "is also outside of this relationship, or exists *in itself.*"[81]

Here I find myself asking how can it be the case that something that consciousness determines can also be outside of this relationship? For Hegel, this is possible by virtue of the difference in consciousness between something that appears to consciousness as other (in-itself) and not merely for it, but is also at the same time for it at another moment of truth. This difference allows the otherness of being-in-itself to be a standard which consciousness sets up for itself and by which it measures what it knows. Hegel puts it this way: "If we designate *knowledge* as the Notion, but the essence or the *True* as what exists, or the *object*, then the examination consists in seeing whether the Notion corresponds to the object."[82] In short, Hegel posits a kind of correspondence theory of truth, not between consciousness and some mind-independent object, but a coherence that exists within a revised Notion of consciousness itself. Thus, for Hegel, the object we are investigating is knowledge-consciousness, a consciousness that can posit an essence or thing-in-itself.

Ultimately, what consciousness examines is its own Self, a re-envisioned Self no longer simply understood in the traditional sense of the "subject" examining an "object." What Hegel seems to have in mind is an intrinsic relationship of two moments of consciousness in which one moment is to perceive something in itself and in another the recognition that the in-itself is for consciousness. In Hegel's description to this point, it is hard to overcome the Kantian idea that the thing-in-itself cannot be something for consciousness, though for Kant it is something that can be thought. But Hegel seems to have something different in mind than the thought of the thing-in-itself. He notes that it does not seem possible to "get behind the object as it exists for consciousness so as to examine what the object is *in itself.*"[83] If we cannot do this, we have no standard by which to test our knowledge and say that we know something. But Hegel again makes the point that the distinction we have been concerned about – between the in-itself and knowledge of it – is already inherent "in the very fact that consciousness knows an object at all. Something is *for it* the *in-itself*; and knowledge, or the being of the object for consciousness," characterizes the very essence of consciousness as a free-flowing movement between moments of its truth.[84] It is on the basis of these moments as the movement between them that the examination rests. If the comparison between these two moments reveals that they do not correspond with one another, it would seem that "consciousness must alter its knowledge to make it conform to the object."[85]

So, it would seem to be the case that even though both moments of consciousness, knowledge, and object-in-itself are within consciousness, they may well be out of tune with each other. Consciousness can mistake itself for what it is not or can recognize itself accurately. For Hegel, it is also the case that as knowledge is altered the object itself is altered as well: "as the knowledge changes, so too does the object, for it essentially belonged to this knowledge."[86] In short, Hegel suggests that knowledge and object are co-relative.

This recognition radically changes what was initially (by Kant) taken to be an in-itself. What was previously taken to be an in-itself proves to be not an in-itself, but rather an in-itself that is *for* consciousness. This change of object is part of what Hegel considers the "*dialectical* movement" of consciousness – "which affects both its knowledge and its object" in an unfolding and developmental process "called *experience*."[87] Hegel recognizes that this movement shows the object to be ambiguous. The first object, seen as in-itself, is altered, as a developing knowledge now recognizes this object as an "*in-itself* only *for consciousness*."[88] This new object is for Hegel the "True" object or "*essence*" and it contains the limiting structure or "nothingness of the first."[89] It is now "what experience has made of it."[90]

This way of looking at what we know suggests that "something [is] contributed by *us*, by means of which the succession of experiences through which consciousness passes is raised into a scientific progression."[91] In every case for Hegel the result of a former state or mode of knowing must be seen as the ground out of which the new progression emerges. The essence of the emergent object is now something different from what appeared at the preceding stage. For Hegel, it is this fact that guides the phenomenology of patterns of consciousness in a necessary historical sequence. This process seems to go on unconsciously or, as Hegel puts it, "behind the back of consciousness."[92] What consciousness is aware of is both the "*content . . . of what presents itself to us*" as well as a "movement and a process of becoming."[93] Hegel notes that "[b]ecause of this necessity," the necessity of the unfolding phenomenology of consciousness, "the way to Science is itself already *Science*, and hence, in virtue of its content, is the Science of the *experience of consciousness*."[94]

For Hegel, self-reflective experience, the experiential unfolding which consciousness goes through, is an "entire system" of the unfolding truth.[95] The *Phenomenology of Spirit* is not a series of "abstract moments," but determinate patterns of a consciousness which presses "forward to its true existence."[96] Finally, consciousness can and "will arrive at a point at which it gets rid of its semblance of being burdened [as Kant was] with something alien."[97] At a certain point "appearance becomes identical with essence. . . . [W]hen consciousness itself grasps this its own essence, it will signify the nature of absolute knowledge itself."[98]

Hegel's alchemy: splendid isolation or fullness of soul

The work of complex thinkers lends itself to multiple interpretations. This seems obviously the case for both Jung and Hegel, as well as for Hillman and Giegerich – so much so that it has not been uncommon to hear the queries: "Which Jung?" or "Which Hegel?", "Which Hillman?" or "Which Giegerich?" Cyril O'Regan, in the introduction to his book *The Heterodox Hegel*, refers to Wilhelm Raimund Beyer's "parade of pictures of Hegel, from revolutionary Hegel to fascist Hegel, from a catholic Hegel to an [sic] Protestant evangelical Hegel."[99] Likewise, Jung's work has been subject to multiple interpretations. From critics and debunkers Stern and Noll to classical analysts Edinger and Von Franz, Jung has been seen as devil and saint, Eurocentric racist, and compassionate wise man. It is not surprising that for many readers Jung and Hegel are difficult to understand. Wolfgang Zucker has remarked that in the English-speaking world, Hegel's books "have the reputation of being as abstruse as medieval texts on alchemy or astrology."[100]

While Zucker refers to alchemy/astrology simply in passing as a way of emphasizing the difficulty of reading Hegel, it is ironic that both Hegel and Jung had more than a passing involvement with alchemy and other esoteric subjects. One might even conceive that certain of their texts are really not unlike alchemical treatises in that they are difficult and obscure, and aim at the transformation of a simple substance into a more differentiated and complex one. In this regard, it is interesting that Glenn Alexander Magee, a Hegelian scholar and controversial interpreter of Hegel's work, refers to Eric Voegelin as describing "the *Phenomenology of Spirit* as a grimoire . . . as an alchemical manual, an Emerald Tablet for the modern age."[101] In a similar spirit, Magee provocatively states that:

> Hegel is not a philosopher. He is no lover or seeker of wisdom – he believes he has found it. Hegel writes in the preface to the *Phenomenology of Spirit*, "To help bring philosophy closer to the form of Science, to the goal where it can lay aside the title of '*love* of knowing' and be actual knowledge – that is what I have set before me." By the end of the *Phenomenology*, Hegel claims to have arrived at Absolute Knowledge, which he identifies with wisdom.[102]

For Magee:

> Hegel's claim to have attained wisdom is completely contrary to the original Greek conception of philosophy as the love of wisdom, that is, the ongoing pursuit rather than the final possession of wisdom.[103]

For Magee, Hegel's claim to wisdom is "fully consistent with the ambitions of the Hermetic tradition."[104] He finds many parallels between Hegel's thoughts and alchemy noting that "[a] systematic parallel can be drawn between each aspect of the [alchemical] opus and Hegel's philosophical project."[105] The goal of working through Hegel's philosophy is for Magee what is necessary for the achievement of Absolute Knowing, which like the Philosophers' Stone "will constitute a perfected form of living in the world; in the words of H.S. Harris [a Hegel scholar], 'an actual experience of living in the light of the eternal day.'"[106] The achievement, Magee notes, draws the adepts to the opus.

> All philosophy, including Hegel's, presupposes that at least some men yearn to know themselves and the world fully. Just as the magicians of old – men such as Agrippa and Bruno – believed that knowledge of the right incantations could give one tremendous power, so Hegel

believes that knowledge of the "magic words" that evoke the Absolute can empower the individual by reconciling him with the world. Kojève defines the Hegelian wise man as the man of both perfect self-consciousness and perfect self-satisfaction. Wisdom and self-satisfaction do not consist, however, in ego-aggrandizement, but in the transcendence of ego and identification with Spirit as such. Kojeve writes: "For Self-consciousness to exist, for philosophy to exist, there must be *transcendence* of self with respect to self as given." H.S. Harris notes that "In [Hegel's] view we have to annihilate our own selfhood in order to enter the sphere where Philosophy herself speaks."[107]

Magee does not want to suggest a simple or magical attainment of wisdom. On the contrary, he sees Hegel's philosophy "as a real experience, stretching all the capacities of those who embark upon it: 'for it is an extremely tortuous way, to abandon what one is used to and possesses now, and to retrace one's steps toward the old primordial things."[108] Magee emphasizes how working through both Hegel and alchemy is like an initiation that "can stretch all of one's capacities and be . . . a highway of despair."[109]

In Hegel's philosophy, as in alchemy, the adepts must purify themselves by passing through the fire of negation. Magee makes an analogy to the phenomenological crucible, where "Spirit is separated from its impurities and, literally, perfected."[110] In each phase, there is impurity and imperfection, a flawed seed that is the *prima materia* necessary for the work to lead to Absolute Spirit. For Hegel, the purification process is, in part, catalyzed by the mystical process, but, in addition, there is for Hegel a

> secret ingredient necessary to synthesize Absolute Spirit. . . . [H]e has placed the historical forms of Spirit into his alembic and, through the fire of dialectic, has caused them to reorganize into a form that reveals the necessity within their apparent contingency. The *Phenomenology* is the *nigredo*, the stage in which the material (man) has its imperfections burned off. In Hegel the *albedo*, the pure white stone from which the Philosopher's Stone can be made, is Absolute Knowing, the pure aetherial consciousness from which the entire system develops.[111]

If I read this passage correctly, Magee appears to be saying that the achievement of purity in and through the forms of the *Phenomenology* and in which all imperfections are "burned off" is a *prima materia* for the development of both the Philosophers' Stone and Absolute Knowing, which he defines as a "pure aetherial consciousness," which is similar to Giegerich's understanding of the spirit of Mercurius. It would appear that there are two levels of purity described in this passage: (1) the *albedo/* white stone and a furthering of the process leading to (2) the Philosophers' Stone and pure aetherial consciousness. In both cases, the results appear to privilege purity. It will be important to differentiate these levels between the white stone and the Philosophers' Stone in order to further evaluate Hegel's notion of Absolute Knowing.

For Jung, as for many alchemists, the stage of purity of thought lacks differentiation and is called a *unio mentalis*, a united mental condition that remains pure and rises above difference. Perhaps it is a condition in which "living in the light of the eternal day" (Harris) is living in a light where all cows are white and where all darkness has been purged from consciousness.

For Hillman, too, such states of purity might be conceived to take place in the *unio mentalis*. Such a whitened consciousness leads to the conviction of the "mental" world as separate and pure. He writes: "In this tepid and shadowless lunar light, everything seems to fit. . . . Having absorbed and unified all hues into the one white, the mirror of silvered subjectivity expands to reflect all things at the expense of differentiation of itself."[112] Hillman notes that the *albedo* should not be confused with the innocent whiteness of the *prima materia* or of virgin's milk, "the *candida* of unmarked and unremarking innocence" since the "*albedo* whiteness [is] achieved after the soul's long exile in [the darkness of the] *nigredo*. . . . In alchemy, *albedo* refers to both a complete separation and a complete conjunction: the separation between sulfur (concrete urgency) and mercury (psychic fusibility and intellectual volatility)," but still "[t]he conjunction *occurs in mind*, in the *unio mentalis* of soul and spirit."[113]

The condition of *mind*, the *unio mentalis*, appears in alchemy as a necessary but insufficient stage of the *opus*. According to Dorn, the *unio mentalis* is significant in overcoming the instinctual pull of internal bodily desires and the influence they have on the mind.[114] According to Jung,

the aim of this separation [then] was to free the mind of the influence of "the bodily appetites and the heart's affections," and to establish a spiritual position which is supraordinate to the turbulent sphere of the body.[115]

Edinger, quoting Jung, notes: "This leads at first to a dissociation of the personality and a violation of the merely natural man."[116] He points out that this separation is only a "preliminary step, in itself a clear blend of Stoic and Christian psychology. . . [and it] is indispensable for the differentiation of consciousness."[117] Thus, for Edinger, "the *unio mentalis* corresponds precisely to the philosophers who make dying their profession."[118] It is the accomplishment of this necessity that Jung captures in his statement, "*the experience of the self is always a defeat for the ego.*"[119] The importance of this process of separation is taken up by Edinger in Chapter 7 of *Anatomy of the Psyche* entitled "*Separatio.*"[120]

At the end of Edinger's chapter, he notes that the "*separatio* is not a final process."[121] It is rather an "intermediate operation that is a prerequisite for the greater *coniunctio*."[122]

Figure 10.3 Image of the alchemical *separatio*. From Michael Maier, *Atalanta Fugiens*, Emblem 8, 1617.

Source: Public domain.

The move to separate and purify soul and body has a long history. I will follow Edinger here in quoting a long passage from Plato's *Phaedo*:

"But does not purification consist in this, as was said in a former part of our discourse, in separating as much as possible the soul from the body, and in accustoming it to gather and collect itself by itself on all sides apart from the body, and to dwell, so far as it can, both now and hereafter, alone by itself, delivered, as it were, from the shackles of the body?"

"Certainly," he replied.

"Is this, then, called death, this deliverance and separation of the soul from the body?"

"Assuredly," he answered.

"But, as we affirmed, those who pursue philosophy rightly are especially and alone desirous to deliver it; and this is the very study of philosophers, the deliverance and separation of the soul from the body, is it not?"

"It appears so."

"Then, as I said at first, would it not be ridiculous for a man who has endeavored throughout his life to live as near as possible to death, then, when death arrives, to grieve? Would not this be ridiculous?"

"How should it not?"

"In reality, then, Simmias," he continued, "those who pursue philosophy rightly, study to die; and to them, of all men, death is least formidable. Judge from this. Since they altogether hate the body and desire to keep the soul by itself, would it not be irrational if, when this comes to pass, they should be afraid and grieve, and not be glad to go to that place where, on their arrival, they may hope to obtain that which they longed for throughout life? But they longed for wisdom, and to be freed from association with that which they hated. . . . and shall one who really loves wisdom, and firmly cherishes this very hope, that he shall nowhere else attain it in a manner worthy of the name, except in Hades, be grieved at dying, and not gladly go there? We must think that he would gladly go, my friend, if he be in truth a philosopher; for he will be firmly persuaded of this, that he will nowhere else than there attain wisdom in its purity; and if this be so, would it not be very irrational, as I just now said, if such a man were to be afraid of death?"

"Very much so, by Jupiter!" he replied.[123]

For Hillman as for Jung, in the condition of the *albedo*, in which purity is attained by separation and rising above worldly matters, something is still missing. Jung had noted that in the "state of 'whiteness' one does not *live* in the true sense of the word."[124] The *unio mentalis* is an "abstract, ideal state."[125]

> In order to make it come alive it must have "blood," it must have what the alchemists call the *rubedo*, the "redness" of life. Only the total experience of being can transform this ideal state of the *albedo* into a fully human mode of existence. Blood alone can reanimate a glorious state of consciousness in which the last trace of blackness is dissolved, in which the devil no longer has an autonomous existence but rejoins the profound unity of the psyche. Then the *opus magnum* is finished: the human soul is completely integrated.[126]

Edinger likewise refers to the Philosophers' Stone as associated with redness and as such "was not only the *prima materia*, but also the goal of the *opus*."[127]

For Hillman what is notably absent from the whiteness of the *albedo* "is the solar power of sophic sulfur, which gives body to the clarified mind and is necessary for the *rubedo*."[128] For Hillman, the whiteness of the albedo resists change. Once an intellectual paradigm is established and all things fit together, a rigidity sets in against external impurities; and yet, for Hillman, such "impurities" are a necessary part of "purity," so that a system does not become dogmatic and lifeless. Hillman's way of speaking about it is that the "whiteness" needs to be spoiled, needs to yellow, to rot and putrify, and in so doing to take on "body, flavor, fatness."[129] "White resists this physical substantiation, for it feels like a regression to the vulgar drivenness of earlier moments in the work" which reflection has "finally sophisticated and pacified."[130] For the alchemist Figulus, says Hillman, "whiteness remains imperfect unless it be brought by heat to highest redness and, in fact, remains 'dead' until that occurs."[131] Reddening brings into existence an imperfect perfection, a perfection that is not perfect. For Hillman then, as well as for other alchemical authors, "yellowing is more than a spoiling of the white. It is also its brighter, more vivifying illumination, a richer, more expansive clarity."[132] The yellowing for Hillman is not a simple return to the unilluminated bodily emotion, but a "transmutation of the mind, a change in the intellect," a change that "cannot be captured by whitened reflection."[133] The change in the intellect brought about by yellowing is described by Hillman as:

> not the usual intellect, dried with concepts, abstracted, pulled away; this is the fat intellect, physical, concrete, emotional, fermenting with instinctual interiority, an unctuous passion. Having first been whitened, its desire is not simple and driven, but desire aware of itself through intellectual fervor – an *intellectus agens* – dawnings of the winged mind, sure as gold. No longer that separation between mercury and sulfur, between fantasy flights and dense emotional body. In the carcass of the lion a new sweetness, thick and yellow and sticking to all things, like honey, like oil, flowing like wax and gilding as it touches. One's nature goes through a temperamental turn, a change in humors from choleric to sanguine, which the dictionary defines as confident, optimistic, cheerful. So does *citrinitas* become the reddening.[134]

As Hillman's reflections approach the *rubedo*, his descriptions appear to overlap with our understanding of the Philosophers' Stone. He notes that reddening, like the Stone, has

> many names and equations, it indicates the inseparability of visible and invisible, psyche and cosmos, a *unus mundus*. It requires the most intense heat: "The spirit is heat." The operations coincident to the reddening are exaltation, multiplication, and projection, according to the fifteenth century English alchemist George Ripley. These expansions together perform the tincturing, staining all things. . . .[135]

Like yellowing, "[t]he rubedo as purple-red is also called in Greek terms *iosis* [poisoning]. It would seem that the *rubedo*" is deconstructive and

> signifies a final dissolution of sunlit consciousness and all distinctions – all the stages, phases, operations, and colors. It is a moment of the *rotatio*, a turning and turning like the cosmos itself, requiring endless numbers of eyes to see with.[136]

For Hillman, before healing can take place, one must be able to see through multiple eyes and from many perspectives. From one point of

Figure 10.4 Multiple views of psychic reality. Artist unknown.

Source: From author's personal collection.

view, the emergence of the white earth leaves the blackness behind, but as we have seen in numerous ways, the *terra alba* and the darkness against which it defines itself form an intimate and indissoluble relationship so that the white earth "is not sheer white in the literal sense but a field of flowers . . . a peacock's tail, a coat of many colors."[137]

The idea of multiple eyes and colors is also imaged in alchemy as the *cauda pavonis*, the peacock's tail, an image associated with the Philosophers' Stone.

Hillman explains that the multiple eyes of the peacock's tail reflect their

> full flowering of imagination [that] shows itself as the qualitative spread of colors so that imagining is a coloring process, and if not in literal colors, then as the qualitative differentiation of intensities and hues which is essential to the *unio mentalis*"[138] and "to the act of imagination."[139]

Ultimately, for Hillman, these colors are not the same as in the subjectivist philosophies of Newton and Locke or of Berkeley and Hume, where colors are considered as only secondary qualities brought about by the mind and senses of the observer. Rather, for Hillman, colors are something more fundamental – a *phainoumenon* on display at the heart of the matter itself prior to all abstractions. For Hillman, with the emergence of the *rotatio* and a Ouroboric consciousness,

> The work is over; we no longer work at consciousness, develop ourselves, or possess a distinct grid by means of which we recognize where we are, how we are, maybe even who we are. "The dissolution of Sol should be effected by Nature, not by handiwork," concludes Figulus. Psyche is life; life, psyche.
>
> Psyche is also death, an equation investigated in my writings on the Underworld. The "death" in this moment of the alchemical work is the "dissolution of Sol," which occurs "by Nature," as if a homeostatic self-correction of solar optimism. This process is similar to the insidious dark strength of Yin afflicting bright Yang from within. The sure optimism of solar clarity is the blind spot itself. Sol dissolves in the darkness of its own light. Or, to put it another way: yellow at this moment is nothing other than the visible presence of the black in its depth.[140]

In these statements, I believe Hillman attempts to deconstruct any vestiges of metaphysical realism, though he has been accused by Giegerich of not going far enough, while Hillman, as we have seen, accuses Giegerich of going too far into the "poisonous state of splendid isolation," a state that for Giegerich needs to be faced and understood. The philosophical and alchemical question remains: to what extent does such a pure state of thought fall short of including the depth of alchemical darkness described by Jung and Hillman. I will attempt to show, in a later chapter, how a reading of Hegel in spite of the movement of idea beyond image includes the full body of historical richness and embeddedness in the depths of soul that Jung and Hillman speak of. If such an interpretation is successful, it challenges the divide between Hillman and Giegerich.

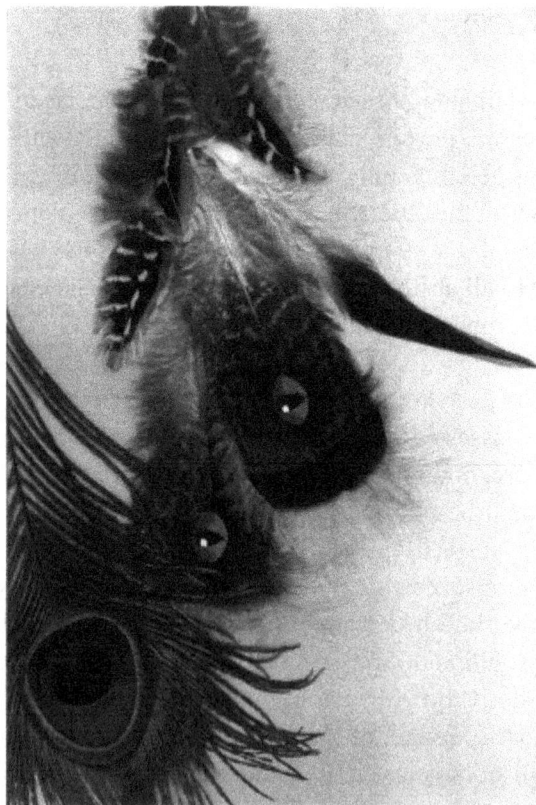

Figure 10.5 Variation of the peacock tail. Artwork by analysand.
Source: Used by permission.

Notes

1 Giegerich, "The Unassimilable Remnant," 198.
2 Ibid.
3 Ibid., 199.
4 Marlan, "From the Black Sun," 7.
5 Hillman, *Alchemical Psychology*, 240.
6 Giegerich, "The Unassimilable Remnant," 201.
7 Ibid., 202; emphasis mine.
8 Rockmore, *In Kant's Wake*, 19.
9 Ibid., 168.
10 Kitcher, "Introduction," xxv.
11 Ibid.
12 Ibid.
13 Kant, *Prolegomena*, 9.
14 De Voogd, "C.G. Jung: Psychologist of the Future," 179.
15 Mendelsohn, quoted in Zweig, "Kant: Philosophical Correspondence," 15.
16 Bishop, *Syncronicity and Intellectual Intuition*, 77; brackets in original.
17 Hillman, *A Blue Fire*, 155.
18 Ibid.
19 Hillman, *Alchemical Psychology*, 69.
20 Kant, *Dreams of a Spirit-Seer*, 37.
21 Kant, *Critique of Pure Reason*, 303.
22 Ibid.
23 Ibid.
24 Ibid., 303–304.
25 Kitcher, "Introduction," xxviii.
26 Bair, *Jung: A Biography*, 35.
27 Bishop, *Synchronicity and Intellectual Intuition*, 179.
28 Bair, *Jung: A Biography*, 508.
29 Bishop, *Synchronicity and Intellectual Intuition*, 4.
30 Ibid.
31 Ibid.
32 Ibid., 5.
33 Ibid.
34 Ibid., 5–6.
35 De Voogd, "C.G. Jung: Psychologist of the Future," 176.
36 Rockmore, *Before and After Hegel*, 20. See also Rockmore, *In Kant's Wake*, 39–40.
37 Rockmore, *In Kant's Wake*, 34.
38 Jung, *Alchemical Studies (CW13)*, §82.
39 Rockmore, *Cognition*, 3. Rockmore notes that, "[i]n reaction to Kant, Hegel maintains that a coherent account of the relation of an appearance to an independent external object is impossible."
40 Rockmore, *Before and After Hegel*, 21.
41 Nagy, *Philosophical Issues*, 149.
42 Caygill, *A Kant Dictionary*, 393.
43 Ibid.
44 Ibid.
45 Ibid.
46 Ibid.
47 Ibid., 393. See Kant, *Critique of Pure Reason*, B 28, footnote 103 and Rockmore, *Before and After Hegel*, 35.
48 Barker, "Appearing and Appearances in Kant," 286.

49 Ewing, *A Short Commentary on Kant's Critique of Pure Reason*, 195.
50 Ibid., 187.
51 Ibid.
52 Schrader, "The Thing in Itself in Kantian Philosophy," 172.
53 Rockmore, *Before and After Hegel*, 35.
54 Watkins, "Review of Daniel Warren."
55 Nagy, *Philosophical Issues*, 62.
56 Kant, *Critique of Pure Reason,* 50.
57 Rockmore, *Before and After Hegel*, 21.
58 Kant, *Critique of Pure Reason*, 67.
59 Wood, "Reiterating the Temporal Toward a Rethinking of Heidegger on Time," 142.
60 Kant, *Critique of Pure Reason*, 343.
61 Jung, *The Structure and Dynamics of the Psyche (CW8)*, §261.
62 Kant, *Critique of Pure Reason*, 774.
63 Rockmore, *In Kant's Wake*, 168.
64 Ibid., 168–169.
65 Hegel, *Phenomenology*, 46, §73.
66 Ibid.
67 Ibid., 47, §74.
68 Ibid.
69 Ibid., 48, §75.
70 Ibid., 48, §76.
71 Ibid., 49, §76; emphasis mine.
72 Ibid., 49, §77.
73 Ibid., 51, §80.
74 Ibid.
75 Ibid., 52, §80.
76 Ibid., 52, §81.
77 Ibid., 52, §82.
78 Ibid., 53, §83.
79 Ibid., 53, §84.
80 Ibid.
81 Ibid.
82 Ibid.
83 Ibid., 54, §85.
84 Ibid.
85 Ibid.
86 Ibid.
87 Ibid., 55, §86.
88 Ibid.
89 Ibid.
90 Ibid.
91 Ibid., 55, §87.
92 Ibid., 56, §87.
93 Ibid.
94 Ibid., 56, §88.
95 Ibid., 56, §89.
96 Ibid.
97 Ibid.
98 Ibid., 57, §89.
99 O'Regan, *The Heterodox Hegel*, 2.

100 Zucker, "Historicism and Relativism," 2.
101 Magee, *Hegel and the Hermetic Tradition*, 187.
102 Ibid., 1.
103 Ibid.
104 Ibid. Magee goes on to define the Hermetic tradition as:

> a current of thought that derives its name from the so-called *Hermetica* (or *Corpus Hermeticum*), a collection of Greek and Latin treatises and dialogues written in the first or second centuries A.D. and probably containing ideas that are far older. The legendary author of these works is Hermes Trismegistus ("Thrice-Greatest Hermes"). "Hermeticism" denotes a broad tradition of thought that grew out of the "writings of Hermes" and was expanded and developed through the infusion of various other traditions. Thus, alchemy, Kabbalism, Lullism, and the mysticism of Eckhart and Cusa – to name just a few examples – became intertwined with the Hermetic doctrines. (Indeed, Hermeticism is used by some authors simply to mean alchemy.) Hermeticism is also sometimes called theosophy, or esotericism; less precisely, it is often characterized as mysticism, or occultism.

(Ibid.)

105 Ibid., 211.
106 Ibid., 129.
107 Ibid.
108 Ibid.
109 Ibid.
110 Ibid., 211.
111 Ibid.
112 Hillman, *Alchemical Psychology*, 212.
113 Ibid., 211; emphasis of "occurs in the mind" is mine.
114 Edinger, *Anatomy*, 171–172.
115 Jung, *Mysterium Coniunctionis (CW14), §670ff.*; quoted by Edinger, *Anatomy*, 171.
116 Ibid.
117 Ibid.
118 Edinger, *Anatomy*, 171.
119 Jung, *Mysterium Coniunctionis (CW14)*, §778.
120 An alchemical illustration of this process can be found in Michael Maier's *Atalanta fugiens* (1618). The image is called "Cutting the Philosophical Egg."
121 Edinger, *Anatomy*, 207.
122 Ibid., 207–209.
123 Although Edinger does quote this passage from Plato's *Phaedo*, please note that this particular translation was retrieved from Project Gutenberg.
124 Jung, *C.G. Jung Speaking*, 229.
125 Ibid.
126 Ibid.
127 Edinger, *Anatomy*, 72.
128 Hillman, *Alchemical Psychology*, 211.
129 Ibid., 213.
130 Ibid.
131 Ibid.
132 Ibid.
133 Ibid.
134 Ibid., 216.

135 Ibid.
136 Ibid., 217. A criticism of Hillman's view of yellowing is taken up by Giegerich in *The Soul's Logical Life*, 194–201.
137 Hillman, *Alchemical Psychology*, 114.
138 Ibid., 112.
139 Hillman, "Alchemical Blue and the Unio Mentalis," 41.
140 Hillman, *Alchemical Psychology*, 217.

Chapter 11

A reflection on the black sun and Jung's notion of self[1]

In my own earlier work *The Black Sun*, I refer to the visible presence of the black in its depth as the light of darkness itself or the *lumen naturae*, the light of nature. I do not believe that what the alchemists called the "light of nature" is easily reducible to any metaphysical realism or notion of nature as a mind independent reality, nor to a self-referential subjectivity. It is both visible and invisible, present and absent. It is in its complexity both the *prima materia* and the Philosophers' Stone, another expression of an ouroboric circle and so both at the beginning and end of the work. In this way, the Black Sun/Philosophers' Stone is another way of imagining what we have earlier called one of the most enigmatic statements of the goal of alchemy – the idea of the Philosophers' Stone – as "a stone that is not a stone." If, for Jung, the Philosophers' Stone is an expression of the Self, then it is important to view the Self in an equally complex way, a self that is not a Self. Such ideas are the height of paradox, linking and transcending what we think of as opposites in such a way that ordinary consciousness is radically challenged and subverted.

In "Silver and White Earth," (Chapter 6 in *Alchemical Psychology*) Hillman speaks of such madness alchemically as a process in which solar brilliance and moon madness are marvelously conjoined. The *mysterium coniunctionis* then is an "illuminated lunacy."[2] In "Concerning the Stone: Alchemical Images of the Goal" (Chapter 8 in *Alchemical Psychology*), Hillman discusses the complexity of images and refuses to break them into hard and fast binaries or opposites. The "grit and the pearl, the lead and the diamond, the hammer and the gold are inseparable."[3] For Hillman, "[t]he pain is not prior to the goal, like crucifixion before resurrection;" rather, "pain and gold are coterminous, codependent, corelative. The pearl

DOI: 10.4324/9781003215905-12

is also always grit, an irritation as well as a luster, the gilding also a poisoning."[4] It is hard to keep these opposite dimensions of experience in consciousness, but, for Hillman, such a description fits with life, "for we are strangely disconsolate even in a moment of radiance."[5] Our golden experience "again and again will press for testing in the fire, ever new blackness appearing, dark crows with the yellow sun."[6]

It was on such a basis that I proposed that the "light of darkness itself" is such a complex image and that the idea of regeneration was better seen in a deeper consciousness of this paradox than in a moving through and beyond it. The paradox holds the "opposites" of light/dark, visible/invisible, and self and no-self (or, as Fichte says, not-self) together, and in so doing there is a "light," an effulgence, or a "shine" that is hard to define or capture in any metaphysical language or traditional binaries. In this sense, if, with Hillman, we have ended in being out of our minds with lunacy, it is only fair to say that it is a higher kind of lunacy. That harkens back to what has been called Jung's madness and his strange visionary experiences that led him to write *Seven Sermons of the Dead*, an outcome of his confrontations with the unconscious described earlier.

Self and no self

In these experiences, Jung heard the following words, which he transcribed:

> Harken: I begin with nothingness. Nothingness is the same as fullness. In infinity full is no better than empty. Nothingness is both empty and full. As well might ye say anything else of nothingness, as for instance, white is it, or black, or again, it is not, or is it. . . . This nothingness or fullness we name the PLEROMA.[7]

This pleroma was a Gnostic name given to Jung's experiential prefiguration of what later became his hypothesis of the Self. This concept was elaborated throughout many of the *Collected Works*, but most fully expressed in *Aion: Researches into the Phenomenology of the Self*. According to Jung, the Self was a concept difficult to define, and, in spite of all of his warnings, it is often taken as a substantialized entity. Perhaps it would be of use to remind ourselves that Jung's Self is not a metaphysical entity. Psychologist and scholar Roger Brooke makes a useful contribution by asserting that to think of the Self as a "something" is less accurate than to understand it as a "no-thing," "a fertile and hospitable emptiness within which the things of the world could shine forth."[8]

In an article that has received too little attention, "Nothing Almost Sees Miracles!: Self and No-Self in Psychology and Religion," scholar of religion and Jungian psychology David Miller writes what amounts to a deconstructive reading of Jung's idea of the Self. He claims that even though Jung ultimately rejects the idea of a No-Self doctrine, in essence what he means by the idea of the "Self" "has the same ontological status as the desubstantialized and deconstructed notion of the 'no-self' in the apophatic religious traditions. 'Self' is no-self."[9] Turning to the margins of Jung's ideas, beyond the formulations of his ideas as an empirical scientist, Miller recalls Jung's comment:

If you will contemplate [your nothingness,] your lack of fantasy, [lack] of inspiration, and [lack] of inner aliveness, which you feel as sheer stagnation and a barren wilderness, and impregnate it with the interest born of alarm at your inner death, then something can take shape in you, for your inner emptiness conceals just as great a fullness, if you allow it to penetrate into you.[10]

An emptiness that is also a fullness resonates with figures such as Pseudo-Dionysius, Meister Eckhart, Lao Tzu, and other masters of Asian or Western philosophies and religions that hold the concept of Nothingness at the core of psychological and religious life. In essence, this is true for Jung, too. For, beyond the scientific Jung is the alchemical Jung, for whom the so-called Self is "in principle unknown and unknowable" to the ego.[11] This Jung follows the alchemical *dictum ignotium per ignotius* (the unknown [is explained] by the more unknown). In short, for Jung the Self "is tantamount to religion's no-self."[12]

The paradoxical tension between Self and No-Self that Miller describes is a point of philosophical debate and doctrinal complexity that reaches a high point in Asian philosophy and religion – in the dialogue between Hindu and Buddhist perspectives. The debate is relevant for understanding Jung's idea of the Self since this idea was modeled in part on the ancient Hindu notion of Atman/Brahman.

The Upanishadic perspective holds that beneath and/or above the flux of the empirical world is an unchanging and eternal Self at the core of the universe. Buddhist philosophy, on the other hand, rejects such an idea

of an unchanging Self and considers any idea of the Self to be an imper-
manent construction that must be seen through. In the place of the Self/
Atman, the Buddhists see Anatman (or No-Self) and Sunyata (Nothingness or Voidness) as a mark of the "real."

The theme of this debate has been taken up by transpersonal psychologist Sean Kelly.[13] He contributes to this debate, positing what he calls
"complex holism," a view in part influenced by Hegel's, Jung's, and Morin's idea of a dialectic that is a "symbiotic combination of two [or more]
logics in a manner that is at once complementary *and* antagonistic." What
is important in Kelly's position is not just the idea of bringing the two perspectives together in unity, but also giving importance to their differences.
This gives his vision nuance and complexity. In other words, the doctrine
that holds the Self (the Hindu Atman/Brahman) as the supreme principle
and the doctrine that holds the No-Self (the Buddhist Annata) as a supreme
principle are complementary while *at the same time* remaining antagonistic. Kelly relativizes each fundamental idea by noting that both principles
"must negate the truth of the other in order to point out its onesidedness
and its missing complement."[14]

It appears that Kelly's idea is parallel to Jung's. Jung's psychology was
originally called complex psychology, and later, as it developed, an important component of it was the idea that the unconscious compensates for the
one-sided attitudes of the conscious mind with the intent of achieving balance and wholeness. For Jung, the "Self" was also a complex (w)holism,
a self-regulating and balancing principle, but what is interesting in Kelly's
argument is that he applies the idea of complementarity to the idea of the
Self itself.[15] He observes that the concept of the Self as Atman is prone
to the kind of sterile hypostatization that impedes rather than facilitates
psychic life. On the other hand, without the stability of the atmanic Self,
the No-Self Annata doctrine is also prone to a sterile nihilism that leaves
psychic life adrift.

It is worth noting here that for each perspective, Hindu or Buddhist, the
idea of a complementarity principle can be accounted for from within. The
Atman/Brahman perspective has its own way of understanding the flux of
the No-Self, just as the No-Self perspective of the Buddhists has its own
way of understanding stability. Those who are committed to one perspective or another are likely to feel that the antagonistic other does not *really*
understand its perspective, which from within its own point of view the
ideas of its critics have already addressed. Those who hold to their own

perspectives alone are traditionally considered orthodox, whereas those who seek to break with tradition may be seen as iconoclastic or even heretical, like Jung himself. The history of ideas and cultures seems to move by virtue of such a dialectic, though ultimately this may be a too-limited way to imagine the complexity of history.

Kelly's perspective of complex holism embraces both perspectives, Self and No-Self. To this dialogical complementarity he adds the either/or of dialogic antagonism, which gives the debate a dynamic thrust that both affirms and relativizes at the same time. If we then imagine Jung's idea of the Self as being subject to a similar critique, the Self would call for the complementarity principle of No-Self to keep it from stagnating into a hypostasized and fixed idea of order, as Hillman has observed.

For Jung as well as Hillman, the Self as the archetype of meaning requires the anima or archetype of life to keep it from stagnation. Hillman, however, prefers not to speak of the Self at all because of its tendency as a transcendental concept to lose connection with the body. For him, the problem with Jung's idea of the Self is that it moves toward transcendence, both mathematical and geometric. Its analogies tend to be drawn from the realm of spirit, abstract philosophy, and mystical theology. Its principles tend to be expressed in terms such as self-actualization, entelechy, the principle of individuation, the monad, the totality, Atman, Brahman, and the Tao.[16]

For Hillman, all of this points to a vision of Self that is removed from life, and so it enters psychology "through the back door, disguised as synchronicity, magic, oracles, science fiction, self-symbolism, mandalas, tarot, astrology and other indiscriminations, equally prophetic, ahistorical and humorless."[17] Here Hillman brings together a variety of ideas and images sacred to the orthodox Jungians, which, while not well differentiated, serves the purpose of painting a vision of the Self as an unconscious, abstract structure that has lost touch with the dynamics of the soul. This is a view of the Self that is not acceptable to the orthodox Jungian, for whom the Self is structural, dynamic, and deeply connected to life.

It is not surprising to find that fundamental concepts such as the Self are open to multiple interpretations. As noted, there are those who regard Jung's Self as anything but static and others for whom it too easily loses itself in a hypostasized, outmoded, out-of-touch, and abstract conception that calls out for revision. As I interpret Kelly's perspective of "complex holism," the importance of the tension is to reveal how every fundamental concept has a shadow even when the concept is as wide-ranging as the Self. In this sense, the complementary/antagonistic idea of the No-Self reveals the Self's shadow as an esoteric and invisible other that is necessary to the animation of psychic life. Traditionally the shadow is considered to be the counterpart of consciousness, but the Self is said to embrace both the conscious and the unconscious dimensions of psychic life.

However, if one follows Jung in the most radical sense while simultaneously giving credence to the perspectives of Miller and Kelly and to the importance of the idea of the No-Self as being both complementary and antagonistic to Jung's idea of the Self, then it is reasonable to imagine the Self as having a shadow, a dynamic and invisible Otherness, that is essential to it. The whole is both Self and Not Self.

Often for alchemy, Sol is the most precious thing, while Sol niger as its shadow is like Lacan's "petit a."[18] This *petit a* is "more worthless than seaweed."[19] Yet without Sol niger there is no ring to consciousness, no dynamic Other that taints and tinctures the brilliance of the Sun. Following the alchemical tradition, Jung writes that

> Consciousness requires as its necessary counterpart a dark, latent, non-manifest side. . . . So much did the alchemists sense the duality of his unconscious assumptions that, in the face of all astronomical evidence, he equipped the sun with a shadow [and stated]: "The sun and its shadow bring the work to perfection."[20]

Ultimately, I believe the notion of a shadow of the Self is supported by the paradoxical play of opposites in alchemy.

Depth psychology and the negated self: the strategy of "sous rature"

We have been grappling with the idea of antinomies, with the paradoxical play of light and dark, life and death, spirit and matter. The *coincidentia oppositorum* and *mysterium coniunctionis* are expressions of paradox and monstrosity, maddening negations and attempts at understanding the unity of identity and difference.

As we have seen, the problem is how can we speak about whatever it is that is referred to in the preceding? How can we address that invisible or absent presence that we call the Self or no-Self? It has been challenging for the ancient philosophers, religious mystics, and alchemists, as well as for modern and contemporary post-structuralist philosophers and psycho-analysts to grapple with expressing what is often felt to be inexpressible. For poststructuralist sensibilities, one difficulty that is often expressed is that in every attempt to name that absent presence, there remains a vestige of metaphysical speculation, a transcendental signified (for our purposes read as Self) that is not deconstructed.

Applying Heidegger's idea of "sous rature" to the notion of the Self in Jung's psychology opens a way of imagining the ~~Self~~ as under erasure. Imagining such a ~~Self~~ psychologically is an attempt to think about some-thing that can never be simply identified with any one side of a binary pair – light or dark, black or white, spirit or matter, masculine or feminine, imaginary or real, conscious or unconscious – or with any hypothesized, transcendental notion that attempts to supersede or lift itself up above these oppositions as if language referred in some nominalist or substan-tialist way to some literal "thing" or entity.

As we have seen, terms such as Self, Being, and God cannot be privi-leged or given status outside the language system from which they have been drawn. For Derrida, following twentieth-century linguist Ferdinand de Saussure, these terms derive their meaning in a diacritical way, each making sense only in relation to other signs in a synchronic system of signifiers and having meaning only in relationship to other signs among which none is privileged. Nevertheless, philosophy, psychology, and reli-gion all have a long history of master tropes or metaphors that appear and are understood to refer to something beyond the ordinary images of famil-iar words, such as Being, God, and Self. These "words" are like arche-traces that refer more to mystical than to literal reality and, like Hermes, stand at the crossroads of "différance," a neologism that Derrida coined from the French word for "difference" and which carries the meaning of both difference and deferral.[21] What is continually deferred is the idea that a word arrives at a literal destination, indicating a one-to-one correspond-ence and representation of reality.

So, for example, the idea of the Self can never be separated from its invisible counterpart, the No-Self, against which it derives its meaning. Since an insight is marked by placing it under erasure, the line drawn through the word ~~Self~~ indicates its negation, its shadow. This ensures that an idea will not be taken literally and reminds us that ideas will continue to disseminate throughout time and culture. No concept, master trope, or metaphor can ever finally complete the play or totality of psyche, which, like Mercurius, always escapes our grasp. The ~~Self~~ under erasure is always in a process of continual deconstruction, and, like the Philosophers' Stone of alchemy, it slips away from our ability to grasp it. Hillman's reading of alchemy imagines the Philosophers' Stone as soft and oily, countering both those images that point to its strength, solidity, and unity and also our tendency to crystallize the goal in terms of fixed positions and doctrinal truth. For him, the Philosophers' Stone is waxy and can "receive endless literalizations without being permanently impressed."[22] Perhaps it is useful to imagine the ~~Self~~ under erasure as a kind of contemporary Philosophers' Stone marking a mystery that has long been sought and continues to remain elusive.

Contemporary poststructuralist thought has proceeded toward "if not a liquidation [or *solutio*], then at least a displacement of the subject from the center of philosophical or theoretical activity."[23] Lacan and philosopher Paul Ricoeur speak of decentering the subject and Foucault of the erasure of man "like a face drawn in sand at the edge of the sea."[24] The removal of the subject from the center of psychic life also resonates with Jung's displacement and relativization of the ego. For Jung, the structures of the Self likewise transcend the individual, and its essence "lies beyond the subjective realm."[25]

Just as for Derrida the subject is an effect of language, so for Jung the ego is the product of an all-embracing totality. In short, the "Self is paradoxically *not* oneself."[26] However, insofar as Jung's Self as a totality rises above and beyond the subjective realm and is seen as constituted by impersonal, collective forces, it is consistent with the poststructuralist contention that the subject is likewise primarily an effect of larger collective forces: historic, economic, or linguistic. The poststructuralist view of such forces is quite different from the more mysterious idea about archetypes and the collective unconscious, but for some philosophers (e.g., Levinas) and some post-Jungian psychoanalysts (e.g., Hillman), the distancing from subjectivity has become problematic. The question remains as to what extent such a subject is dissolved in structure and function, with a loss of body and sensibility. In both Levinas and Hillman, the problem of the body and sensibility remains an important theme in the constitution of the Self/soul and resists abstraction[27] while, at the same time, paradoxically, it must move beyond the idea of a reified subject and/or an abstract transcendence.

The entrance problem

To this point, I have considered the paradox of the Self that is not a Self as a circular relation within which one finds the beginning and the end of the work. The paradoxical relation of Self to Self or Self to No Self reiterates the play of opposites reminiscent of the Philosophers' Stone; the Stone as Sol niger or black sun in its mercurial doubleness was said to *shine*, as a *lumen naturae*, a light of nature that is a light different from all other lights because it is not simply visible to a naturalist look, not an appearance of some metaphysical object, but rather an imaginal lumination that is also not reducible to simple subjective fantasy either. I have imagined such a light as an imaginal effulgence of the Philosophers' Stone as the experience of the Self under erasure.

Still, the question of the ~~Self~~ under erasure calls for further clarification, perhaps continuing clarification. To place an X or line through any master trope to assure that it is not simply read in the spirit of metaphysical realism is an interesting heuristic. However, I still find myself asking what such a cut implies at a lived level. Wolfgang Giegerich has in his own way addressed what has been called the entrance problem.[28] Entering into something like the complexity of the Self requires the recognition of a dividing line that runs through every individual. For him, to really recognize the Self in this way requires a radical break with one's old identity, "[a] rupture [to] one's identity is the only entrance requirement."[29] For Giegerich, "[T]he Self is real only to the extent that the ego has been negated, [crossed out], overcome; stretching the point, one might even say it exists only as a reality 'over the ego's dead body.'"[30] Here one might imagine that the "sous rature" of Heidegger and the dividing line that runs through the ~~Self~~ requires a hurtful cut, a narcissistic offense that introduces the not-Self into the Self. In this way, for Giegerich, "sous rature" becomes an existential violence; a discontinuity has entered into identity.[31] This violence implicit in the ~~Self~~ is life's existential price for a larger personality, what the alchemists have called the *opus contra naturam*, the work against nature that is also the dissolution of the *unio naturalis*.[32]

It is interesting that for the alchemists both the establishment and the overcoming of the *unio mentalis* have been gruesomely symbolized by the act of beheading. Jung writes:

> Beheading is significant symbolically as the separation of the "under-standing" from the "great suffering and grief" which nature inflicts on the soul. It is an emancipation of the "cogitation" which is situated in the head, a freeing of the soul from the "trammels of nature." Its pur-pose is to bring about, as in Dorn, a *unio mentalis* in the overcoming of the body.[33]

In addition, and evidently as a later operation, beheading also sym-bolizes the complete man and a movement beyond the *unio mentalis*. Edinger notes that "beheading extracts the *rotundum*, the round, com-plete man, from the empirical man. The head or skull becomes the round vessel of transformation."[34] Edinger refers to such a transformation: "In one text it was the head of the black Osiris or Ethiopian that, when boiled, turned into gold."[35] Here the golden head anticipates the "completeness," or, perhaps more accurately, the complexity of the Philosophers' Stone.

For Giegerich following Hegel, such a move of negation of the ego "is not to be confused with a simple, undialectical subversion, which is some-thing that modern man delights in."[36] Giegerich writes,

> Being on the edge of a sword or having settled on the very threshold implies to also be on the other side of the threshold. What I am talking about is the *accomplished* negation . . . the negation of the natural self already *having taken* place, and secondly it refers to the perfection or completion of the negation, i.e., to a negation that goes all the way and therefore does not even stop at negating itself (in the sense of 'nega-tion of the negation' [Hegel]).[37]

This negation of negation requires "a fundamental shift of the center of gravity . . . from the habitual personality to a *non*-ego, a real Other *in us*."[38] Giegerich sees this existential shift in the sense of Self as requiring a break in our ordinary comfortable "logic" and a move to a greater complexity of thinking. What is required is "a much more complex dialectical logic, such as developed by HEGEL in his *Science of Logic*, which might serve as a model for the kind of abstract thought required to do justice to the

Figure 11.1 Image of the skull as representing the *mortificatio* process in this use of Eve. From the "Miscellanea d'alchimia," 14th century manuscript.

Source: Public domain.

complexities of the plight of the modern soul."[39] For Giegerich, psychology needs the "labor of the concept" to do justice to alchemy and psychology.

Magee amplifies the importance of Hegel's contribution by noting that he was "the World-Historical Alchemist" as the producer of "the

Philosopher's Stone, the *lapis aethereus* or, as it was known to the Germans, *der Stein der Weisen*."[40] He notes that "[t]he place of transformation is represented in the *Phenomenology* as Golgotha, the Place of the Skull (*die Schädelstätte*)."[41] Magee further states that "the alchemical retort was sometimes a skull, and the *caput mortuum* was symbolized by the skull."[42]

Hegel uses the term *caput mortuum* several times in both the *Encyclopedia Logic* and the *Philosophy of Nature*. Edinger notes that the *caput mortuum* "was used to refer to the residue left after the distillation or sublimation of a substance."[43] O'Regan notes that it refers to the "precipitate that remains after spirit has been extracted."[44] This extract appears to correspond with the *unio mentalis*. Hegel also uses the term *caput mortuum* to describe what he calls Essence (*unio mentalis?*), but also points out that Essence (like the *unio mentalis*) is still

> a stepping-stone on the way to Concept and Absolute Idea. Essence itself is indeed a *caput mortuum* insofar as it is a *negated* provisional definition for the Absolute Idea. It "dies" or falls away, yet it is at the same time "material" used in the process of dialectic that presses on to Absolute Idea. Hegel's use of *caput mortuum* to describe Essence taken abstractly (i.e., taken on its own, in isolation from the other categories) indicates that he recognized the parallel between dialectic and alchemical transmutation: determinate negation is the *nigredo* that precedes the synthesis of *rubedo*, the philosopher's stone, or the Absolute.[45]

As such, the Absolute becomes a "goal" of the process like the Philosophers' Stone. Hegel describes his idea of the goal in the *Phenomenology of Spirit*:

> The *goal*, Absolute Knowing, or Spirit that knows itself as Spirit, has for its path the recollection of the Spirits as they are in themselves and as they accomplish the organization of their realm. Their preservation, regarded from the side of their free existence appearing in the form of contingency, is History; but regarded from the side of their [philosophically] comprehended organization, it is the Science of Knowing in the sphere of appearance: the two together, comprehended History, form alike the inwardizing and the Calvary of absolute Spirit, the

actuality, truth, and certainty of his throne, without which he would be lifeless and alone. Only

> from the chalice of this realm of spirits
> foams forth for Him his own infinitude.[46]

The absolute

In a complex and difficult passage leading to "Absolute Knowing." Hegel writes:

> In this knowing, then, Spirit has concluded the movement in which it has shaped itself, in so far as this shaping was burdened with the difference of consciousness [i.e., of the latter from its object] a difference now overcome. Spirit has won the pure element of its existence, the Notion. The content, in accordance with the *freedom* of its *being*, is the self-alienating Self, or the immediate unity of self-knowledge. The pure movement of this alienation, considered in connection with the content, constitutes the *necessity* of the content. The distinct content as *determinate*, is in relation, is not "in itself," it is its own restless process of superseding itself, or *negativity*; therefore, negativity or diversity, like free being, is also the Self; and in this self-like *form* in which existence is immediately thought, the content is the *Notion*. Spirit, therefore, having won the Notion, displays its existence and movement in this ether of its life and is *Science*.[47]

If I understand these passages as he intended, it is interesting to compare the ideas of "sous rature," the rature, the beheading, the self-negation, the self that is not the Self, with Hegel's idea of the "self-alienating self" and knowledge of the Notion. The *Notion* is not a static moment, but rather what he calls a pure moment of an "alienation" and restlessness that is also a vitality, a sublation that is also a continuing dialectical moment. The achievement of Absolute Knowing can also know itself as Spirit and as a mimesis of spirits that in memory can be recollected and organized.

It appears that for Hegel this mimetic organization can be preserved and as such can both appear contingently as a historical process, but also philosophically as "Absolute Knowing," as a "Science" of appearances. For Hegel at the end of the *Phenomenology*, it appears that these "two" perspectives of historical Science can be brought together and understood as "Absolute Spirit." Hegel uses the word Absolute in many different contexts with different meanings. Often he uses it adjectively, "for example in 'Absolute Idea,' 'Absolute Knowing,' 'Absolute Religion,' 'Absolute Spirit,'"and so on.[48] "He utilizes the substantive, 'the Absolute' less frequently."[49] The adjectival and substantive uses of the Absolute have important philosophical implications. Magee points out:

> The term "absolute" has a long history in German philosophy. Nicholas of Cusa in his *Of Learned Ignorance* (*De Docta Ignorantia*, 1440) used the term *absolutum* to mean God, understood as a being that transcends all finite determinations: the *coincidentia oppositorum* (coincidence of opposites). Schelling's use of "Absolute" is remarkably similar to Cusa's. For Schelling, the Absolute is the "indifference point" beyond the distinction of subject and object, or any other distinction. In the famous Preface to *The Phenomenology of Spirit* Hegel rejects this conception of the Absolute [as noted above], referring to it derisively as "the night in which all cows are black." Hegel means that when the Absolute is conceived simply as the transcendent unity of all things (or as the cancellation of all difference) it really amounts to an idea devoid of all content. It is terribly easy to say "in this world definite distinctions abide – but in the Absolute all is one." But what does this really mean?[50]

Rockmore points out that in spite of the many ways Hegel uses the term "Absolute," that his position

> convey[s] a single, central insight: philosophy culminates in the comprehension of experience as a structured whole, or totality, whose interrelations are known with necessity. As early as the *Differenzschrift*, he defends a normative view of philosophy intended to "overcome" difference through speculative unity. This same basic approach runs throughout his later thought, in the treatments of absolute knowing in the *Phenomenology of Spirit*, of the absolute idea in the *Encyclopedia Logic*, and of absolute spirit in the *Philosophy of Spirit*.
>
>   He depicts the absolute differently in these different texts as a function of what he is doing in each of them. In his account of the science of the experience of consciousness in the *Phenomenology of Spirit*, he

describes the stages leading from sense certainty to absolute know-ing, from the poorest, most abstract, unmediated or immediate experi-ence to the richest, most concrete, fully mediated experience. In the *Encyclopedia Logic*, he characterizes the abstract form of science. In the *Philosophy of Spirit*, at the end of the *Encyclopedia*, he portrays the concrete result of the process whose moments traverse logic, then nature, before ending in spirit that knows and knows that it knows, a process which culminates in philosophy as the highest, final, and unsurpassable form of absolute spirit.[51]

Rockmore goes on to point out some presuppositions of Hegel's position, notably that "the subject is free, and reason is universal." It presupposes as well that the subject-object identity specifically includes subjective, objec-tive, and absolute perspectives.[52] On this basis, Rockmore like Magee asks: "How are we to interpret Hegel's understanding of the absolute?"[53]

Rockmore sets the stage for understanding the complexity of the Abso-lute by placing Hegel's philosophy in relation to Kant. He cites Hegel's "own reluctance to separate philosophy from the history of philosophy"[54] and goes on to compare Kant's idea of the thing-in-itself to Hegel's abso-lute idealism. He notes that absolute idealism, like Kant's thing-in-itself, "combines epistemological and ontological dimensions."[55]

Kant, however, maintains that we do not know things as they are, as merely objects of thought, but only as they appear. For Kant, "the thing-in-itself functions in two ways: epistemologically as a limit to knowledge, and ontologically as a causal principle that can without contradiction be understood as giving rise to the phenomena of experience."[56] Kant claims "that although we cannot *know* these objects as things-in-themselves, we must yet be in a position at least to *think* them as things-in-themselves; otherwise we should be landed in the absurd conclusion that there can be appearance without any*thing* that appears."[57] Rockmore then goes on to make a most important distinction in ways of interpreting Hegel's view of Absolute Knowing that the idea of the absolute can be interpreted in two ways: "either ontologically or epistemologically."[58]

For Rockmore, "[a]n ontological reading of Hegel makes the absolute into an ultimate ontological principle" comparable "to the late Heidegger's reading of being."[59] For Hegel as for Heidegger, history is intelligible only because it is literally constituted by the unfolding of an absolute.[60] Read-ing Hegel ontologically, the Absolute might be understood "as the ultimate ground or source of all being."[61] For Magee, it was this approach that was present in the search for the *archē*. This search for absolute ground existed "right from the beginning of the Western philosophical tradition in the Pre-Socratic philosopher Thales who declared that 'water' is the source of all that is."[62]

For Rockmore, reading Hegel ontologically is "erroneous" and he rejects it citing three reasons, the first of which is that the ontological reading is "out of date."[63] Second, that an ontological reading of Hegel interpreting "the absolute as a hidden cause of history implies that Hegel intended to describe the world as it really is, what James calls the really real and Putnam calls the furniture of the universe."[64] For Rockmore, in our time we can "no longer defend any reading of Hegel's theory resembling a claim to tell us about the world in independence of us."[65] Thirdly, Rockmore claims that any ontological reading of Hegel

> is inconsistent with Hegelian theory itself. If absolute idealism, like philosophy itself, can make no presuppositions, if it cannot admit merely postulated entities, Hegel cannot consistently assert that the absolute is the final cause of history. Now it may be that this is the case, that history in fact records the unfolding of the absolute which is known as its result. Yet were that the case, that fact about history could not be known. For we cannot know this on a priori grounds, and no experience is sufficient to teach us that the absolute is at the basis of experience.[66]

Ontologically implying the basis of our experience outside experience remains for Rockmore unintelligible. In another place, Rockmore makes the point even more poignantly. For Rockmore, "[u]nlike [Kant's] critical philosophy, and unlike its rationalist and empiricist predecessors, philosophical reflection, in which speculation takes itself as its object, has nothing to do with making indefeasible cognitive claims," such as *the absolute*'s existing in some transcendental way outside of time and place.[67]

For Rockmore, then, any ontological interpretation must address the relationship between thought and being. With regard to this issue, Rockmore has noted that in the above regard, Hegel's thought is incomplete in a significant sense; manifestly "unable to demonstrate the required unity of thought and being in terms of circularity."[68] If philosophical knowledge is "presuppositionless, it cannot yield knowledge in the full sense."[69] For

Rockmore, "if knowledge is apodictic, it cannot result from presuppositionless theory."[70]

> The assumption of the inquiry into knowledge has always been
> that thought knows being, although as Hegel knew, this assump-
> tion never has been demonstrated. Hegel's own attempt to provide
> this demonstration fails, since as we have seen, it is in tension with
> his view that philosophy is necessarily presuppositionless, therefore
> circular, and accordingly unable to escape from the circle of thought
> and being.
>   It is perhaps paradoxical, but unquestionably the case, that a striking
> consequence of Hegel's endeavor to demonstrate that reason can be
> self-subsistent, that thought is identical with being, is to show that this
> result cannot be established through reason. Hegel, the archrational-
> ist, unwittingly but definitively puts an end to the rationalist form of
> the epistemological enterprise as concerns the full emancipation of
> reason. For he shows the necessity of assuming the indemonstrable
> validity of the claim of thought to know being as an unavoidable pre-
> supposition of all epistemology.[71]

The inability to complete the circle between thought and being is also
held by noted Hegelian scholar Donald Phillip Verene. Verene notes that
"Once the world of the Idea is entered, there is no exit back to what is there
before and outside the Idea." Nature will always lose its independence
and "remain a function of the Idea, no matter how cleverly the dialectics
of its reality are explained."[72] Verene focuses on one sentence of Hegel's
corpus that for him remains suspect. "It is a sentence that has bothered me
since I first read it thirty-four years ago."[73] It is Hegel's claim in the last
moments of the *Science of Logic* that

> The passing over [of the Idea into nature] is thus to be grasped here in
> this way, that the Idea *freely releases* itself in its absolute confidence
> and calm.
>   Das Übergehen ist also hier vielmehr so zu fassen, daß die Idee sich
> selbst *frei entläßt*, ihrer absolut sicher und in sich ruhend.
>   Or, as he puts it in the *Encyclopedia Logic*, the Idea resolves freely
> to *release out of itself* . . . the *immediate Idea* as its reflection, or itself
> as nature.

Die *unmittelbare Idee* als ihren Widerschein, sich als *Natur* frei *aus sich zu entlassen.*[74]

For Verene, "[i]f light can be thrown on how the Idea becomes nature, the whole of the system will be illuminated."[75] He thinks these sentences are too often passed over by commentators and no commentary has solved it to his satisfaction. He calls attention to two statements: namely, that "Hegel says that something is *for* consciousness – namely, the *in-itself* – and the knowing (*Wissen*), or the being (*Sein*) of the object for consciousness, is itself *for consciousness* another moment."[76] For Verene, there are simply two "objects" of consciousness and "there is no specifiable relationship or principle that can be used to describe the passage from one moment to the other."[77] Verene struggles with this "twoness," wanting to speak of them together as a whole, but realizing that to do so does not constitute a "unity."[78] He notes: "The object for consciousness, the object with being-for-itself, is just as ambiguous because its being is immediately transposed into a new in-itself." A third thing, a moment that would truly hold all together, is always just out of reach.[79] For Verene, consciousness lives in this kind of ambiguity which is in continuous motion. We live in the fantasy that this ambiguity can be resolved. But such hopes, as we learn from Hegel's *Phenomenology* are in a continuing play between hope and despair and we live with the illusion of wholeness. Then, for Verene, comes the wisdom of absolute knowing.

For Verene, "[t]he achievement of absolute knowing is the realization that all the stages up to it have refused to accept the ambiguity of experience."[80] Absolute Knowing then for Verene is the acceptance of ambiguity that the conjunction of opposites, "the two-in-the-one, and the one" are an equally necessary "andness."[81] For Verene, Absolute Knowing is thus an "ironic and melancholic wisdom."[82]

Verene then considers Hegel's movement from the *Phenomenology* to the *Logic*, a move "in which consciousness freely goes forth as thought."[83] The Logic attempts to be a pure science that overcomes the "and" and the "two" "through the power of the Idea."[84] Verene asks: "Can the 'and,' if not overcome on the level of phenomena, be grasped in thought such that the doubleness, the ambiguity that is present in experience, is surmounted?"[85] While the *Logic* seems to be an asylum for the philosopher from experience, "there is still nature to worry about."[86] Verene notes "that the movement from Idea to nature . . . is not '*a process of becoming*' (*ein Gewordensein*), nor is it properly a 'transition' (*Übergang*) such as exists within the dialectic of the *Logic*, e.g., as when '*the subjective end becomes life*.'"[87] For Hegel, the movement "to nature is an absolute liberation. . ., a freedom . . . that the [Idea] . . . commands."[88] For Verene, however, the question remains just how the idea "goes forth freely as nature?" He notes

> [j]ust when the forms of spirit seem to be getting on so well, nature reminds us of its own free existence in its primal scene of space and time. Within the human animal itself is always the day of the locust, the "labor of the negative" come to dinner, always an unwelcome guest.[89]

Following Rockmore, and with Verene's recognition of the limits of the dialectic to complete the circle of thought and being, we return to what we have called the yellowing of the work, the spoiling of the *unio mentalis*, the cut, wound, the line, and the always dark aspects of life itself – the gap, abyss, unconscious from which there is no complete shadowless freedom. For Verene it is "[t]he reality of nature" which "has been there from the beginning, as the double of spirit – the ever-present *Ansich* to spirit's reality 'for us.'"[90]

Finally for Verene, the failure to resolve the twoness, if it is claimed to be "resolved" at all, seems to depend on an ancient attitude not unlike the one held by the Plato of the *Timaeus* – "the ancient *techne* of a 'likely story,'"[91]

> that old humanist faculty of *ingenium* [ingenuity] – the ability to perceive a resemblance between two things, which in science results in the formation of hypotheses, in the arts results in the formation of the metaphor, and in philosophy results in the formation of dialectic.[92]

For Verene, without this attitude which he sees as essential for wit, humor, and irony, we could not understand Hegel.[93]

> Without the sense of the incongruous, Hegel has no science. His dialectic depends upon the presence of humor in the reader's own existence. *Ingenium* makes the incongruous congruous, without eliminating its ambiguity. What I have called "doubling" is no mystery to anyone

who has developed the capacity of *ingenium*. But it is not a feature of literal-mindedness.[94]

For Verene,

> *Ingenium* connotes at once the power both to form imagistically and to form through an intellectual principle. It contains *both* a sense of imagistic and conceptual forming. Through ingenuity a new and needed object is produced through a reshaping of what is already at hand. In other words ingenuity is a way of doing something that gets its method immediately from the content before it. Each time it makes up its method immediately. It is always doing something for which there is no method. Yet each time such a thing is done it is grasped as a result of ingenuity. Hegel's method of the double *Ansich* is like this.[95]

For Jung, like for Hegel and Verene, the attempt to make the incongruous congruous without losing ambiguity and real difference is found in his notion of Mercurius duplex. Jung describes his view of Mercurius in the following passage:

> He is *duplex* and his main characteristic is duplicity. It is said of him that he "runs round the earth and enjoys the company of the good and the wicked." He is "two dragons," the "twin," made of "two natures" or "two substances." He is the "giant of twofold substances." . . . The two substances of Mercurius are thought of as dissimilar, sometimes opposed; as the dragon he is "winged and wingless."[96]
>
> Because of his united double nature Mercurius is described as hermaphroditic. Sometimes his body is said to be masculine and his soul feminine, sometimes the reverse. The *Rosarium philosophorum*, for example, has both versions. As *vulgaris* he is the dead masculine body, but as "our" Mercurius he is feminine, spiritual, alive, and life giving.[97]

Just as for Hegel, the lifeless universality perishes into self-consciousness; so self-consciousness exhibits a life-giving spirit. The relationship of Jung's "imagistic" version of Mercurius to Hegel's complex notion of self-consciousness needs further elaboration, but I believe the parallel is compelling. Is it possible that Hegel's notion of self-consciousness could be seen as a concept of what Jung calls Mercurius duplex, and that Mercurius

duplex is an image of what Hegel calls self-consciousness? Both are dialectical and circular notions, and the circle was an important archetypal
structure for both Hegel and Jung. I believe the complex circularity of
"image" and "idea" requires further reflection. One might say that Jung's
version of a dialectic process is described in his notion of the transcendent
function. Sanford Drob, a Jungian scholar, writes:

> Hegel's dialectic and Jung's transcendent function each endeavor to
> unify opposites that remain unreconciled within everyday thought and
> in what Hegel refers to as the "understanding." The simple distinc-
> tion between these thinkers is that while for Hegel the reconciliation
> occurs in *thought*, for Jung it occurs and can only occur unconsciously
> via the *imagination*.[98]

It would appear that the "dialectical" approach of both Jung and Hegel
each emphasized one side of the *ingenium*. However, for Drob, the contrast between Hegel and Jung is more complex. Drob turns to Hegel's
Introduction to his "Lectures on Aesthetics," where Hegel adopts a view
of the artistic image that comes quite close to Jung's understanding of the
role of symbols and the imagination in the transcendent function. Drob
writes:

> In the *Lectures [on Aesthetics]*, Hegel holds that *art expresses ideas in
> sensuous, material form*. Indeed, he holds that art expresses the *Abso-
> lute Idea* of *Geist* (mind/spirit) alienating itself in nature (matter and
> sensuous form) and then returning to itself self-consciously as spirit.
> For Hegel, in art, as in religion and philosophy, mind comes to recog-
> nize itself. However, while art expresses the Idea in sensuous form,
> art cannot result from a conscious, "thinking" process. Hegel writes:
>
> > it would be possible in poetical creation to try and proceed by first
> > apprehending the theme to be treated as a prosaic thought, and then
> > by putting it into pictorial ideas, and into rhyme, and so forth; so
> > that the pictorial element would simply be hung upon the abstract
> > reflections as an ornament or decoration. Such a process could only
> > produce bad poetry, for in it there would be operative as two sepa-
> > rate activities that which in artistic production has its right place
> > only as undivided unity.

For Hegel, in "artistic *imagination* . . . the rational element . . . extrudes itself into consciousness, but yet does not array before it what it bears within itself till it does so in sensuous form."[99]

Hegel puts it this way, according to Drob:

the productive imagination of the artist is the imagination of a great mind and heart, the apprehension and creation of ideas and of shapes, and, indeed, the exhibition of the profoundest and most universal interests in the definite sensuous mode of pictorial representation.[100]

For Hegel, however, thought and reflection have moved us only beyond art and a religious, mythological view of the world. "Hegel considers and rejects the notion, later endorsed by Jung, that the life of the mind is 'disfigured and slain' by thought. . . 'as the means of grasping what has life, man rather cut himself off from . . . his purpose.'"[101]

For Hegel, "thought – to think – is precisely that in which the mind has its innermost and essential nature. In gaining this thinking consciousness concerning itself and its products, the mind is behaving according to its essential nature. . . .

Drob concludes:

While Jung clearly held that the "transcendent function" is a religious/ psychological as opposed to an artistic function, I believe that the issue between Hegel and Jung . . . rests on the role of the "image" (artistic, symbolic, mythological) in the contemporary (post-Hegelian) development of *Geist*. Jung was wrong to accuse Hegel of failing to grasp the role of the imagination in psychic development – Hegel grasped it, I think, but held that the imagination, which expressed nascent thought in the form of art and religion, had been largely superseded by philosophy, by thought in its "purest" form.[102]

This is Hegel's position, but for Drob it is insufficiently dialectical. I am not exactly sure what Drob means here, but for me, as noted above, the dialectic continues – beyond art and religion is thought, but then from thought back into the images of art and religion and symbolic thinking.

The idea of a circular rather than a linear dialectic is closer to what for me remains a non-reducible function of the imaginal life. At the end of her book *Hegel's Theory of Imagination*, Jennifer Bates writes:

> If imagination is central to the movement of *Aufhebung* – if it is, indeed, the inception of it – then we never get beyond it. What the imagination holds, and what it *is* today, is the key to understanding the depth of our time. And if we have learned anything from Hegel, we must think it through carefully.[103]

If I have interpreted Bates correctly, and I'm not sure I have or that she would agree with me, her position would be close or parallel to Kathleen Magnus.

Magnus states that "Hegel conceives of a wholly self-determining spirit that is *at once* open to the difference of the 'other,'"[104] but "does not leave its sensuous dimension behind as a mere preliminary stage to its fulfillment; spirit actually incorporates the sensuous into its absolute dimension through its various acts of symbolization."[105] In addition, the "symbolic element remains in tension with the clarity of philosophical thought."[106]

Paul Ricoeur had already noted that "Hegel fights against any conception of the Absolute which would 'lack the seriousness, the suffering, the patience, and the labour of the negative.'"[107] For him as for Magnus, a close reading of Hegel suggests the need for "mediation which entails the dialectic between determinate shapes, the identifiable patterns, and the flux which shatters all fixed forms. We have *both* to dwell in determinate shapes and also accompany their dissolution into further different shapes."[108] Ricoeur raises the question of whether it is "possible for a human mind to 'cease to think in pictures' and to keep for philosophy the inner thrust which projects figurative thinking toward speculative thought? Such is the quandary that the philosophy of religion of the *Phenomenology* left unsolved and that" Hegel took up in the Berlin *Lectures* "by following a less antagonistic stance as regards picture-thinking."[109] Ricoeur understands

> the last pages of the 1831 Berlin *Lectures* in this sense: becoming more and more aware of the mutual relevance of religion and philosophy, Hegel had to overcome his own distrust for picture-thinking in order to secure the future of philosophy itself. Finally, absolute knowledge

affords no supplement of thought, but is no less and no more than the conceptual light within which each cultural context, and finally each religious representation, thinks itself.[110]

Ricoeur notes that absolute thought "is less a final stage than" it is "the process thanks to which all shapes and all stages remain thoughtful. Absolute knowledge, consequently, is the thoughtfulness of picture thinking."[111] Is this what imagistically we earlier called the "light of darkness itself"?

At the end of my essay in *Spring*,[112] I noted that, perhaps in the end, idea and image may best be spoken about in a couple of ways: as an alchemical *circulatio* or a monstrous *coniunctio*. Both might be thought of as metaphors that attempt to speak the unspeakable. The need to attempt this speech is a continuing historical process, a process undertaken by Hegel. Absolute Knowledge, therefore, is not a supplement of knowledge, but the thoughtfulness of all modes that generate it. "As a result, we have the possibility of reinterpreting the hermeneutics of religious thinking as an endless process thanks to which representative and speculative thought keep generating one another."[113] This leads to a focus on "the inner dynamism which keeps directing figurative thought towards speculative thought, without ever abolishing the narrative and symbolic features of the figurative mode."[114] For the sake of completing the circle, I would add that speculative thought also always discovers metaphor in its midst.

It is this tension that continues to animate Hegel's notion of Absolute Knowing. For Ricoeur, as it was for Magnus, spirit never literally "reaches the point of 'simply being' absolute."[115] Rather "[i]ts absoluteness lies *within* its self-creating, self-determining act. Spirit *becomes* absolute," but the emphasis is on the dynamic of becoming.[116] "It is never absolute 'once and for all.'"[117] That is, it can never "sustain its absoluteness on the level of immediacy, but must continually create and recreate, present and *represent*, itself. In other words, *in order to preserve its self-identity*, spirit must remain in self-differentiating motion."[118] If one takes seriously that Absolute Knowing is never literally absolute "once and for all" and always remains in "self-differentiated motion," then one must also conclude with Rockmore that Absolute Knowing "points toward the historical nature of the process of knowledge."[119] For Rockmore, Hegel's understanding and knowing is "a thoroughly historical conception of knowledge claims indexed to time and place, hence to the historical moment."[120] "Claims to know are always dependent on theories which are relative to the *historical* moment."[121] And again, for Hegel, "we cannot understand knowledge other than from the perspective of human being. . . . [and] if we understand the subject as a real human being, hence as *historical*, then we must understand knowledge as a historical process"[122] in which image and thought are intimately interrelated, co-dependent, and necessary for the generative movement of the historical soul.[123]

It seems to me that if, on the one hand, the circularity of self-consciousness and of image and idea are archetypal structures, they are also always historical. "The realized concept of spirit is precisely this paradox"[124] and Absolute Knowing, while it is absolute, is always also historical. Rockmore's emphasis on history is echoed by James Hillman who states: "I shall ride this horse of history until it drops, for I submit that history has become the Great Repressed."[125]

Notes

1 Portions of this chapter are modified from sections of my book, Marlan, *The Black Sun*.
2 Ibid., 125.
3 Ibid., 239–240.
4 Ibid., 240.
5 Ibid.
6 Ibid.
7 Jung, *Memories*, 379.
8 Brooke, *Jung and Phenomenology*, 99.
9 Miller, "Nothing Almost Sees Miracles!," 15.
10 Jung, *Mysterium Coniunctionis (CW14)*, §190; quoted by Miller, "Nothing Almost Sees Miracles!," 14.
11 Miller, "Nothing Almost Sees Miracles!," 13.
12 Ibid., 15.
13 Kelly, "Atman, Anatta, and Transpersonal Psychology," 188–199.
14 Ibid., 198.
15 Jung also uses the word "complementarity," which for him was a bit too mechanical and functional and for which compensation is "a psychological refinement." (Jung, *The Structure and Dynamics of the Psyche [CW8]*, §545, footnote 3).
16 Hillman, *The Myth of Analysis*, 207–208.
17 Hillman, "Peaks and Vales," 67.
18 Lacan's *petit a* is a profoundly polyvalent concept and the subject of literally thousands of pages of exegesis in Lacan's work. That said, Bruce Fink discusses it in terms of

the residue of symbolization – the real that remains, insists, and exsists after or despite symbolization – as the traumatic cause, and as that which interrupts the smooth functioning of law and the automatic unfolding of the signifying chain. (Fink, The Lacanian Subject, 83)

19 Jung, *Mysterium Coniunctionis (CW14)*, §117.
20 Ibid.

21 Sim, *Derrida and the End of History*, 33.
22 Hillman, *Alchemical Psychology*, 253.
23 Critchley, "Prolegomena to Any Post-Deconstructive Subjectivity," 25.
24 Foucault, *Order of Things*, 387.
25 Stein, *Jung's Map of the Soul*, 152.
26 Ibid.
27 Levinas, for instance, criticizes Heidegger's transsubjective concept of Dasein by not-
    ing that "Dasein is never hungry" (Critchley, "Prolegomena," 30), and Hillman chooses
    to rely on the word "soul" as opposed to Self because it retains a connection with the
    body, with physical and emotional concerns above love and loss, life and death. "It is
    experienced as a living force having a physical location" and is more easily expressed
    in psychological, metaphoric, and poetic descriptions (Hillman, *The Myth of Analysis*,
    207). Both Levinas and Hillman share a number of overlapping concerns. Both are
    critical of the primacy of a theoretical model of consciousness in which the subject
    maintains an objectifying relation to the world mediated through representation. Both
    support a movement toward a re-envisioned subject as an embodied being of flesh and
    blood, a subject who is fully sentient and in touch with sensation and who is "vulner-
    able" and "open to wounding" (Levinas, *Otherwise Than Being or Beyond Essence*,
    15), filled with "*jouissance* and *joie de vivre*" (Critchley, "Prolegomena," 29). In addi-
    tion, both Levinas and Hillman share a unique, ethical sensibility. For Levinas, ethics
    is fundamental, and the entire thrust of his *Otherwise than Being* is to "found ethical
    subjectivity in sensibility and to describe sensibility as a proximity to the other"(Ibid.,
    30). What this means for Levinas is very different from our usual understanding of eth-
    ics. For him, "Ethics is not an obligation toward the other mediated through" formal
    principles or good conscience: Moral consciousness is not an experience of values but
    an access to exterior being – to what he calls the Other. From a psychological point
    of view, this begins to sound like the capacity to see beyond our narcissistic self-
    enclosure and to actually have contact with something outside of our own egos. The
    subject is subject to something that exceeds us (Ibid., 26). The "deep structure of sub-
    jective experience" – the responsibility or responsivity to the other – is what Levinas
    calls Psyche (Ibid., 31). Likewise, the thrust of Hillman's archetypal psychology is a
    movement beyond the narcissistic enclosure in which the aim is a "psychotherapeutic
    cure of 'me,'" in which all the me-ness has been cooked out of our emotions (Hillman,
    Alchemical Psychology, 255). This comparison of Levinas with Hillman is not meant
    in any way to equate their thought. A real comparison of their work would require an
    independent study of what each thinker means by terms they use in common.
28 See Giegerich, *The Soul's Logical Life*, 13–38.
29 Ibid., 17.
30 Ibid., 18.
31 Ibid., 18–19.
32 Ibid., 20.
33 Jung, *Mysterium Coniunctionis (CW14)*, §730.
34 Edinger, *Anatomy*, 167.
35 Ibid.
36 Giegerich, *The Soul's Logical Life*, 22.
37 Ibid.
38 Ibid., 26; emphasis of "in us" is mine.
39 Ibid.
40 Magee, *Hegel and the Hermetic Tradition*, 211.
41 Ibid., 212.
42 Ibid.
43 Edinger, *Anatomy*, 167.
44 Magee, *Hegel and the Hermetic Tradition*, 165.

45 Ibid.
46 Hegel, *Phenomenology*, 493, §808; brackets in original.
47 Ibid., 490–491, §805; brackets in original.
48 Magee, *The Hegel Dictionary*, 19.
49 Ibid.
50 Ibid.
51 Rockmore, *On Hegel's Epistemology*, 62.
52 Ibid., 62–63.
53 Ibid., 63.
54 Ibid.
55 Ibid.
56 Ibid.
57 Kant, *Critique of Pure Reason*, B xxvi–xxvii, 27; quoted by Rockmore, *On Hegel's Epistemology*, 63; emphasis of "thing" is mine.
58 Rockmore, *On Hegel's Epistemology*, 63.
59 Ibid.
60 Ibid.
61 Magee, *The Hegel Dictionary*, 19.
62 Ibid.
63 Rockmore, *On Hegel's Epistemology*, 63.
64 Ibid., 64.
65 Ibid.
66 Ibid.
67 Rockmore, *Kant and Idealism*, 78.
68 Rockmore, *Hegel's Circular Epistemology*, 178.
69 Ibid.
70 Ibid.
71 Ibid., 180–181.
72 Verene, "Hegel's Nature," 212.
73 Ibid.
74 Ibid.; brackets in Verene's text.
75 Ibid., 213.
76 Ibid., 215.
77 Ibid., 216.
78 Ibid.
79 Ibid.
80 Ibid., 218.
81 Ibid.
82 Ibid.
83 Ibid.
84 Ibid., 219.
85 Ibid.
86 Ibid.
87 Ibid., 220.
88 Ibid.
89 Ibid., 221.
90 Ibid.
91 Ibid., 215.
92 Ibid., 223.
93 Ibid.
94 Ibid. For Verene as for others before him, humor remains a quality valuable for coming to terms with Hegel. I cannot engage this issue in this context, but a fuller reflection on this theme can be found in Flay, *Hegel and His Critic*. See particularly the essay

"Hegel, Derrida and Bataille's Laughter," by Joseph C. Flay with a Commentary by Judith Butler, 163–178.
95 Verene, "Hegel's Recollection," 20; emphasis mine.
96 Jung, *Alchemical Studies (CW13)*, §267.
97 Ibid., §268.
98 Drob, personal communication, May 12, 2014.
99 Ibid.
100 Ibid.
101 Ibid.
102 Ibid.
103 Bates, *Hegel's Theory of Imagination*, 153.
104 Magnus, *Hegel and the Symbolic Mediation of Spirit*, 25; emphasis mine.
105 Ibid., 241.
106 Ibid., 242.
107 Ricoeur, "The Status of Vorstellung," 81.
108 Ibid.; emphasis mine.
109 Ibid., 84.
110 Ibid., 86.
111 Ibid.
112 Marlan, "From the Black Sun."
113 Ricoeur, "The Status of Vorstellung," 86.
114 Ibid.
115 Magnus, *Hegel and the Symbolic Mediation of Spirit*, 245.
116 Ibid.
117 Ibid.
118 Ibid.
119 Rockmore, *In Kant's Wake*, 169.
120 Ibid., 168.
121 Ibid., 169; emphasis mine.
122 Rockmore, *Cognition*, 216. Emphasis mine.
123 For a further discussion, see Rockmore, *Cognition*, 210.
124 Magnus, *Hegel and the Symbolic Mediation of Spirit*, 245.
125 Hillman, "Peaks and Vales," 62.

Chapter 12

Spirit and soul

Image and idea, spirit and soul, have been imagined in different ways and in differing constellations. What has become clear to me is that they are not clear-cut opposites. In the Introduction to Karin de Boer's study of Hegel, she notes that Hegel denounced

> the tendency of modernity to treat contrary determinations and clear-cut oppositions. Whereas modern thought, in his view, unduly assumed the relative independence of contraries such as necessity and freedom, the inner and the outer, essence and appearance, he believed that "the sole intent of philosophy consists in resolving such rigidified oppositions." Only thus might it achieve insight into the *dynamic unity* constitutive of thought, nature, and history.[1]

De Boer's thesis sheds additional light on a number of my own concerns raised above, namely, the circular process of Spirit and Soul, image and thought, and the optimism of Hegel's march to the absolute as a linear view of history, as necessary progress. For me, progress remains a highly ambivalent notion and is always in need of a disclosure of values and context.

In my study of the black sun, I challenged the optimistic idea that oppositions can always be overcome, surpassed, or sublated. The tragic dimension of Sol niger showed, at least in individual lives if not in culture, that the tragic dimensions of life resisted, if not refused, to be uplifted. I also noted above that my interpretation of Hegel was that he was not naïvely optimistic in bypassing tragedy, that he did existentially suffer the impact of the negative. As Desmond has noted, for Hegel, "[t]he human spirit is

DOI: 10.4324/9781003215905-13

an agony before evil"[2] and yet, for Hegel, and Desmond as well as for De Boer, the "sway of the negative" demands further, if not continuing, reflection with regard to the tragic sides of life.[3] De Boer writes:

> Hegel's speculative science as a whole testifies to a deep tension between two different strands, namely, a tragic and a dialectical strand. Whereas, as I hope to show, the dialectical strand allowed Hegel to develop a comprehensive philosophical system, this book deploys its tragic strand to develop a contemporary criticism of Hegel's philosophy, and modernity alike.[4]

For De Boer,

> Hegel could only resolve the conceptual oppositions constitutive of modern thought by recoiling, as it were, from the implications of his early conception of tragic conflicts.[5]

While I don't think recoiling is a fair word, I think De Boer is referring to the optimism of Hegel's dialectic which for her is in tension with another aspect of Hegel's awareness which she believes is not given enough recognition as playing an equal role in the dialectic itself. This aspect is Hegel's recognition of the "tragic," which for De Boer cannot be fully sublated, but remains "entangled" with the "advance" of spirit and constitutes an equal principle, a "logic of entanglement" on par with Hegel's notion of "absolute negativity." De Boer's view of "tragic negativity"[6] fits with my original concerns about the tragic aspects of the black sun, while Hegel's more optimistic view of logical negativity, which drives the dialectic, expresses the shine of Sol niger and its illumination in spirit, which inspired me to continue my reflection beyond the black sun to the shine of darkness itself and to the Philosophers' Stone.

Tarrying with the negative

Perhaps De Boer's contribution in my terms would be to recognize that as the Philosophers' Stone moves toward a shining whiteness, it bears its darkness; brings its darkness with it as an essential aspect of its differentiated wholeness. In this sense, the Stone truly tarries with the negative and continues to "hesitate before the magical power that turns death into being."[7] Tarrying here has less the meaning of a temporal hiatus and more of an archetypal principle of hesitancy of "being of two minds" which should not be identified with stasis as such or with any fixed principle. Without trying to elaborate the philosophical structure of tarrying or hesitation, I would simply like to suggest that an attitude of hesitation enriches the dialectical process and theoretical speculation. It also deepens interiority and psychological space – which for James Hillman increases through slowness. In accord with the alchemists, Hillman refers to "patience as a first quality of soul."[8] Now this psychological recognition does not yet address the fundamental place of tarrying or hesitation with the problematics of the dialectic raised by De Boer and others, but it is important to note that "[w]e live in a time of rush."[9]

"[C]ontemporary societies have little or no time for metaphysical pondering. . . . even the privileged, academic philosopher is often caught in the hurry, too harried by professional obligations to have enough time or inclination to think."[10] Even philosophers have been infected by what Carl Honoré has called the "cult of speed."[11] Honoré quotes British psychologist Guy Claxton who states: "We have developed an inner psychology of speed, of saving time and maximizing efficiency. . . "[12] In his book, *In Praise of Slowness*, Honoré describes his own life as having "turned into an exercise in hurry" and notes that American physician Larry Dossey "coined the term 'time-sickness' to describe the obsessive belief that 'time is getting away, that there isn't enough of it, and that you must peddle faster and faster to keep up.'"[13]

Desmond notes that in our time philosophers

> risk the seduction of what I will call "thought-bites:" positions ready prepared for speed reading, prepackaged for mental digestion. Our quick attention to ideas, more or less familiar, offers a satisfaction but this is short-lived. Little nourished, we seek the stimulus of more quick "thought-bites" to keep the hunger of spirit at bay. A philosopher has to be prepared to stand aside in the rush – and to let that hunger of spirit speak. The willingness to think long, with a discerning taste for what sustains thought – these are necessary for philosophy. To have the freedom to think one must have the time to savor thought. There is no quick or easy solution to philosophical perplexity that would give to the mind an undemanding rush of conceptual ecstasy. Philosophy can be urgent but need not be hurried. Philosophy requires the patience of

thinking. Patience of thought is especially required when, as we often find, philosophy does not dispel our perplexity but deepens it.[14]

For Desmond, philosophy must acknowledge its own plurivocity. "It does not just have one voice, say, that of a dominating univocal logicism."[15] Here Desmond is referring to his multiple reflections on Hegel and dialectics in his book, but this plurivocity as well can be seen to refer to the dialectical tensions implicit in both philosophical and psychological dialectics – personal, cultural, and historical voices that, in their dialogue with the philosopher or psychologist, slow the pace to reach ontological convictions.

Following Jung and Hillman, plurivocity can be imagined as a daimonic process, an engagement with what they have called the "little people" who want their say and have a story to tell. Engagement with them is a complex dialectic that drives one to the limits of one's understanding and relativizes one's point of view, and in so doing continues to open new horizons and broadens one's vision. Such a dialogue challenges stale ideas and helps to give meaning to what initially appears as nonsense. It opens a fertile abyss and connects the subject to a larger world. Such dialogue provokes hesitation and such tarrying can help us to reserve judgment and to resist quick one-sided formulations. It may allow us to stand firm against the pressure for clear and distinct ideas that devitalize our reflections and foreclose an openness and ambiguity on the threshold of meaning that enriches us. When this open space collapses, our theories can become stultified, and we lose something essentially human.

For Desmond, there is no quick and easy solution to the conundrums of philosophy. Philosophy requires patience and a resistance to any easy "univocal logicism."[16] While Desmond is very sympathetic to Hegel, he resists seeing philosophy as standing over other modes of discourse in a hierarchical fashion. Philosophy for Desmond has limits in the face of other forms of discourse to which it must open itself beyond its own familiar categories not reducing otherness "to its own categorial self-mediation."[17]

For Desmond, Hegel is a master philosopher who takes the time to think things through to the end, but as noted above there are many ways to read Hegel. Desmond struggles with a reading of Hegel not unlike the ones Rockmore criticizes, basically a reading that literalizes the Absolute and reduces it to an ontology of spirit. For Desmond, this happens when spirit encompasses all other modes of thought and subordinates them to its own purpose.

At the end of the *Phenomenology*, Desmond finds an example of this in the way the dialectic subordinates both art and religion. Pointing to this moment in the dialectic has not been an uncommon criticism and Hegel has been fairly or unfairly accused of "a hubris of reason, a disrespect for what is other to thought, and a will to subordinate all being to philosophical speculation."[18] However, Desmond suggests that if systematic philosophy is to take account of art and religion as "other" to philosophy, in the sense of "their proximity to ultimacy, then what we mean by philosophical science is itself made problematic."[19] For Desmond, there is no easy solution to this problem. Unlike many other critics, he does not simply dismiss Hegel's handling of this issue. He does, however, underline what he considers paradox, "thought provoking ambiguities," and "fundamental tensions inherent in the philosophical enterprise itself."[20]

For Desmond, these ambiguities call for a different way of reading Hegel "to think otherwise than Hegel did."[21] Here it appears that Desmond is not simply reading Hegel differently, but actually proposing a different way of engagement of philosophy with other disciplines. Desmond cites his contribution as reinterpretation, a "'metaxological understanding' of the interplay of philosophy and its others."[22] Giving credit to Hegel, he notes that in Hegel's thought we also find both "the coexistence of an inexorable will to systematic reason *and* philosophical respect for modes of mind that normally are taken as recalcitrant to rational systematization."[23] In short, Hegel "wants to think the dialectical togetherness of philosophical reason and its recalcitrant others."[24]

The paradox Desmond points to centers around the question: What is other to philosophy? Desmond again returns to the seeming divide between the task of systematic philosophy and subordinating all otherness to the self-mediation of philosophical thought and yet maintaining a genuine openness to other modes of mind – a seeming contradiction, an either/or. In Desmond's view, "Hegel rejects this either/or. . . . [in] his desire to respond to both these requirements."[25] Ultimately, Desmond claims that Hegel reduces "this double requirement to a singular, all-embracing process of dialectical self-mediation."[26] For Desmond, it is undeniable that Hegel "gives philosophical priority to *thought thinking itself*."[27] This paradoxical way of thinking challenges us to "rethink what it is to think philosophically. It forces us to rethink the others of philosophy, not only in their continuity with philosophy, but also in their discontinuity."[28]

In this moment, Desmond is critical of Hegel, but he is relentless in his attempt to give Hegel as fair a reading as he can. Following his first line of criticism, he notes that self-mediation leads to a continuity between philosophy and its others, which is valorized by Hegel's admirers, while the gap between philosophy and its other, the discontinuity, remains important to those who see Hegel's thought as reductive. Desmond finds it important to reflect on both ways of reading Hegel, a balanced reading. In this double reading, Desmond both praises and criticizes Hegel in an attempt to hear Hegel's complex voice, noting that he himself has been criticized by some as being "too Hegelian," by others as being "not Hegelian enough," and by still others as getting "the balance right."[29]

In Desmond's ongoing reflections, he leans toward continuity, but also allows for more discontinuity than is often the case with Hegelians. This approach is fitting to Desmond's "concern with what is other to system at the limits of philosophical reason."[30] Desmond considers himself to be a generous reader of Hegel, but his reading does not lay fully to rest his "pervasive unease" and "suspicion."[31] While "Hegel occupies a certain intermediate position between continuity and discontinuity,"[32] the mediating between these two moments is itself dialectical for Hegel while for Desmond it is "metaxological," and he argues that this "takes us beyond Hegel and dialectic."[33]

What and how then does Desmond's approach differ from Hegel's? Like Hegel, Desmond realizes that "the relation of thought and what is other to thought" requires a "complex balance of unity and plurality, identity and difference, sameness and distinction."[34] For Desmond, the middle between these divergences is not adequately "interpreted either by totalizing holisms" (as some attribute to Hegel) or by "the discontinuous plurality" of deconstructionism and the pluralism of Wittgenstein and others.[35] While Desmond's perspective acknowledges the contemporary appreciation of the importance of "dissents from any sterile obsession with discontinuity," he also notes that "[O]therness itself asks us to think through the meaning of the community of being. A community of being that sustains otherness distances us from merely asserted difference, as well as from any equally unfruitful sense of totalizing unity."[36]

At first, it is hard to distinguish Desmond's dialectics from Hegelian dialectics. Toward the end, however, Desmond finally notes that for him the limitation he finds with Hegel's dialectics is the "tendency to interpret *all* mediation primarily in terms of *self-mediation* . . . . The thought of everything other to thought risks getting finally reduced to a moment of thought thinking *itself*."[37] Desmond attempts to remedy this with his idea of a metaxological approach. This approach, he claims, "is not so much hostile to dialectic as it is to any such reduction of otherness, and to the reduction of a pluralized intermediation to a singular self-mediation."[38] The metaxological approach seems to complement dialectics in so far as "[i]t wants to articulate the togetherness with a different accent on otherness," a way of seeing that is

> open to a double mediation . . . that is no dualistic opposition. The middle is plurally mediated: it can be mediated from the side of the dialectical self; but also it can be mediated from the side of an otherness that is not reduced to a moment of self-mediation.[39]

Again, Desmond points out the singularity that can be found with a careful reading of Hegel who "also believes that the other mediates the middle," but for Desmond there are many places

> that this mediation from the side of the other invariably turns out to be a penultimate, hence subordinate moment of a more ultimate process of dialectical self-mediation . . . a mediation of the self in the form of its *own* otherness, and hence not the mediation of an irreducible other at all.[40]

A metaxological approach intends even more than Hegel to grant "otherness its irreducible otherness."[41] It is hard to understand how, if "otherness" is to be "mediated," it remains "irreducible." Desmond states that otherness "must" indeed be mediated, but it has to do so "in terms other than dialectical self-mediation."[42] The metaxological approach

> is itself plural. . . [in] an affirmative sense of the double that cannot be spoken of simply as a dualistic opposition. Nor is the other simply the self in the form of its own otherness. . . . The mediation of the metaxological between cannot be exhausted either by the mediation of the self or the mediation of the other. Neither side can claim entirely to mediate the complex between. The "whole" is not a whole in the sense of a conceptual monologue with itself; it is a plurivocal community of voices in interplay just in their genuine otherness.[43]

In elaborating the metaxological sensibility, Desmond hopes to counter the dangers of "spiritual" and "mental" reductionism and to reinforce that "[t]he deepest openness of the speculative mind is the impossibility of the ultimate closure of thought by itself and in itself."[44]

Speculative thought in Desmond's sense both self-mediates and inter-mediates "between thought and what is other than thought."[45] Therefore, the metaxological way of thinking may discover that "honest speculative reflection may find its self-mediations broken or ruptured on forms of otherness that its categories cannot entirely master."[46] Put another way, a metaxological approach opens itself beyond monologue, goes to the edge of logos and beyond to hear the voices of otherness on their own terms. The relationship between self and other is still "held together" as "a sense of 'wholeness' that is not closed."[47] Examples of such open wholeness can be found for Desmond in works of art. In his recognition of such whole-ness, the metaxological is seen as closer to Hegel than to deconstruction-ist thinkers who, Desmond feels, "disdain any suggestion of wholeness," which they identify "with a closed totality."[48] Rather than leave Hegel and dialectics behind, Desmond proposes that Hegel can be "fruitfully reinterpreted as trying to stand dialectically in the middle."[49] In this con-text, Hegel's "dynamic interplay of the self and other, unity and differ-ence, sameness and otherness" exhibits the "power of dialectical thinking" which is not surpassed in either Heidegger or Derrida.[50] "Its power is not completed or exhausted, but still stands before us a promise."[51] To philoso-phize in Desmond's sense requires a patient dwelling with and mediating attitude toward what is "other" than philosophy.

An example of such mediation can be found in the work of Casey who engages one of philosophy's "others" – psychology. The otherness of phi-losophy and psychology have been thought of as two different, exclusive enterprises, but for Casey they may actually be more closely related then typically imagined. For Casey, they may in fact show themselves not sim-ply needing to be brought into relationship, but as already co-joined. In order to take up the relationship between philosophy and psychology, he first draws them apart, pointing to the way these "fields" have been char-acterized and marked respectively in terms of spirit (philosophy) and soul (psychology).

Casey characterizes philosophy as emphasizing spirit, pure reason, sepa-ration, division, diakrises, analysis, form, logos. Psychology is, in contrast, characterized by soul, as synthetic, syncretic, fusing, and lively spirit, with body and world, in concrete places. While philosophy, according to Casey, classically divides, psychology refuses dichotomies. Psychology emphasizes feeling rather than thought and argues that feeling links opposites and sits at the border between them. For Casey, psychology's syncretic style extends to the divides between philosophy and psychology, spirit and soul, though he recognizes how difficult this divide is for the modern mind characterized as it is by Cartesian dualism.

Casey continues to refine his reflections on the interplay between philosophy and psychology by noting the tension between reason and perception. Reason attempts to unify from above, while psychology, more rooted in perception, attempts to unify from below. For Casey, neither reason nor perception can close the gap between the two perspectives or between thought and feeling, spirit and soul. For Casey, moving further toward the integration of these divides is facilitated by his focus on imagination and memory. At a subtle level, it appears as if imagination and memory mirror the contrast between philosophy and psychology in that imagination appears to move upward toward spirit, while memory seems to move down toward feeling.

Casey describes the power of imagination as moving up from body to soul, "an essential step to corporeal action," and "Up from Soul to Spirit."[52] This process is a moving from inarticulate feeling toward expression in "categories, concepts, and words," but he also notes the subtler and progressive move in the direction of " 'verbalization' . . . that has not yet found words adequate to its level of insight."[53] What Casey has in mind here appears to be a progressive active imagination, including "pondering" and "meditating" that takes place "without yet crystalizing our thought in language – not even in inner speech."[54] Casey gives the example of the sequential processes in both Hegel's *Phenomenology* and the *Logic*, processes that he says (much like Bates) "would not be possible without the intervention of an imagination that inspired the soul to think abstractly."[55]

For Casey, philosophy itself would not be possible without the imagination. Like emotion, imagination is "a spontaneously unifying factor in human experience, first linking body with soul . . . and then connecting soul with spirit."[56] For Casey, like for Hegel and Giegerich, this linking is not an external process that starts with two different objective entities: body and soul, "but of an indefinite plurality of modes of existing between which imagination moves in its Mercurial manner."[57] If, for Casey, imagination is an upward linking already in process, a binding adhesive that is active at a subtle level, it is also not the only process at work as a synthe-sizing force. Imagination's upward movement is matched by memory's downward movement from spirit to soul. "Memory brings spirit down to feeling. . . [and] to its . . . troubled body that is re-membered in mind."[58]

For Casey, "soul seeks its own substance."[59] The two operations of imagination and memory, the upward and downward movement are not the same. They are complimentary and both work as connecting princi-ples and are necessary to each other. "[W]ithout the continual and conjoint operations of imagination and memory human existence would indeed fall apart into warring factions, divided against itself."[60]

An interesting and important aspect of Casey's description of imagina-tion and memory is that they do not simply operate on an inward level. He notes that in imagining and remembering we move out of simple interior-ity extending beyond ourselves and "out of our skin and into places of the world."[61] The notion of "place" is one of Casey's creative contradictions to both philosophy and psychology which I cannot further explore in this context. However, with the idea of "place," there is a movement beyond the expression of either idea and image, spirit or soul – in separation. "The twain between spirit and soul not only will meet but has already met in the continual collusions of imagery and remembering, which, tied to each other, tie soul and spirit together."[62]

For Casey, this "co-constitution" and coherence "of spirit and psyche"[63] are "held together in a bodily mode . . . above all, by the *images* which imagining and remembering share."[64] Here "image" must be understood not simply as a representation in mind of some outer physical reality, but rather as "essential features of phenomena" or "*structures of presenta-tion.*"[65] For Casey, both imagining and remembering share images and operate as " 'intentional threads' by which a life comes to composition and compresence with itself."[66] Casey notes:

> Language is no more a matter of an individual speech act (*la parole*) than primordial images are affairs of the isolated ego. Each proceeds from a level of the psyche that is profoundly impersonal: "collective" in Jung's preferred term, "institutionalized" in Saussure's answering notion. In this way, image and word come together in the end after all – despite Jung's sometimes heroic efforts to hold them apart. But they come together at a level of human being that has been given full recognition only in postmodernist thought. Jung and Saussure are not

alone in their insistence on the collective basis of image and word that earlier modernists failed to acknowledge. They are joined by thinkers as diverse as Lévy-Bruhl and Chomsky, both of whom also assert the transpersonal foundation of imagination and language, whether in the guise of collective representations or universally shared rules of generative grammar. What matters, however, is not the history of the trend, or who in particular belongs to it. What matters is the vision it embodies. This is a vision that gives back to images, as it gives back to words, a grounding in the spontaneous action of the psyche, which *is* image as it *is* word, and, in being both at once, transcends the ecological confines – in sign and copy – of the modernist conception of the human self, a conception that renders the self incapable of the symbolic activity of the psyche in its cosmic and collective dimensions.[67]

For Casey, "[i]mages also serve to specify. They occupy places in psyche. . . . It is with images, then, that the ultimate rapprochement is to be made between" philosophy and psychology.[68] More particularly the kind of philosophizing and psychology that Casey has in mind and has been concerned with is phenomenological philosophy and archetypal psychology. He draws both "fields" together by virtue of their mutual concern with "manifestation," where what matters to both "is the manifest image and the world in which it is set."[69] In both fields, the world as *anima mundi* is a notion of world that goes out beyond "the entrapment of personalized consciousness."[70] Both fields "step into the light of place . . . a diffusely lighted, amorphously luminous place whose proper name is 'landscape.'"[71] With this notion, Casey offers a philosophical setting "for archetypes as well as for structures of presentation."[72] Casey imagines the linking of phenomenological philosophy with archetypal psychology as a three-sided discipline which he calls "arche-pheno-topology" and which he sees as "a region within which philosophy and psychology can commingle more fully and freely than they have allowed themselves to do thus far in the modern and post-modern era."[73] In such a place, Casey imagines images can play back and forth between imaging and remembering.

they are the free play of their enactments. They also furnish the *Spielraum*, the very play-space, for a psychology conceived archetypally and a philosophy considered as phenomenology. Images allow these two "fields" to *take place together*, to find a common ground – a shared placescape – and even on occasion to take each other's place.[74]

The work of bringing philosophy and psychology together is also taken up by David Morris who, inspired by Casey's idea to "get back with things into place," argues that this is an unending process.[75] It is unending because, as Morris suggests, "place" in Casey's sense "is never fully here"[76] and requires what he calls a "vagabond," "subliminal," or "peripheral approach to things."[77] The method by which one may approach such a place or landscape is to "turn from determinate objects to indeterminate horizons, from the more to the less, [which] *is at work within experience itself*, prior to reflection."[78]

To "capture," or perhaps better, to enter, into such awareness requires differentiating between gazing and glancing. "Glancing opens [us] onto the non-givenness of place" to indeterminate horizons "let[ting] things catch our glance before we have objectified [them] with our gaze."[79] This lets us see what Casey calls periphenomenon "that can reveal, within the phenomena themselves, tell tales of a non-appearing, non-givenness that nonetheless appears and is given in each and every phenomenon."[80] For Morris,

Casey's phenomenology is subliminal in its topic, since what it reveals is that the condition of appearance of delimited things is place as not itself susceptible of full delimitation, since such delimitation always, inherently, and endogenously proceeds into further moves of delimitation. Casey shows us how there is no bottom to place, as there is no end to time. Place is both beneath and beyond delimitation.[81]

Casey's distinction between the gaze and the glance and his refusal to separate spirit from soul, psychology from philosophy, renders his thought resonant with a number of contemporary interpreters of Hegel and sets the stage for a non-traditional understanding of Hegel's notion of Spirit. For these interpreters of Hegel, Spirit itself must be intimately connected with soul and the psychological ground important in an understanding of the idea of the Absolute that is grounded in history, in time and place, and is a complex unity. As such, it can serve as an important way to deepen our understanding of the alchemical project of creating a unified vision of the Philosophers' Stone not split into the binaries discussed throughout this work.

Notes

1 De Boer, *On Hegel*, 1–2; emphasis mine.
2 Desmond, *Beyond Hegel*, 230.
3 I cannot here adequately discuss the important challenges Desmond raises for speculative thought. See his chapter entitled "Dialectic and Evil," 189–250, for a fuller discussion.
4 De Boer, *On Hegel*, 2.
5 Ibid., 7.
6 Ibid., 4.
7 Hegel *Phenomenology of the Spirit*, 19.
8 Hillman, *Revisioning Psychology*, 94.
9 Desmond, *Beyond Hegel*, xi.
10 Ibid.
11 Honoré, *In Praise of Slowness*, 11.
12 Ibid., 4.
13 Ibid., 3.
14 Desmond, *Beyond Hegel*, xi.
15 Ibid.
16 Ibid.
17 Ibid., 1.
18 Ibid., 2.
19 Ibid., 3.
20 Ibid., 4.
21 Ibid.
22 Ibid.
23 Ibid.
24 Ibid.
25 Ibid.
26 Ibid., 5.
27 Ibid.
28 Ibid.
29 Ibid.
30 Ibid.
31 Ibid.
32 Ibid.
33 Ibid., 6. Whether Desmond succeeds in going beyond Hegel or rather offers an alternative reading of Hegel's dialectic requires further discussion.
34 Ibid.
35 Ibid.
36 Ibid.
37 Ibid., 7.
38 Ibid.
39 Ibid.
40 Ibid., 7–8.
41 Ibid., 8.
42 Ibid.
43 Ibid.
44 Ibid.
45 Ibid., 9.
46 Ibid.
47 Ibid., 10.
48 Ibid.

49 Ibid., 11.
50 Ibid., 12.
51 Ibid.
52 Casey, *Spirit and Soul*, xv.
53 Ibid., xvi.
54 Ibid.
55 Ibid.
56 Ibid.
57 Ibid.
58 Ibid., xvii.
59 Ibid.
60 Ibid., xviii.
61 Ibid.
62 Ibid.
63 Here Casey alters his conjunction between "spirit and soul" to "spirit and psyche." I am unsure if he is using the term "psyche" as congruent with "soul" in this context.
64 Casey, *Spirit and Soul*, xix.
65 Ibid.
66 Ibid.
67 Casey, "Jung and the Postmodern Condition," 323.
68 Casey, *Spirit and Soul*, xx.
69 Ibid.
70 Ibid.
71 Ibid.
72 Ibid.
73 Ibid.
74 Ibid., xxi.
75 Morris, "Casey's Subliminal Phenomenology," 54.
76 Ibid.
77 Ibid., 56.
78 Ibid., 57.
79 Ibid., 61.
80 Ibid.
81 Ibid.

Chapter 13

The self, the absolute, the stone

Throughout this work, I have pointed to the importance of Hegel for an understanding of the Philosophers' Stone and the Self. Previously I have touched upon the idea of the Absolute, which is perhaps the most complex and difficult of Hegel's ideas. In the *Phenomenology of the Spirit*, Hegel's idea of Absolute Knowing is described in the last and perhaps most enigmatic chapter of his work. Rockmore comments that this is Hegel's "most cryptic chapter" and though it "still retains a large portion of mystery after almost two centuries," it is "not impenetrable."[1] If Derrida is correct, and I believe that he is, "we will never be finished with a reading or rereading of Hegel"[2] – and this, I would add, is also the case for Jung.

As noted, Jung's works are likewise difficult, particularly his notion of the "Self" as it developed over time out of his alchemical studies and as it was discussed in his work *Aion* and ultimately in his last major work, *Mysterium Coniunctionis*. The classical analyst Edward Edinger, in his *The Mysterium Lectures*, calls reading Jung's *Mysterium* "a very sizable enterprise. . . . It is likely that you will all fall into confusion. . . . This is absolutely inevitable because *Mysterium* is like the psyche itself. It's oceanic and to take it seriously means to run the risk of drowning."[3] He states that "What makes *Mysterium* so exasperating is that every paragraph, every sentence, confronts us with material with which we are unfamiliar, and that's very hard on one's vanity." Similar to Rockmore's and Derrida's comments on Hegel, Edinger maintains that the *Mysterium* "will be a major object of study for centuries."

If Jung and Hegel are difficult and complex, it seems even more problematic to attempt any comparison between their thought, but Sean Kelly, an academic researcher in the fields of philosophy and religion, attempts

DOI: 10.4324/9781003215905-14

such a dialectical encounter between them. Kelly's book *Individuation and the Absolute* attempts to synthesize the core ideas of Jung and Hegel and to explore the dialectical tensions between their concepts of Self and other, ego and unconscious, and the individual and the Absolute. Here, I will focus particularly on Hegel's notion of the "Absolute" and Jung's idea of the "Self" and the way these notions have been interpreted.

Kelly has noted that a comparison of Hegel and Jung at first glance seems an unlikely encounter in that Hegel is known as a speculative philosopher while Jung, on the other hand, is a depth psychologist who has again and again proclaimed that he is an "empiricist," "with eyes trained on those aspects of human experience which manifest a hypothetical pre-rational and unconscious ground."[4] On closer inspection, however, Kelly finds a number of grounds which make a comparison not only viable, but also fruitful. Most particularly, Kelly notes that "Jung's understanding of Self-actualization as the quest for meaning and wholeness" resonates with Hegel's "dialectically self-articulating totality."[5] That is, Kelly makes an effort to set the stage for a deeper exploration of both Jung's notion of the Self (the outcome and goal of Jung's process of individuation) and the culmination of Hegel's system in the *Phenomenology of Spirit*.

Even though Jung himself has stated that he had not "been influenced by Hegel, nor to have studied him properly," he admitted that there was "a remarkable coincidence between certain tenets of Hegelian philosophy"[6] and his own findings. Jung himself goes on to see a parallel between Hegel's conclusions and his own conception of a collective unconscious. The collective unconscious is said to be composed of archetypal structures and the Self as an archetype is central among them. For our purposes here, let me begin by noting that both the "Self" and "Absolute Knowing" can be said to be outcomes of Jung's and Hegel's respective systems of thought.

Both notions emerge from the achievement of having passed through a profound transformation process of historical and psychological development. Jung called this the process of individuation, by which he meant, in the simplest terms, a person's self-actualization or becoming whole. This simple statement is a thread that runs through Jung's *Collected Works*. It is a notion that is often misunderstood merely as the development of the individual ego. Jung makes it clear that it has more to do with the working through of various archetypal patterns of the "psyche" to the point where the constellation of the "Self" is a defeat for the ego. This is a point in development where the ego is relativized and the central meaning-making function of the "soul" becomes visible. The typical outlines of this process have been characterized as a movement of differentiation through a series of archetypal patterns or forms of the Spirit.

The unfolding individuation process has been described in terms of the ego's encounter with what Jung has called the shadow, the anima or animus, the animal trickster, the wise old man or woman, and the Self, but there is no precise order of archetypal unfolding, and some consider the process to be more circular. The shadow, usually encountered early in the individuation process but not always, can be described "as the negative side of the personality, the sum of all the unpleasant qualities one wants to hide, the inferior, worthless and primitive side of man's nature, the 'other person' in one, one's own dark side."[7]

To recognize the shadow side of one's "self" is to acknowledge a complexity, split, or tension in one's own identity. We discover that we are more than we thought and/or would like to be. We carry in ourselves a sense of otherness with which we are often in conflict. We are divided in ourselves in a way reminiscent of what Hegel called the "unhappy consciousness." For Jung, because the shadow makes the ego uncomfortable, he hypothesized that this inner otherness is projected out and not seen as part of the Self, but rather is seen in others. Part of the task of individuation is to reclaim this otherness, internalizing what has been projected outward until it can be seen and felt to be one's own. This move Jung calls the withdrawing of projections and it seems to roughly correspond to what Hegel sees as happening in the move from Stoicism to Scepticism. For Hegel, the negative is experienced as out in the world, and the subject reacts to it. The Stoic subject

> keeps the poles of this its self-contradiction apart and adopts the same attitude to it as it does in its purely negative activity in general. . . . Its talk is in fact like the squabbling of self-willed children, one of whom says *A* if the other says *B*, and in turn says *B* if the other says *A*.[8]

A move out of Stoicism to what Hegel calls "Scepticism" is similar to what happens in Jungian analysis when a person experiences the shadow as their own internal reality.

> In Scepticism, consciousness truly experiences itself as internally contradictory. From this experience emerges a *new form* of consciousness

which brings together the two thoughts which Scepticism holds apart. Scepticism's lack of thought about itself must vanish, because it is in fact *one* consciousness which contains within itself these two modes. The new form is, therefore, one which *knows* that it is the dual consciousness of itself, as self-liberating, unchangeable, and self-identical, and as self-bewildering and self-perverting, and it is the awareness of this self-contradictory nature of itself.[9]

In short, it becomes a more complex subject. Hegel called this the "*Unhappy Consciousness*," which "is the consciousness of self as a dual-natured, merely contradictory being."[10] This description could also easily be applied to Jung's idea of discovering the shadow.

A literary example of the dual nature of the unhappy consciousness might be drawn from Goethe. When Faust speaks to his assistant Wagner he says:

> One impulse art thou conscious of, at best;
> O, never seek to know the other!
> Two souls, alas! reside within my breast,
> And each withdraws from, and repels, its brother.
> One with tenacious organs holds in love
> And clinging lust the world in its embraces;
> The other strongly sweeps, this dust above,
> Into the high ancestral spaces.[11]

Then Faust proclaims, as if to call out for Hegel's sublation or Jung's transcendent function:

> If there be airy spirits near,
> 'Twixt Heaven and Earth on potent errands fleeing,
> Let them drop down the golden atmosphere,
> And bear me forth to new and varied being![12]

It is to this "new and brighter life" that we now turn to consider the further unfolding of the individuation process and the development of Hegel's dialectic. The integration of the shadow and the move from stoicism to skepticism with its unhappy consciousness sets the stage for the further unfolding respectively described by Jung and Hegel. The journey of consciousness toward its goal in the respective systems of Jung and Hegel is long and arduous and, while the paths to their goals have many resonances, they cannot be discussed here. However, we can consider some possible parallels between the outcome of both systems, in terms of Jung's notion of the Self and Hegel's Absolute Knowing.

Self and absolute knowing

It is said of the Philosophers' Stone that it is a great "reconciler of opposites." This is relevant to both the Self and Absolute Knowing, which becomes more and more complex as the "soul" moves toward self-consciousness in its ultimate shape. At the level of the Shadow, consciousness begins a recognition of its dual complexity and, in the development of the dialectics in Jung and Hegel, the principle of overcoming one-sidedness and movement toward wholeness is an ongoing theme. Rockmore put it this way: "Philosophy's task consists in reconciling, or uniting, such aspects as being and non-being, infinity and finitude, necessity and contingency within a structured whole."[13]

As we have seen, for Jung "the self has a paradoxical, antinomial character . . . a true 'complexio oppositorum.'"[14] As such, the Self is the fullest expression of the actuality of the archetype. It "has somewhat the character of a result, of a goal attained, something that has come to pass gradually and with much travail. So too the self is our life's goal, for it is the completest expression of the fateful combination we call individuality . . ."[15] For Jung, the seed of this individuality is present at the beginning as well as at the end.

Similarly, for Hegel, the Self "is the process of its own becoming, the circle that presupposes its end as its goal, having its end also as its beginning; and only by being worked out to its end, is it actual."[16] And again: ". . . the self is like that immediacy and simplicity of the beginning because it is the result, that which has returned into itself, the latter being similarly just the self. And the self is the sameness and simplicity that relates itself to itself."[17] For both Jung (mandala) and Hegel (circle), the circle is a powerful indicator of the Self and, in speaking about goal images and the Philosophers' Stone, Jungian analyst James Hillman writes: "The goal images correlate precisely with this motion of circularity, since the *iteratio* . . ., *circulatio*, and *rotatio* are often considered among the last operations of the *opus*."[18]

So, what does it mean to come to an end in light of the notion of a circle? The Self and Absolute Knowing have been interpreted in static and essentialist ways, but where is the end of a circle? Or, as Rockmore put it, "[t]here is the problem of the absolute character of so-called absolute knowledge."[19]

An example of the problem is present in Magee's book entitled *Hegel and the Hermetic Tradition*. As we've discussed, Magee states that "Hegel is not a philosopher. He is no lover or seeker of wisdom – he believes he has found it."[20] To support his view, he quotes Hegel from the Preface of the *Phenomenology of Spirit*: "to help bring philosophy closer to the form of Science, to the goal where it can lay aside the title of love of knowing and be actual knowledge – that is what I set before me."[21]

For Magee, this aim is interpreted in the context of the Hermetic tradition in which Absolute Knowledge appears in gnostic, if not ontological, fashion. He states: "If Hegel departs from the metaphysical tradition in anything, it is in dispensing with its false modesty. Hegel does not claim to be merely searching for truth. He claims that he has found it."[22] While Hegel does say the things Magee emphasizes, interpretation of just what Hegel has found remains at issue.

As noted earlier, Jung, like Hegel, has also been interpreted in gnostic and ontological fashion on the basis of comments that might understandably be interpreted in such a manner. As noted earlier, in an interview Jung once stated when asked if he believed in God:

> All that I have learned has led me step by step to an unshakable conviction of the existence of God. I only believe in what I know. And that eliminates believing. Therefore, I do not take His existence on belief – I *know* that He exists.[23]

One can see how, on the basis of such statements, one might conclude Jung was also a gnostic thinker and came to be interpreted metaphysically, but this single statement is overshadowed by many others in which Jung again and again demonstrates a far greater reserve. For example, in a typical self-assessment, Jung states: "I am and remain a psychologist. I am not interested in anything that transcends the psychological content of human *experience*."[24] He goes on to say:

> Speaking always as a psychologist, I affirm that the presence of God is manifest, in the profound experience of the psyche, as a *coincidentia*

oppositorum, and the whole history of religion, all the theologies, bear witness to the fact that the *coincidentia oppositorum* is one of the commonest and most archaic formulas for expressing the reality of God.[25]

Further, Jung states "[t]he designation of my 'system' as 'Gnostic' is an invention of my theological critics."[26]

It seems to me that Jung's statements taken in context might best be understood in light of Rockmore's differentiation of the interpretation of the idea of the absolute as "the absolute for human being," as opposed to "claiming [ontological] knowledge in some absolute sense beyond time and place."[27] This interpretation also fits well for Jung who notes: "[t]he goal is important only as an idea; the essential thing is the *opus* which leads to the goal: *that* is the goal of a lifetime."[28] Post-Jungian Hillman notes that "[t]he *rotatio*, like a turning wheel, announces that no position can remain fixed . . . no end place achieved."[29] Rockmore's interpretation is also supported by Jon Mills who notes that:

> Hegel shows that spirit comes to know itself as spirit by coming to understand its historical progression of encountering contingencies and this constitutes an absolute position insofar as spirit understands its process, but nowhere does he say that spirit ends, only perhaps that spirit has reached the zenith of the pure form of its understanding which is always open to the introduction of new experiences and novelties. Hegel even ends his *Phenomenology* with an adapted reference to Schiller underscoring the significance of "infinitude." Spirit lives on; it must continue in the lives of individual minds.[30]

Previously, we alluded to the complexity of Absolute Knowing as a historical and ongoing process while nevertheless remaining absolute. This seeming paradox is more fully discussed by Rockmore in his book on Hegel's epistemology. He asks: "What can be said for absolute idealism today?"[31] In reflecting on this question, he suggests two possible approaches: the traditional approach claims that Absolute Knowledge can be seen "as truth beyond time" or, in a non-traditional sense, as a claim for knowledge and "truth as relative to a particular theoretical framework."[32] For Rockmore, the first claim asserts a version of foundationalism which has been forcefully reflected in modern times. The more interesting and promising approach for him is interpreting absolute knowledge in terms of an "historically-linked, contextualized analysis of claims to know."[33]

Rockmore finds hints in Hegel's *Phenomenology* and in his *Philosophy of Right* to support the non-traditional view and evidence for a perspectival position and "various models of knowledge."[34] Such a position recognizes Absolute Knowing and spirit as "impure."[35] In part this position recognizes both knowledge and reason as historical and notes that each philosopher is a child of a particular time and place. As such, Absolute Knowing cannot claim to be "a perspective without perspective, surpassing other perspectives."[36] And yet, for Rockmore, there is a way that the Absolute is absolute in that, as a perspective, it "depicts the proper attitude of thought to objectivity."[37] He states that if Hegel is right about this, then "[f]rom the metatheoretical vantage point, absolute knowing, which is itself part of the knowing process, is itself absolute as the form for fully *mediated* claims to know."[38]

I think, to make this more explicit, consciousness comes to realize that the nature of any knowledge (of what we mean by knowledge) must be mediated. This truth is absolute; it is what the meaning of knowledge must be. However, such a recognition appears as a paradox in which what is absolute is also mediated and historically contingent. In this sense, as Rockmore then notes, "absolute idealism is not only absolute but relative as well, or *absolutely relative*."[39] Rockmore then asks whether or not holding both the Absolute and the relative as properly characterizing Absolute Knowing constitutes an inconsistency. He states that it is not, and resolves the issue by pointing out that both of these aspects refer to differing aspects of Hegel's theory.

> [A]bsolute knowledge is absolute when it functions as the metatheoretical criteria of what it means to know, as a relative a priori that conditions any analysis of experience. Yet it is also relative in its dependence on the historical movement. In fact, all such criteria depend for their acceptance on the historical moment and all are subject to revocation at some future time.[40]

Rockmore ironically underlines this "impure" statement by further noting that "the truth of absolute idealism . . . is that knowledge is never absolute and always relative to time and place."[41]

An interesting gloss on this point is made by Slavoj Žižek with regard to post-Kantian German Idealism. Like Rockmore in *In the Wake of Kant*, Žižek argues that the implication of the subject in any quest for knowing is fundamental and as fundamental (Absolute?). This linking or co-relation is an "unsurpassable horizon, the mark of the finitude of the human condition."[42] For Žižek, the *"gap (between For-us and In-itself) must be part of the Absolute itself,* so that the very feature that seemed forever to keep us away from the Absolute is the *only* feature which *directly* unites us with the Absolute."[43]

From a Lacanian point of view, the gap that separates us as human beings from the "In-itself" is "correlative to Lacan's move from desire to drive."[44] For Lacan, the lack of access to the in-itself is a void, a lost primordial object or thing. The desire for this thing Žižek considers Kantian, while the drive enacted in its absence is Hegelian. Absence is related to the absence of the impossible object as thing-in-itself. Lacan posits the *object a*, which overlaps with the loss of the Kantian object. This "new" *object a* emerges at the very same moment of its loss – and the movement from desire to drive opens up a transcendental space in which "fantasy" fills the void of the lost primordial object. In short, the drive in Lacan's sense shows itself "in fantasmatic incarnations, from breast to voice and gaze," as "metonymic figurations of the void, of nothing. . . . [I]n the shift from desire to drive, we pass from the *lost object* to *loss itself as an object*," to the concreteness of the void.[45] Thus the work of drive and fantasy is not aimed simply at "the 'impossible' quest for the lost [Kantian] object [an abstract thing in itself]; it is [rather] *a push to directly enact the 'loss' – the gap, cut distance – itself.*"[46] Such an enactment is itself a move away from the abstract to the concreteness of a *new object.*

The living quality of this parallax gap is indispensable to productive thinking. For Žižek, such thinking is itself such a gap that approaches the ultimate Hegelian paradox: "the Spirit is a bone."[47] "The great binary oppositions – subject v. object, [spirit and matter], materialism v. idealism, . . . are all ways of naming this fundamental parallax gap: their tensions and incommensurabilities are indispensable to productive thinking."[48] In regard to these reflections we might also say that spirit is a stone.

The Philosophers' Stone as chaosmos and the dilemma of diversity[49]

The Philosophers' Stone is a strange complexity, difficult to understand and filled with psychological and philosophical contradictions. Perhaps the most paradoxical and enigmatic description of the Stone was *lilthos ou lithos*, the "stone that is not a stone," and as an expression not expressible – manifest yet not manifest. Such paradoxes haunted the alchemists and the Philosophers' Stone was shrouded in darkness, but also continued to provoke an ongoing dissemination of ideas and conundrums.

One such idea was Sol niger, the black sun, expressing itself in a single gesture, both darkness and light. For the alchemist, the Stone as *prima materia* was both at the beginning and end of the work. The realization of the Philosophers' Stone was not simply a move from darkness to light, but a deepening into an illuminated darkness, the light of darkness itself. As such, the work "begins" in chaos and disorder, and yet it ends in order, illumination, and cosmos, but these two moments (order and disorder) are not simply separate. Rather they represent a complex and integral order that is named the Philosophers' Stone. As we have noted, Jung tried to account for such paradoxes with the idea of a *complexio oppositorum*,[50] as an attempt to describe for his psychology what appeared to be incompatible dimensions of the Stone.

Jung writes: "In order to attain this union, [the alchemists] tried not only to visualize the opposites together but to express them in the same breath."[51] *Hierosgamos*, sacred marriage, chemical wedding, *filius philosophorum*, Mercurius duplex, *mysterium conuinctionis*, Anthropos, Abraxas, Adam Kadmon, *coniunctio, lapis philosophorum*, and so on, were Jung's attempts to render complexity and multiplicity in a single gesture.

In his *Mysterium Coniunctionis*, Jung gives his late-life account of grappling with these complexities. The subtitle of his book, "An Inquiry into the Separation and Synthesis of Psychic Opposites in Alchemy," prefigures the focus of this work. Jung opens this book with: "[t]he factors which come together in the coniunctio are conceived as opposites, either confronting one another in enmity or attracting one another in love."[52] It has been traditional to treat Jung as privileging love over enmity, synthesis over separation, convergence over divergence, and to see him as unifying diversity into oneness, chaos into cosmos, and suffering into healing and wholeness. As Jung states: "the desperately evasive and universal Mercurius – that Proteus twinkling in a myriad shapes and colours – is none other than the 'unus mundus,' the original, non-differentiated unity of the world or of Being"[53] or its "equivalent," the Philosophers' Stone.[54]

Jung spent a good part of his later life trying to describe this goal of psychic life, but, despite all of his efforts, the *coniunctio* remains anything but a simple unity. The entire *Mysterium Coniunctio* testifies to the complexity of Jung's vision, and what remains clear is that the unification of opposites requires continuing investigation. Despite all of Jung's attempts to see beyond the opposites and the plurality of psychic life, he recognized that the idea of unity and the *unus mundus* remain a "metaphysical speculation."[55] Elsewhere, he observed that, while the tensions between psychic pairs of opposites "ease off" over time, "the united personality will never quite lose the painful sense of innate discord. Complete redemption from the sufferings of this world is and must remain an illusion."[56]

The forces at work, according to the *Mysterium*, are enmity and love, and it is important to realize that these "energies" are more than personal. They are archetypal phenomena that do not simply give up their force. Love and hate continue to be generators of psychic process, and they spur continuing tensions and remain active in some form, even when relaxed and refined in the production of the lapis. The lapis can then be seen to be as much a multiplicity as a unity.

The symbols that attempt to capture what Edinger called "a transcendent, miraculous substance"[57] are multiple, wide-ranging, and diverse, and as much harmonious as dissonant.

Jung's struggle with unity and multiplicity had an historical and archetypal background. From the Presocratics to the postmoderns, in the philosophies of the East and West, the perennial problems of unity and diversity, the one and the many of monism and pluralism, continue to challenge us to this day.

Mercurius the mediator

Jung proposed a solution to the perennial problem of unity and multiplicity in the figure of Mercurius, who lies between opposites and is the means of bringing them together. As the mercurial body that bridges the divide, he was called a "mediator."[58] Mercurius links heaven and earth and, as such, is both "prima materia" and "ultima materia,"[59] and therefore called "lapis"[60] and "the stone,"[61] as the great principle of unification. But Jung was also aware that this unity was subject to a deconstruction and a division. He notes that Mercurius "is named a unity in spite of the fact that his innumerable inner contradictions can dramatically fly apart into equal numbers of disparate and apparently independent figures."[62]

If the linking of heaven and earth can be said to transcend the opposites, it is not in any kind of transcendental purity beyond the world but rather in the midst of things – in a oneness that is not a oneness, in a multiplicity that is not simply multiple. In his essay on James Joyce, Jung imagines a view of the Self as

> a being who is not a mere colourless conglomerate soul composed of an indefinite number of ill-assorted and antagonistic individual souls, but consists also of houses, street-processions, churches, . . . several brothels, and a crumpled note on its way to the sea – and yet possesses a perceiving and registering consciousness![63]

In short, what seems to express the transcendence of opposites is a world just as it is, conscious of itself in nuance and complexity as a living being in a way that reminds one of Hillman's call to return soul to the world. Like Jung, Hillman finds it particularly strange how personal life reflects the objective psyche. It is a "me-ness that is simply thatness"[64] a deeply subjective expression that is also an objectivity.

Hillman likewise describes the Stone in a spirit not unlike James Joyce's and Jung's: "All that other people are and the world is, from rivers and elephants to teacups and toasters is essentially what I call 'me' as part of an ensouled *anima mundi* and yet utterly depersonalized."[65] And yet what a strange vision of Self! In these, at times, infernal and sacrilegious chants of psychology, literature, and life, we find a variegated multiple world, rich beyond any organizing principle of the ego, a Self who is a dark father and demiurge, a hundred-eyed Argus, and so, for Jung, "a monstrosity [that] drives one to speculation."[66]

For Jung, and perhaps more so for Hillman, alchemy is an art of multiple, careful distillations and tinctures, and the continuing refinement of the play between unifications and differentiations, all of which yield subtle non-essentialist essences and soft rather than hard lines of demarcation, like the Philosophers' Stone itself.

As an alchemical book, *Ulysses* is different from the hard-edged book that Derrida claims is at an end. By being flexible, like wax or soft gold, *Ulysses* as an image of the Philosophers' Stone defeats logocentrism. If the distillation of this new consciousness can be said to reflect the Self and the Stone, or if the Stone and the Self reflect this new consciousness, perhaps we can also imagine that, when it does so mythically and religiously, it parallels images such as Christ, Buddha, Atman-Brahman, and the multi-eyed Argus. But when this new consciousness is seen through the scintilla of these multiple eyes, the demiurgic creativity is expressed in the multiplicity and free play of life as it is in its everydayness. However, when this play is frozen into one or the other of the opposites, it produces a one-sided vision requiring yet another tincture. Unity becomes a Cyclops, and multiplicity, a hundred-eyed Argus. The Cyclops sacrifices heterogeneity, and the hundred-eyed Argus lacks integral unity. Both are monsters. But when unity and multiplicity are both legitimate aspects of the Self, when they are imagined as simple undialectical opposites, the complexity of the Self is lost.

One might imagine this everydayness, this flow of life, like a Heraclitian river, or moving like the Tao of Lao Tse, playful like the Lila of the Hindu sages. It also might be seen as "a paradoxical co-incidence of order and disorder, cosmos and chaos,"[67] a "quantum weirdness"[68] or chaosmos of the natural world – anything but the static frozenness of categories and fixed meaning.

Perhaps then we can add the notion of chaosmos to the effort to express what Jung was after when speaking of the *complexio oppositorum*. Its further exploration can add contemporary nuance to our mercurial understanding of just what we mean by the unity of opposites, which is never a simple unity or stable presence, but rather a dynamic hybridity, a unity that does not require that differences subordinate themselves to a unifying principle. Such a unity "affirms the very heterogeneity that would appear to dissolve it."[69] As such, it is a unity in continuing self-deconstruction and so an errant fugitive that maddeningly continues to escape our grasp while teasing us into conjunctions,[70] usually expressing itself in the spiritualization of language. When these conjunctions fall apart, the Self becomes fixed and rigid, controlled by the senex or abandoned to Dionysus, a split between the stable and dynamic aspects of the soul that affect both theoretical understanding and personal life. I believe it is in the mutual engagement of these archetypal energies that one can find the dynamic hybridity that links chaos and cosmos, an integration that Jung intended but did not always achieve. This linkage between chaos and cosmos is what I have here called chaosmos – another name for the Philosophers' Stone and another perspective through which we can reconsider and reread Jung's idea of the Self.

It is my contention that the most productive way to understand the outcome of Jungian analysis and Hegelian philosophy is in the spirit of the many scholars, philosophers, and analysts who have been referred to in this book and is best understood as an ongoing movement of continuing reconciliation, and that both the Self and Absolute Knowing are always absolute for a concrete, temporal human being in a historical and ongoing process. Clearly, at the end of the arduous journey, in both traditions the human subject has become more complex, refined, and has achieved a structural, self-conscious wholeness. It is this wholeness I believe Hegel indicated in his image of a "chalice" that "foams forth;"[71] it is the creative fullness of Spirit overflowing its containers that constitutes the continuing work of both psychology and philosophy.

Notes

1 Rockmore, *Cognition*, 179.
2 Derrida, *Positions*, 77.
3 Edinger, *The Mysterium Lectures*, 17.
4 Kelly, *Individuation and the Absolute*, 3.
5 Ibid., 4.
6 Ibid.
7 Samuels et al., *A Critical Dictionary*, 138.
8 Hegel, *Phenomenology*, 125–126, §205.
9 Ibid., 126, §206.
10 Ibid.
11 Goethe, *Faust*, Retrieved from Project Gutenberg.
12 Ibid.
13 Rockmore, *Cognition*, 183.
14 Jung, *Aion (CW9i)*, §355.
15 Jung, *Two Essays (CW7)*, §404; quoted by Kelly, *Individuation and the Absolute*, 27.
16 Hegel, *Phenomenology*, 10, §18.
17 Ibid., 12, §22.
18 Hillman, *Alchemical Psychology*, 256.
19 Rockmore, *Before and After Hegel*, 102.
20 Magee, *Hegel and the Hermetic Tradition*, 1.
21 Ibid.
22 Ibid., 16.
23 Jung, *C.G. Jung Speaking*, 251.
24 Ibid., 229; emphasis mine.
25 Ibid., 229–230.
26 Jung, *The Symbolic Life (CW18)*, §1642.
27 Rockmore, *Before and After Hegel*, 101.
28 Jung, *The Practice of Psychotherapy (CW16)*, §400.
29 Hillman, *Alchemical Psychology*, 256.
30 Mills, *The Unconscious Abyss*, 218.
31 Rockmore, *On Hegel's Epistemology*, 64.
32 Ibid.
33 Ibid., 65.
34 Ibid.
35 Ibid.
36 Ibid.
37 Ibid., 66.

38 Ibid.; emphasis mine.
39 Ibid.
40 Ibid., 67.
41 Ibid., 68.
42 Žižek, *Less Than Nothing*, 626.
43 Ibid., 635.
44 Ibid., 638.
45 Ibid., 639.
46 Ibid.
47 Hegel, *Phenomenology*, 208, §343; quoted by Žižek, *Less Than Nothing*, 205.
48 Jameson, "First Impressions."
49 This section and the following one utilize parts of a paper by the author entitled "The Philosophers' Stone as Chaosmos."
50 Jung, *Aion (CW9i)*, §555.
51 Jung, *Mysterium Coniunctionis (CW14)*, §36.
52 Ibid., §1.
53 Ibid., §660.
54 Ibid., §661.
55 Ibid., §660.
56 Jung, *The Practice of Psychotherapy (CW16)*, §400.
57 Edinger, *Anatomy*, 9.
58 Jung, *Alchemical Studies (CW13)*, §283.
59 Ibid., §282.
60 Ibid., §283.
61 Ibid., §282.
62 Ibid., §284.
63 Jung, *The Spirit in Man (CW15)*, §198.
64 Hillman, *Alchemical Psychology*, 248.
65 Ibid.
66 Jung, *The Spirit in Man (CW15)*, §198.
67 Kuberski, *Chaosmos*, 3.
68 Ibid., 2.
69 Evans, *The Multivoiced Body*, 4.
70 Ibid., 28.
71 Hegel, *Phenomenology*, 493, §808.

Conclusion

In this exploration of Jung's Alchemical Psychology and the Philosophers' Stone, we have encountered the problem of many binary oppositions, splits and gaps that are seemingly impossible to close, among them: chemistry and alchemy, scientific positivism and religious esotericism, psychology and philosophy, phenomena and noumena, limit and transcendence, mechanism and vitalism, thought and being, spirit and nature, soul and spirit, ontology and history, absolutism and relativism.

In this reflection, I have considered these binaries in several contexts and among different thinkers, arriving at the conclusion, as noted in the Preface, that none of these divides can easily, if at all, be resolved into a simple unity or oneness. Rather, a complex oneness or irreducible dynamic twoness showed itself in multiple images and thoughts: the "and," the "two," the "gap," "being of two minds," consciousness and unconsciousness," "primordial paradox," "the dual-face of alchemy," "Mercurius duplex," and so on. Throughout history, those struggling with these "divides" and "gaps" have generated many attempts to go beyond them, leading to notions such as the ouroboric circle, the mandala, the wheel or *rota*, "*telos* returning to itself," a circular movement around an "alchemical *mysterium*," a mediatrix of elements, of the "fusing of sense and nonsense," as *übersinn*, supreme or excess of meaning, the syzygy, *coniunctio*, *complexio oppositorum*, the *mysterium coniunctionis*, and the Self.

For the alchemists, these conjunctions happened in stages and in and through complex and, at moments, monstrous imagery such as the hermaphrodite, Abraxas, and Mercurius, conjunctions which have been referred to as an "illuminated lunacy."[1] More palatable rational images of wholeness were also described in geometric terms such as the square of

DOI: 10.4324/9781003215905-15

the circle and in more aesthetically pleasing images such as the "golden flower," "golden castle," and "golden head," reflecting the illuminated philosopher. All of these images attempt to bring the opposites together in some kind of harmonious integration and unity. An early expression of this unity is found in the alchemical idea of the *unio mentalis* – yet, for many alchemists, psychologists, and philosophers, none of these images captures the dynamic and complex conjunction philosophically necessary to do justice to the dynamics of the idea of the Philosophers' Stone.

In alchemy, the *unio mentalis* was known as the white stone and, for many alchemists, it represented a "lesser *coniunctio*" and awaited a more differentiated goal called the "greater *coniunctio*." To reach the "greater *coniunctio*" meant achieving a fuller connection with the "redness" of lived life. As Dorn has challenged his colleagues, "Transform yourself from dead stones into living philosophic stones." Along with Jung's, Hillman's, and Giegerich's ideas of self, soul, and spirit, which unify opposites, Hegel's idea of the "unity of unity and difference" approaches a more complex and dialectical understanding of the struggle with opposites – leading toward "Absolute Knowing." The power of Hegel's formulations of the goal of Absolute Knowing added much to my attempt to understand the goal of alchemy beyond the simpler formulation of the *unio mentalis*.

Taking up Hegel's view of complex unity, I considered to what extent it answers Dorn's challenge and brings dead stones to philosophical life. Here I have turned to Giegerich's work, following Hegel's notion of spirit, which takes us beyond life, self, and soul, into what he called the "logical life of the soul" or spirit. I found that to some extent his formulation leans toward a formalism or ontologizing of syntax over semantics, thought and idea over image, and at a subtle level interprets Hegel in a way that leaves itself open to the charge of philosophical abstraction and to a further refinement of the *unio mentalis* as an outcome of absolute negativity.

Common interpretations of Hegel consider his thought highly abstract and intellectual, and read his view of Absolute Knowing as expressing an ontological if not Gnostic view of knowledge. In my own early reading of Hegel and in response to Giegerich's binary leanings elevating pure spirit above and beyond life, I, too, quickly resonated with postmodern criticisms of Hegel's view of spirit and Absolute Knowing. However, in re-reading Hegel and reconsidering his thought as an expression of a complex rather than simple unity, I began to see what I consider to be a modern philosophical rendering that can shed additional light on notions such as the Self and the Philosophers' Stone. For me, this required reading Hegel in some respects contra-Giegerich and in light of other readers of Hegel, including Verene, who noted that in the attempt to make the incongruous congruous, we must not lose an irresolvable "ambiguity" – what has also been called an "impure entanglement" and "tragic negativity" (De Boer) – that resists and slows down the optimism of absolute negativity (Hegel). De Boer's idea of entanglement resonates with Magnus' recognition of the importance of spirit's connection with the symbolic as a necessary mediating and irreducible factor in the expression of spirit. Thus, entanglement, tragic negativity (De Boer), and symbolic mediation (Magnus) fit well with Desmond's metaxological twoness and Žižek's "parallax gap," all of which emphasize the importance of keeping spirit and the dialectic away from any fantasy of pure and perfect completion.

In this sense, Hegel's dialectic can be seen as a "complex holism" (Kelly), a bringing together of two or more logics in a moment that is at once *complementary* and *antagonistic*. As such, the dialectic can be read as a dynamic hybridity in which the otherness of the other, which threatens the wholeness of spirit, is itself embraced but not reduced to the oneness of mind or spirit as a simple unity, nor left as a thing-in-itself. Rather, the dialectic can be read as a dynamic two-in-oneness and one-in-twoness, in a dual mediation of a bifocal logic. In this way, I re-imagine Hegel's dialectic of spirit and of "Absolute Knowing" as a goal that helps us further differentiate what he means by unity. Hegel describes unity as a Unity (of unity and difference) and to this I would add the Difference (between unity and difference) as mutual yet different ways of seeing the dynamics of the Philosophers' Stone and Jung's concept of the Self. To me, such a reading re-envisions the gaze of the philosopher and rather finds its place in the glance (Casey), in a philosophical psychology and a psychological philosophy, that loosens the pull of ontologizing and releases the Mercurial play between idea and image, spirit and soul, philosophy and psychology.

My way of reading this play resists seeing philosophy as rising above life, but rather as intrinsic to it, present in both image and idea, in history and in the circular play of image and thought. Such a ouroboric vision of soul and spirit gives rise to imagination and imagination shapes the lives that we live, our psychologies and philosophies, and as such is a touchstone to my vision of a contemporary Philosophers' Stone. To my mind, a unity like the Stone is also a multiplicity, a unity and difference. It both aims at a universal and eternal oneness but is also a paradox that yields a startling philosophical illumination.

Note

1 Hillman, *Alchemical Psychology*, 125.

Epilogue

This book has been a reflection on Jung's alchemical work and on the importance of philosophy as a way of understanding it. Alchemy has been viewed in the context of the history of natural science as a precursor to and primitive form of chemistry. Jung's research has shown that this view was far too limited and that a scientific approach to alchemy sheds little light on its mythic, esoteric, and symbolic meanings, which are intrinsic to many alchemical traditions and at the heart of the alchemical imagination. From the broader perspective of the history of the human spirit, these neglected aspects of alchemy can be seen as vital dimensions of the soul and important for our understanding of alchemy and the Philosophers' Stone. Jung's idea of the work was not simply the creation of a literal goal, but rather the transformation of the adept into an illuminated philosopher and the discovery of a new vision of the cosmos. Seeing alchemy in this way led Jung to recognize it as a forerunner of his psychology of the unconscious and as a symbolic process of individuation. Jung's vision revitalized our understanding of alchemy and opened the door to continuing study both within and outside the Jungian tradition.

I have considered a number of classical followers of Jung as well as revisionists, particularly James Hillman and Wolfgang Giegerich. They each set in motion interesting and challenging philosophical and psychological juxtapositions between images and ideas, imagination and thought, and they each consider one or the other term as primary. Hillman sticks to the image and Giegerich absolutizes thought in the spirit of Hegel. These leanings lead them to considerably different viewpoints.

In my own work, I have tended to emphasize the importance of images and imagination. In the end, I have discovered a way of understanding

DOI: 10.4324/9781003215905-16

Hegel that is more compatible with my own orientation in which the imagination is not surpassed by thought or spirit. Ultimately, I have come to link image and idea together, prioritizing the ouroboric and mercurial play between them. Images then give rise to thought and thought gives rise to images – a *circulatio* and *chasmos* – at times a monstrous *coniunctio* and a poetic undecidable, yielding not an absolute spirit rising above, but rather a philosophical illumination essential to life and to the depths of the soul, and resonant with the Philosophers' Stone.

Bibliography

Abraham, Lyndy. *A Dictionary of Alchemical Imagery*. Cambridge: Cambridge University Press, 1998.

Badiou, Alain. *Theoretical Writings*. New York: Continuum International, 2004.

Bair, Deirdre. *Jung: A Biography*. Boston: Little Brown and Company, 2003.

Barker, S.F. "Appearing and Appearances in Kant." In *Kant Studies Today*, edited by Lewis W. Beck. LaSalle, IL: Open Court, 1969, 274–289.

Bates, Jennifer Ann. *Hegel's Theory of Imagination*. Albany: State University of New York Press, 2004.

Bishop, Paul. *Synchronicity and Intellectual Intuition in Kant, Swedenborg, and Jung*. Lewiston, NY: The Edwin Mellen Press, 2000.

Brent, T. David. "Jung's Debt to Kant: The Transcendental Method and the Structure of Jung's Psychology." PhD diss., University of Chicago, Chicago, 1977.

Brooke, Roger. *Jung and Phenomenology*. London: Routledge, 1991.

Căliăn, George Florin. "*Alkimia Operativa* and *Alkimia Speculativa*: Some Modern Controversies on the History of Alchemy." *Annual of Medieval Studies at CEU*, 16, 2010, 166–190.

Cardew, Alan. "The Archaic and the Sublimity of Origins." In *The Archaic: The Past in the Present*, edited by Paul Bishop. East Sussex: Routledge, 2012, 93–146.

Casey, Edward S. *Spirit and Soul: Essays in Philosophical Psychology*. Putnam, CT: Spring Publications, 1991/2004.

Caygill, Howard. *A Kant Dictionary*. Oxford: Blackwell, 1995.

Cheak, Aaron. "Introduction." In *Alchemical Traditions from Antiquity to the Avant-Garde*, edited by Aaron Cheak. Melbourne: Numen Books, 2013.

Coudert, Allison. *Alchemy: The Philosopher's Stone*. Boulder: Shambhala, 1980.

Critchley, Simon. "Prolegomena to Any Post-Deconstructive Subjectivity." In *Deconstructive Subjectivities*, edited by Simon Critchley and Peter Dew. Albany: State University of New York Press, 1995, 13–45.

———. *Very Little: Almost Nothing*. London: Routledge, 2004.

De Boer, Karin. *On Hegel: The Sway of the Negative*. New York: Palgrave Macmillan, 2010.

Derrida, Jacques. *Positions*. Translated by Alan Bass. Chicago: University of Chicago Press, 1972/1982.

———. *Margins of Philosophy*. Translated with additional notes by Alan Bass. Chicago: University of Chicago Press, 1982.

———. "Deconstruction and the Other." In *Dialogues with Contemporary Continental Thinkers*, edited by Richard Kearney. Manchester: Manchester University Press, 1984.

———. "Passages – from Traumatism to Promise." In *Points. . .: Interviews, 1974–1994*, edited by Elisabeth Weber and translated by Peggy Kamuf et al. Stanford: Stanford University Press, 1995, 386–387.

Desmond, William. *Beyond Hegel and Dialectic: Speculation, Cult, and Comedy*. Albany: State University of New York Press, 1992.

———. "Dialectic and Evil: On the Idiocy of the Monstrous." In *Beyond Hegel and Dialectic: Speculaltion, Cult, and Comedy*. Albany: State University of New York Press, 1992, 189–250.

De Voogd, Stephanie. "C.G. Jung: Psychologist of the Future, 'Philosopher' of the Past." *Spring*, 1977, 175–182.

Diamond, Stanley. *Anger, Madness, and the Daimonic: The Psychological Genesis of Violence, Evil, and Creativity*. Albany: State University of New York Press, 1996.

Drob, Sanford. *Reading the Red Book: An Interpretive Guide to C.G. Jung's Liber Novus*. New Orleans: Spring Journal Books, 2012.

Edinger, Edward F. "Alchemy as a Psychological Process." *Quadrant: The Journal of the C.G. Jung Foundation*, 2, Autumn 1968. Précis to the Lectures by Gladys Taylor.

———. *Anatomy of the Psyche: Alchemical Symbolism in Psychotherapy*. LaSalle, IL: Open Court, 1985.

———. *The Mysterium Lectures: A Journey Through C.G. Jung's Mysterium Coniunctionis*. Edited by J. Dexter Blackmer. Toronto: Inner City Books, 1995.

———. *The Aion Lectures: Exploring the Self in C.G. Jung's Aion*. Edited by Deborah A. Wesley. Toronto: Inner City, 1996.

Eliade, Mircea. *The Forge and the Crucible: Origins and Structures of Alchemy*. New York: Harper & Row, 1962/1971.

Evans, F.J. *The Multivoiced Body: Society and Communication in the Age of Diversity*. New York, NY: Columbia University Press, 2009.

Ewing, A.C. *A Short Commentary on Kant's Critique of Pure Reason*. Chicago: University of Chicago Press, 1967.

Fabricius, Johannes. *Alchemy: The Medieval Alchemists and Their Royal Art*. London: Diamond Books, 1976.

Fink, Bruce. *The Lacanian Subject: Between Language and Jouissance*. Princeton: Princeton University Press, 1995.

Flay, Joseph C. "Hegel, Derrida and Bataille's Laughter with a Commentary by Judith Butler." In *Hegel and His Critics: Philosophy in the Aftermath of Hegel*, edited by William Desmond. Albany: State University of New York Press, 1989, 163–178.

Foucault, Michel. *The Order of Things: An Archeology of the Human Sciences*. New York: Vintage Books, 1970.

Giegerich, Wolfgang. *The Soul's Logical Life: Towards a Rigorous Notion of Psychology*. Frankfurt am Main: Peter Lang, 1998/2001.

———. "The End of Meaning and the Birth of Man: An Essay About the State Reached in the History of Consciousness and an Analysis of C.G. Jung's Psychology Project." *Journal of Jungian Theory and Practice*, 6(1), 2004, 1–66.

———. "Afterword." In *Dialectics and Analytical Psychology: The El Capitan Canyon Seminar*, edited by Wolfgang Giegerich, David Miller, and Greg Mogenson. New Orleans: Spring Journal Books, 2005, 107–112.

———. "'Conflict/Resolution,' 'Opposites/Creative Union' Versus Dialectics, and the Climb Up the Slippery Mountain." In *Dialectics and Analytical Psychology: The El*

Capitan Canyon Seminar, edited by Wolfgang Giegerich, David Miller, and Greg Mogenson. New Orleans: Spring Journal Books, 2005, 1–24.

———. "The Ego-Psychological Fallacy: A Note on 'the Birth of the Meaning Out of a Symbol'." *Journal of Jungian Theory and Practice*, 7(2), 2005.

———. "Closure and Setting Free: Or the Bottled Spirit of Alchemy and Psychology." *Spring Journal*, 74, Alchemy, 2006.

———. "Once More 'the Stone Which Is Not a Stone': Further Reflections on the 'Not'." In *Disturbances in the Field: Essays in Honor of David Miller*, edited by Christine Downing. New Orleans: Spring Journal Books, 2006, 127–141.

———. "Psychology – The Study of the Soul's Logical Life." In *Who Owns Jung?*, edited by Ann Casement. London: Karnac, 2007, 247–264.

———. *Soul-Violence, Collected English Papers, Volume III*. New Orleans: Spring Journal Books, 2008.

———. "The Unassimilable Remnant: What Is at Stake?: A Dispute with Stanton Marlan." In *Archetypal Psychologies: Reflections in Honor of James Hillman*, edited by Stanton Marlan. New Orleans: Spring Journal Books, 2008, 193–223.

———. "Liber Novus, That Is, the New Bible: A First Analysis of C.G. Jung's *Red Book*." *Spring: A Journal of Archetype and Culture*, 83, Spring 2010, 361–411.

———. *What Is Soul?* New Orleans: Spring Journal Books, 2012.

———. "Jung's Betrayal of His Truth: The Adoption of a Kantian-Based Empiricism and the Rejection of Hegel's Speculative Thought." In *Dreaming the Myth Onwards: C.G. Jung on Christianity and on Hegel, Collected English Papers, Volume VI, Part 2 of the Flight into the Unconscious*. New Orleans: Spring Journal Books, 2013.

Goethe, Johann Wolfgang von. *Faust [Part 1]*. Translated into English in the Original Metres by Goethe. Urbana, IL: Project Gutenberg, January 4, 2005. Free Ebook. gutenberg.org.

Gratacolle, William. "The Names of the Philosophers Stone." In *Five Treatises of the Philosophers' Stone*, republished, restored and compiled by Adam Goldsmith. London: Vitriol Publishing, 2011. Originally published in London, 1652.

Grossinger, Richard. *Alchemy: Pre-Egyptian Legacy, Millennial Promise*. Richmond, CA: North Atlantic Books, 1979.

Hanegraaff, Wouter J. *Esotericism and the Academy: Rejected Knowledge in Western Culture*. Cambridge: Cambridge University Press, 2012.

Hegel, G.W.F. *Phenomenology of Spirit*. Translated by A.V. Miller. Oxford: Oxford University Press, 1977.

Henderson, Joseph L. and Dyane N. Sherwood. *The Transformation of the Psyche: The Symbolic Alchemy of the Splendor Solis*. Hove: Brunner-Routledge, 2003.

Heym, Gerhard. "Review of Paracelsica, Zwei Vorlesungen über den Arzt und Philosophen Theophrastus," *Ambix*, 2(3), December 1946, 64–67.

Hillman, James. "On Senex Consciousness [Lead and Saturn]." *Spring*, 1970, 146–165.

———. *The Myth of Analysis: Three Essays in Archetypal Psychology*. New York: Harper & Row, 1972.

———. *Re-Visioning Psychology*. New York: Harper & Row, 1975.

———. "The Therapeutic Value of Alchemical Language." In *Dragonflies: Studies of Imaginal Psychology*, edited by Robert Sardello. Irving: University of Dallas, 1978, 118–126.

———. *The Dream and the Underworld*. New York: Harper and Row, 1979.

———. "Image-Sense." *Spring*, 1979, 130–143.

———. "Peaks and Vales." In *Puer Papers*. Irving, TX: Spring Publications, 1979, 54–74.

———. "Alchemical Blue and the Unio Mentalis." In *Sulfur*, 1, 1981, 33–50.

———. "Silver and the White Earth (Part Two)." *Spring*, 1981, 21–66.

———. *A Blue Fire*. Introduced and edited by Thomas Moore. New York: Harper & Row, 1989.

———. "The Cure of the Shadow." In *Meeting the Shadow: The Hidden Power of the Dark Side of Human Nature*, edited by Connie Zweig and Jeremiah Abrams. New York: J.P. Tarcher/Putnam, 1991, 242–243.

———. "Salt: A Chapter in Alchemical Psychology." In *Salt and the Alchemical Soul*, edited by Stanton Marlan. Woodstock, CT: Spring, 1995.

———. "A Note for Stanton Marlan." *Journal of Jungian Theory and Practice*, 5(2), 2003, 101–103.

———. *Archetypal Psychology: A Brief Account, Uniform Edition of the Writings of James Hillman, Vol. 1*. Putnam, CT: Spring Publications, 2004.

———. *Alchemical Psychology, Uniform Edition of the Writings of James Hillman, Vol. 5*. Putnam, CT: Spring Publications, 2010.

———. "Carl Gustav Jung & the Red Book." Library of Congress Event: Video (in two parts), June 19, 2010. www.loc.gov/item/webcast-4909 and www.loc.gov/item/webcast-4910.

———. "Divergences: *A Propos* of a Brazilian Seminar on Giegerich/Hillman – Organized by Marcus Quintaes." Unpublished paper, 2011.

Holmyard, E.J. *Alchemy*. Harmondsworth: Penguin Books, 1957.

Honoré, Carl. *In Praise of Slowness: Challenging the Cult of Speed*. San Francisco: Harper, 2004.

Jameson, Fredric. "First Impressions [Review of *The Parallax View* by Slavoj Žižek]." *London Review of Books*, 28(17), September 7, 2006. www.lrb.co.uk/v28/n17/fredric-jameson/first-impressions (Used with the kind permission of the *London Review of Books*.)

Jung, C.G. *Psychology and Alchemy, the Collected Works of C.G. Jung, Vol. 12*. Edited by Gerhard Adler and translated by R.F.C. Hull. Princeton: Princeton University Press, 1935/1944/1968.

———. *The Practice of Psychotherapy, the Collected Works of C.G. Jung, Vol. 16*. Edited by Gerhard Adler and translated by R.F.C. Hull. Princeton: Princeton University Press, 1946.

———. "The Psychology of the Transference." In *The Practice of Psychotherapy, the Collected Works of C.G. Jung, Vol. 16*, edited by Gerhard Adler and translated by R.F.C. Hull. Princeton: Princeton University Press, 1946, 163–323.

———. *Aion: The Collected Works of C.G. Jung, Vol. 9ii*. Edited and translated by Gerhard Adler and R.F.C. Hull. Princeton: Princeton University Press, 1951/1969.

———. *Alchemical Studies: The Collected Works of C.G. Jung, Vol. 13*. Edited by Gerhard Adler and translated by R.F.C. Hull. Princeton: Princeton University Press, 1953/1968.

———. "The Philosophical Tree." In *Alchemical Studies: The Collected Works of C.G. Jung, Vol. 13*, edited by Gerhard Adler and translated by R.F.C. Hull. Princeton: Princeton University Press, 1953/1968, 251–349.

———. *Two Essays on Analytical Psychology: The Collected Works of C.G. Jung, Vol. 7*. Edited by Gerhard Adler and translated by R.F.C. Hull. Princeton: Princeton University Press, 1953/1966/1970.

———. *Mysterium Coniunctionis: The Collected Works of C.G. Jung, Vol. 14*. Edited by Gerhard Adler and translated by R.F.C. Hull. Princeton: Princeton University Press, 1954/1963/1970.

————. *The Archetypes and the Collective Unconscious: The Collected Works of C.G. Jung, Vol. 9i.* Edited by Gerhard Adler and translated by R.F.C. Hull. Princeton: Princeton University Press, 1959/1968/1971.

————. *The Structure and Dynamics of the Psyche: The Collected Works of C.G. Jung, Vol. 8.* Edited by Gerhard Adler and translated by R.F.C. Hull. Princeton: Princeton University Press, 1960/1969.

————. "Commentary." In *The Secret of the Golden Flower: A Chinese Book of Life*, translated from the Chinese and explained by Richard Wilhelm and translated from the German by Cary F. Baynes. New York: Harcourt Brace & Company, 1962, 81–138.

————. *Civilization in Transition: The Collected Works of C.G. Jung, Vol. 10.* Edited by Gerhard Adler and translated by R.F.C. Hull. Princeton: Princeton University Press, 1964/1970.

————. *Psychological Types, the Collected Works of C.G. Jung, Vol. 6.* Edited by Gerhard Adler and translated by R.F.C. Hull. Princeton, NJ: Princeton University Press, 1970.

————. *C.G. Jung Speaking: Interviews and Encounters.* Edited by William McGuire and R.F.C. Hull. Princeton: Princeton University Press, 1977.

————. *The Spirit in Man, Art, and Literature: The Collected Works of C.G. Jung, Vol. 15.* Edited by Gerhard Adler and translated by R.F.C. Hull. Princeton: Princeton University Press, 1977.

————. *The Symbolic Life: The Collected Works of C.G. Jung, Vol. 18.* Edited by Gerhard Adler and translated by R.F.C. Hull. Princeton: Princeton University Press, 1977.

————. *Memories, Dreams, Reflections.* Recorded and edited by Aniela Jaffé and translated by Richard and Clara Winston. New York: Vintage Books, 1989.

————. *The Red Book: Liber Novus.* Edited by Sonu Shamdasani and translated by Mark Kyburz, John Peck, and Sonu Shamdasani. New York: W.W. Norton & Co., 2009.

Kant, Immanuel. *Dreams of a Spirit-Seer.* London: New-Church Press Limited, 1915.

————. *Prolegomena to Any Future Metaphysics.* Indianapolis: The Bobb's-Merrill Company, 1950.

————. *Critique of Pure Reason.* Translated by Werner S. Pluhar with Introduction by Patricia W. Kitcher. Indianapolis: Hackett Publishing, 1996.

Kelly, Sean M. "Atman, Anatta, and Transpersonal Psychology." In *Buddhist-Hindu Interactions from Sakyamuni to Sankaracarya*, edited by V. Subramaniam. New Delhi: Ajanta Books International, 1993. www.cejournal.org/GRD/Kelly.htm (accessed September 21, 2014).

————. *Individuation and the Absolute: Hegel, Jung and the Path Toward Wholeness.* New York: Paulist Press, 1993.

Kirsch, Thomas B. *The Jungians: A Comparative and Historical Perspective.* London: Routledge, 2000.

Kitcher, Patricia. "Introduction." In *Critique of Pure Reason*, edited by Immanuel Kant and translated by Werner S. Pluhar. Indianapolis and Cambridge: Hacket Publishing Co., 1996, xxv–lix.

Kuberski, P. *Chasmos: Literature, Science and Theory.* Albany, NY: State University of New York Press, 1994.

Kugler, Paul. *Raids on the Unthinkable: Freudian and Jungian Psychoanalysis.* New Orleans: Spring Journal Books, 2005.

Kuspit, Donald. "Negatively Sublime Identity: Pierre Soulage's Abstract Paintings." www.artnet.com/magazine_pre2000/features/kuspit/kuspit10-7-96.asp (accessed October 19, 2021).

LaCapra, Dominick. "Who Rules Metaphor? Paul Ricoeur's Theory of Discourse." *Diacritics*, 10(4), Winter 1980, 15–28.

Levinas, Emmanuel. *Otherwise Than Being or Beyond Essence*. Translated by Alphonso Lingis. The Hague: Martinus Nijhoff, 1981.

Magee, Glenn Alexander. *Hegel and the Hermetic Tradition*. Ithaca: Cornell University Press, 2001.

———. *The Hegel Dictionary*. London: Continuum, 2010.

Magnus, Kathleen Dow. *Hegel and the Symbolic Mediation of Spirit*. Albany: State University of New York Press, 2001.

Main, Roderick. "Numinosity and Terror: Jung's Psychological Revision of Otto as an Aid to Engaging Religious Fundamentalism." In *The Idea of the Numinous: Contemporary Jungian and Psychoanalytic Perspectives*, edited by Ann Casement and David Tacey. London: Routledge, 2006, 153–170.

Marlan, Stanton. "A Blue Fire: The Work of James Hillman." *Psychologist-Psychoanalyst, Official Publication of Division 39 of the American Psychological Association*, 9(4), Fall, 1989, 5–8 (Reused by permission of James W. Barron, PhD, then Editor of the *Psychologist/Psychoanalyst*).

———. *The Black Sun: The Alchemy and Art of Darkness*. College Station: Texas A&M University Press, 2005 (Used with the kind permission of Texas A&M University Press).

———. "Alchemy." In *The Handbook of Jungian Psychology: Theory, Practice and Applications*, edited by Renos Papadopolous. London: Routledge, 2006, 263–295 (Reused by permission of Taylor & Francis Ltd. www.tandfonline.com, on behalf of C.G. Jung Institute of San Francisco).

———. "From the Black Sun to the Philosopher's Stone." *Spring: A Journal of Archetype and Culture*, 74, 2006, 1–30 (Reused with the kind permission of Spring Journal, Inc).

———. "Archetypal Alchemy: Transformation of the Psyche/Matter Continuum." Paper presented at the International Alchemy Conference, Las Vegas, NV, October 6, 2007.

———. "Facing the Shadow." In *Jungian Psychoanalysis: Working in the Spirit of C.G. Jung*, edited by Murray Stein. Chicago: Open Court Publishing, 2010, 5–13 (Used with the kind permission of Open Court Publishing/Cricket Media).

———. "Foreword." In *Reading the Red Book: An Interpretive Guide to C.G. Jung's Liber Novus by Sanford Drob*. New Orleans: Spring Journal Books, 2012, ix–xv (Reused with the kind permission of Spring Journal, Inc).

———. "The Philosophers' Stone as Chaosmos: The Self and the Dilemma of Diversity." *Jung Journal: Psyche and Culture*, 7(2), 2013, 10–23. Copyright © 2013 C.G. Jung Institute of San Francisco. DOI:10.1080/19342039.2013.787525 (Reused by permission of Taylor & Francis Ltd. www.tandfonline.com, on behalf of C.G. Jung Institute of San Francisco).

———. "Colors of the Soul – Alchemy and the Aesthetic Imagination: A Review of James Hillman's *Alchemical Psychology*." *Jung Journal: Culture & Psyche*, 8(1), Winter 2014, 71–79.

———. "The Psychologist Who's Not a Psychologist: A Deconstructive Reading of Wolfgang Giegerich's Idea of Psychology Proper." *Journal of Analytical Psychology*, 61(2), 2016, 223–238.

Merleau-Ponty, Maurice. *The Visible and the Invisible*. Evanston, IL: Northwestern University Press, 1969.

Micklem, Niel. "I Am Not Myself: A Paradox." In *Jung's Concept of the Self: Its Relevance Today*. Papers from the Public Conference organized in May 1990 by the Jungian Postgraduate Committee of the British Association of Psychotherapists.

Miller, David. "The 'Stone' Which Is Not a Stone: C.G. Jung and the Post-Modern Meaning of 'Meaning'." *Spring*, 49, 1989, 110–122.

———. "Nothing Almost Sees Miracles! Self & No-Self in Psychology & Religion." *Journal of Psychology of Religion*, 4(5), 1995, 1–25.

———. "The End of Ending: A Response to Wolfgang Giegerich." *Journal of Jungian Theory and Practice*, 6(1), 2004, 85–93.

Mills, Jon. *The Unconscious Abyss: Hegel's Anticipation of Psychoanalysis*. Albany: State University of New York Press, 2002.

———. *Origins: On the Genesis of Psychic Reality*. Montreal: McGill-Queen's University Press, 2010.

Mogenson, Greg. "Different Moments in Dialectical Movement." In *Dialectics and Analytical Psychology: The El Capitan Canyon Seminar*. New Orleans: Spring Journal Books, 2005, 77–106.

Mookerjee, Ajit. *Kali: The Feminine Force*. Rochester, VT: Destiny Books, 1988.

Morris, David. "Casey's Subliminal Phenomenology: On Edging Things Back into Place." In *Exploring the Work of Edward S. Casey: Giving Voice to Place, Memory, and Imagination*, edited by Donald A. Landes and Azucena Cruz-Pierre. London: Bloomsbury, 2013, 53–61.

Morris, Marla. "Archiving Derrida." In *Derrida, Deconstruction and Education: Ethics of Pedagogy and Research*, edited by Peter Pericles Trifonas and Michael A. Peters. Malden: Blackwell Publishing, 2004, 43–57.

Nagy, Marilyn. *Philosophical Issues in the Psychology of C.G. Jung*. Albany: State University of New York Press, 1991.

Newman, William. "*Decknamen* or Pseudochemical Language? Eirenaeus Philalethes and Carl Jung." *Revue D'Histoire des Sciences*, 49(2), 1996, 159–188.

Noll, Richard. *The Jung Cult*. Princeton: Princeton University Press, 1994.

———. *The Aryan Christ*. New York: Random House, 1997.

O'Hara, D.T. "The Irony of Being Metaphorical." *Journal of Postmodern Literature*, 8(2), 1980, 324–345.

O'Regan, Cyril. *The Heterodox Hegel*. Albany: State University of New York Press, 1994.

Pagel, Walter. "Jung's Views on Alchemy," *Isis*, 39, 1948, 44–48.

Panisnick, George David. "The Philosophical Significance of the Concept of the Philosopher's Stone as Used in the Hermetic and Alchemical Writings of Paracelsus." PhD diss., University of Hawaii, Honolulu, 1975.

Papadopolous, Renos (editor). *The Handbook of Jungian Psychology: Theory, Practice and Applications*. London: Routledge.

Patai, Raphael. *The Jewish Alchemists*. Princeton: Princeton University Press, 1994.

Pernety, Dom. *Dictionaire Mytho-Hermetique*. Paris: E.P. Denoël, 19 Rue Amélle, 1972, reprint.

Plato. *Phaedo*. Urbana, IL: Project Gutenberg, October 12, 2004. Apology, Crito, and Phaedo of Socrates by Plato – Free Ebook (gutenberg.org).

Plutarch. *On the Face Which Appears on the Orb of the Moon: Translation and Notes, with Appendix* (Classic Reprint). London: Forgotten Books, 2012.

Principe, Lawrence. "Alchemy I: Introduction." In *Dictionary of Gnosis: Western Esotericism, Vol. I*, edited by Wouter J. Hanegraaff. Boston: Brill Academic Publishing, 2005, 12–16.

———. *The Secrets of Alchemy*. Chicago: University of Chicago Press, 2013.

Principe, Lawrence and William Newman. "Some Problems with the Historiography of Alchemy." In *Secrets of Nature: Astrology and Alchemy in Early Modern Europe*, edited by William R. Newman and Anthony Grafton. Cambridge: MIT Press, 2001.

Ricoeur, Paul. *Freud and Philosophy: An Essay on Interpretation*. New Haven: Yale University Press, 1970.

———. "The Status of Vorstellung in Hegel's Philosophy of Religion." In *Meaning, Truth, and God*, edited by Leroy S. Rouner. South Bend, IN: University of Notre Dame, 1982, 70–88.

Rockmore, Tom. *Hegel's Circular Epistemology*. Bloomington: Indiana University Press, 1986.

———. *Before and After Hegel*. Berkeley: University of California Press, 1993.

———. *On Hegel's Epistemology and Contemporary Philosophy*. Atlantic Highlands, NJ: Humanities Press, 1996.

———. *Cognition: An Introduction to Hegel's Phenomenology of Spirit*. Berkeley: University of California Press, 1997.

———. *In Kant's Wake: Philosophy in the Twentieth Century*. Malden, MA: Blackwell Publishing, 2006.

———. *Kant and Idealism*. New Haven: Yale University Press, 2007.

Roethke, Theodore. "Fourth Meditation." In *Words for the Wind: The Collected Verse of Theodore Roethke*. Bloomington: Indiana University Press, 1970.

Romanyshyn, Robert. "Psychological Language and the Voice of Things." *Dragonflies: Studies in Imaginal Psychology*, Fall 1978, 79–80.

Rosen, David. *Transforming Depression: Healing the Soul Through Creativity*. York Beach, ME: Nicolas-Hays, 2002.

Sallis, John. *Stone*. Bloomington: Indiana University Press, 1994.

Samuels, Andrew, Bani Shorter, and Fred Plaut. *A Critical Dictionary of Jungian Analysis*. London: Routledge, 1996.

Sarton, May. "The Invocation of Kali." http://college.holycross.edu/projects/himalayan_cultures/2006_plans/syoung/The%20Invocation%20to%20Kali.pdf.

Schrader, George. "The Thing in Itself in Kantian Philosophy." In *Kant: A Collection of Critical Essays*, edited by Robert Paul Wolff. New York: Doubleday, 1967, 172–188.

Schwartz-Salant, Nathan. *The Mystery of Human Relationship: Alchemy and the Transformation of Self*. London: Routledge, 1998.

Shakespeare, William. *Hamlet (Act 3, Scene 1)*. Urbana, IL: Project Gutenberg, November 1, 1998 [Most recently updated: October 17, 2021]. Hamlet, Prince of Denmark by William Shakespeare – Free Ebook. gutenberg.org.

Shamdasani, Sonu. *Cult Fictions: C.G. Jung and the Founding of Analytical Psychology*. London: Routledge, 1998.

———. "Introduction." In *The Red Book: Liber Novus, by C.G. Jung*, edited by Sonu Shamdasani and translated by Mark Kyburz, John Peck, and Sonu Shamdasani. New York: W.W. Norton & Co., 2009, 194–221.

Sharp, Daryl. "Tribute for E. Edinger." *Psychological Perspectives*, 39, Summer 1999, 17–18.

Sim, Stuart. *Derrida and the End of History*. London: Totem Books, 1995.

Sinha, Indra. *Tantra: The Cult of Ecstasy*. London: Hamlyn, 2000.

Stein, Murray. "The Aims and Goal of Jungian Analysis." In *Jungian Analysis*, edited by Murray Stein. Chicago: Open Court, 1995, second edition, 29–49.

———. *Jung's Map of the Soul: An Introduction*. Peru, IL: Open Court Press, 1998.

——— (editor). *Jungian Psychoanalysis: Working in the Spirit of C.G. Jung*. Chicago: Open Court, 2010.

———. "Mysterium Coniunctionis: The Mysterious Creation of Unity." Unpublished lecture delivered on September 25, 2021, as part of a 14-week program, The Jungian

Mystery School (co-chaired by Stephen Farrah and Murray Steing), sponsored by the Centre for Applied Jungian Studies, Cape Town, South Africa.

Tarrant, John. *Carl Jung's Red Book*. Santa Rosa, CA: Pacific Zen Institute, September 17, 2021 (Used with the kind permission of the author).

Tilton, Hereward. *The Quest for the Phoenix: Spiritual Alchemy and Rosicrucianism in the Work of Count Michael Maier (1569–1622)*. Berlin: Walter de Gruyter, 2003.

Verene, Donald P. *Hegel's Recollection: A Study of Images in the Phenomenology of Spirit*. Albany: State University of New York Press, 1985.

———. "Hegel's Nature." In *Hegel and the Philosophy of Nature*, edited by Stephen Houlgate. Albany: State University of New York Press, 1998, 209–225.

Vivekananda, Swami. *In Search of God and Other Poems*. Calcutta: Advaita Ashrama, 1968, 25.

Von Franz, Marie-Louise. *Aurora Consurgens: A Document Attributed to Thomas Aquinas on the Problem of Opposites in Alchemy*. Princeton: Bollingen Foundation, Pantheon, 1966.

———. *Alchemical Active Imagination*. Dallas: Spring, 1979.

———. *Alchemy: An Introduction to the Symbolism and the Psychology*. Toronto: Inner City Books, 1980.

———. "Psychological Commentary." In *Corpus Alchemicum Arabicum: Book of the Explanation of the Symbols, Kitāb Ḥall ar-Rumūz by Muḥammad Ibn Umail*, edited by Theodor Abt. Zurich: Living Human Heritage Publications, 2006.

Wagner, S. "A Conversation with Marie-Louise von Franz." *Psychological Perspectives*, 38, Winter 1998–1999, 12–42.

Watkins, Eric. "Review of Daniel Warren: Reality and Impenetrability in Kant's Philosophy of Nature." Notre Dame Philosophical Reviews, University of Notre Dame, February 10, 2002. https://ndpr.nd.edu/news/23403-reality-and-impenetrability-in-kant-s-philosophy-of-nature/ (Used with the kind permission of the *Notre Dame Philosophical Reviews*).

Wood, David. "Reiterating the Temporal Toward a Rethinking of Heidegger on Time." In *Reading Heidegger: Commemorations*, edited by J. Sallis. Bloomington: Indiana University Press, 1993.

Žižek, Slavoj. *Less Than Nothing: Hegel and the Shadow of Dialectical Materialism*. London: Verso, 2013.

Zweig, Arnulf (editor and translator). *Kant: Philosophical Correspondence 1759–99*. Chicago: The University of Chicago Press, 1967.

Zucker, Wolfgang. "Historicism and Relativism." Unpublished Lecture XI, Student Faculty Colloquium, Drew University Graduate School, 1958–1959.

Index

Note: Page numbers in *italics* indicate a figure and page numbers in **bold** indicate a table on the corresponding page. Page numbers followed by 'n' indicate a note.

matter 9–10, 21, 39–40, 100–101, 159;
and *nigredo* 81
memory 242
Mendelssohn, 174
Mercurius 35, 58–59, 69–77, 92; as
caduceus unifying the opposites *38*;
duplex 35–40, 224–225; liquification
of 133; as mediator 257–260; Mercurial
monster *70*; spirit of 52–53, 69;
telos of 127; turning the wheel which
symbolizes the alchemical process 37,
37; as a uniting symbol *36*
metaphysics 131, 175–176, 183
metaxological approach 239–240, 264
Metzger, Hélène 15, 17
Micklem, Neil 64–65, 143
Miller, David 148, 150, 163, 207
Mills, Jon 253
mind-independent reality 185
Mogenson, Greg 148–149, 150
monstrous *coniunctio* 266
monstrous conjunctions *see* benign and
monstrous conjunctions
monstrous hermaphrodite *55*
monstrum 35, 38, 71
Moore 96
moral consciousness 230n27
Moran, Bruce T. 24
Morienus 11
Morin, Edgar 152
Morris, David 244
Morris, Marla 158
mortificatio 141, 156; process *215*;
mortificatio/putrefactio operation, of
alchemy 90–92, *91*
multiple eyes 199, 258
Mutus liber 12
Mysterium Coniunctionis (Jung) 58, 62,
77–82, 142, 156, 210, 247, 256–257
mystical death 157–159
myths 131

Nargarjuna 154
nature 9–10, 223
negativity 152; absolute 234, 264; logical
234; tragic 234, 264
neurosis 131–132, 138, 161
"New Birth, The" 56–57
Newman, William R. 13–15, 17, 19, 21;
see also Principe and Newman's thesis
Nicholas of Cusa 57
nigredo 139; and matter 81;
undifferentiated state of 48, 50
Noll, Richard 20–21, 30n75, 190

no-self 157, 206–211, 213
"not" 146, 152
nothingness 67, 133, 186–187,
206, 207
Notion 109–110, 187, 188, 217
noumena 174, 180

objective psyche 87, 89, 183
Obrist, Barbara 17
oneness 44, 142, 256, 258, 262, 264
opposites 3, 119–120, 205, 206; divine
geometry 74; of the dual face of alchemy
39; God and devil 67; incestuous
unification of 71–72; Jung on 43–44,
50, 77–82, 143, 182–183, 257;
Mercurius as caduceus unifying the *38*;
and Philosophers' Stone 39; and pleroma
67; unification of 4, *38*, 39, 50, 71, *78*,
143, 182–183, 257; *see also coniunctio*
opus 58, 59, 193
opus contra naturam 130, 213
O'Regan, Cyril 190, 216
ouroboros 35, *36*, 37, 39

Pagel, Walter 13, 16
Panisnick, George David 9, 127
Paracelsus, Philippus Aureolus 155, 156
parallax gap 255, 264
patience, and philosophy 235–236
Paton, H.J. 173
peacock's tail 81–82, 199, *200*
perceiving and imagining, difference
between 163
periphenomenon 244
Pernety, Dom 1
personality 101
Phaedo (Plato) 195
phenomena 174, 179–180, 186
Phenomenology of Spirit (Hegel)
184–185, 190, 216–217, 247, 252
Philalethes 17
Philosophers' Stone 1, 4, 6, 8, 145,
153–154, 264; achievement,
cosmological vision of *81*; and black
sun 165; characteristics of 162–163; and
darkness 154, 234–235; divine geometry
74–76, *76*; and goal images 251; Hillman
on 145–146; imagined as speaking 39; as
an initiatory experience 144; linked to the
lumen naturae of *sol niger* 166; *lithos ou
lithos 2*; lumen of 153; and peacock's tail
199, *200*; as *prima materia* 256;
prima materia Mercurius 2; problematic
origin 9; *rotatio* 146; and Self 6, 162,

For Product Safety Concerns and Information please contact our EU
representative GPSR@taylorandfrancis.com
Taylor & Francis Verlag GmbH, Kaufingerstraße 24, 80331 München, Germany

9 781032 105444